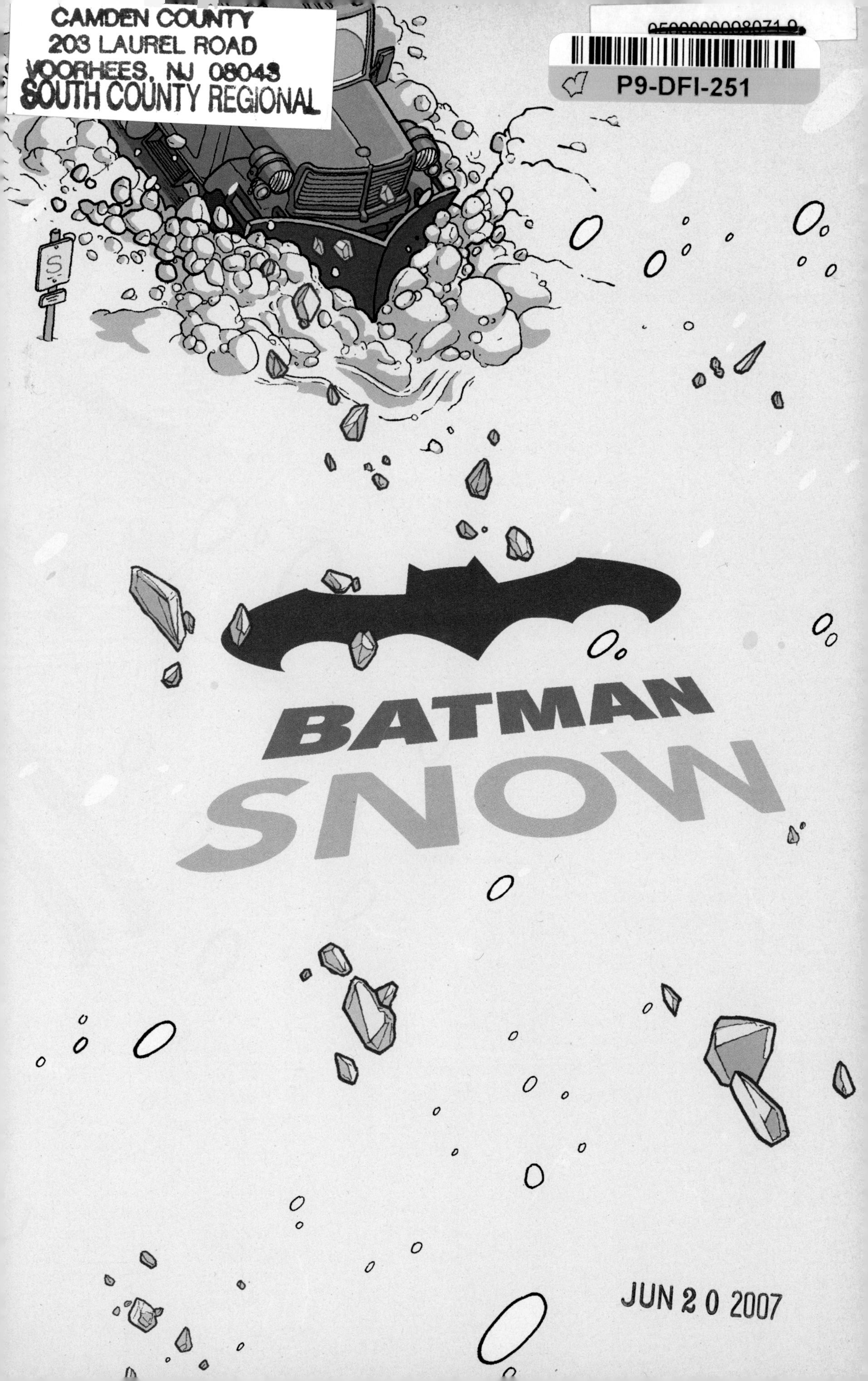
BATMAN
SNOW

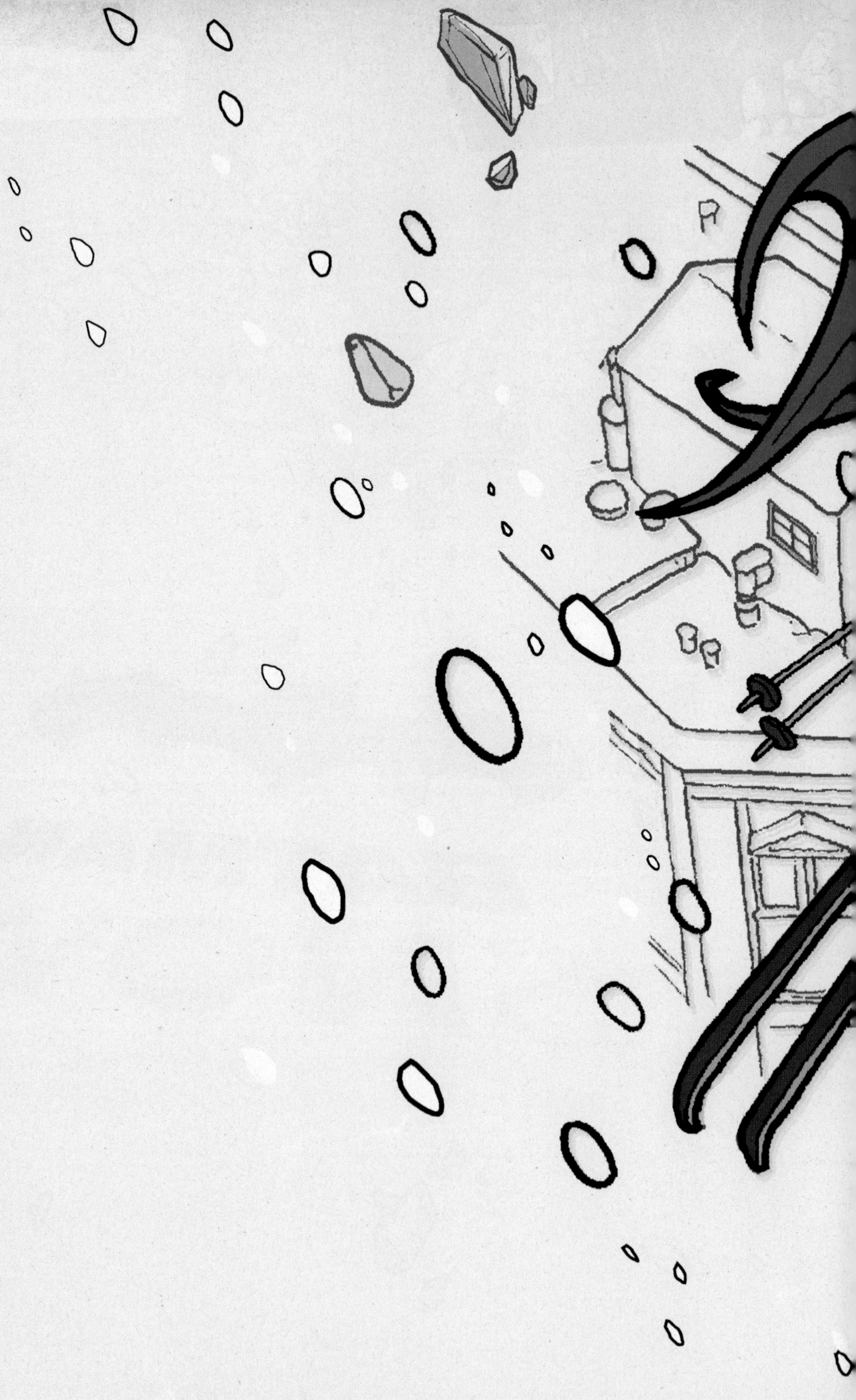

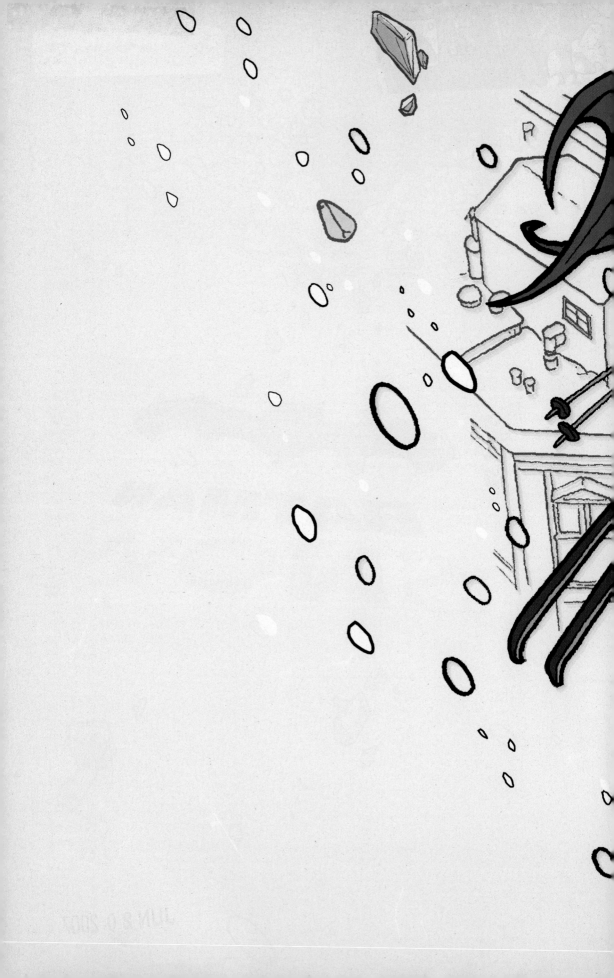

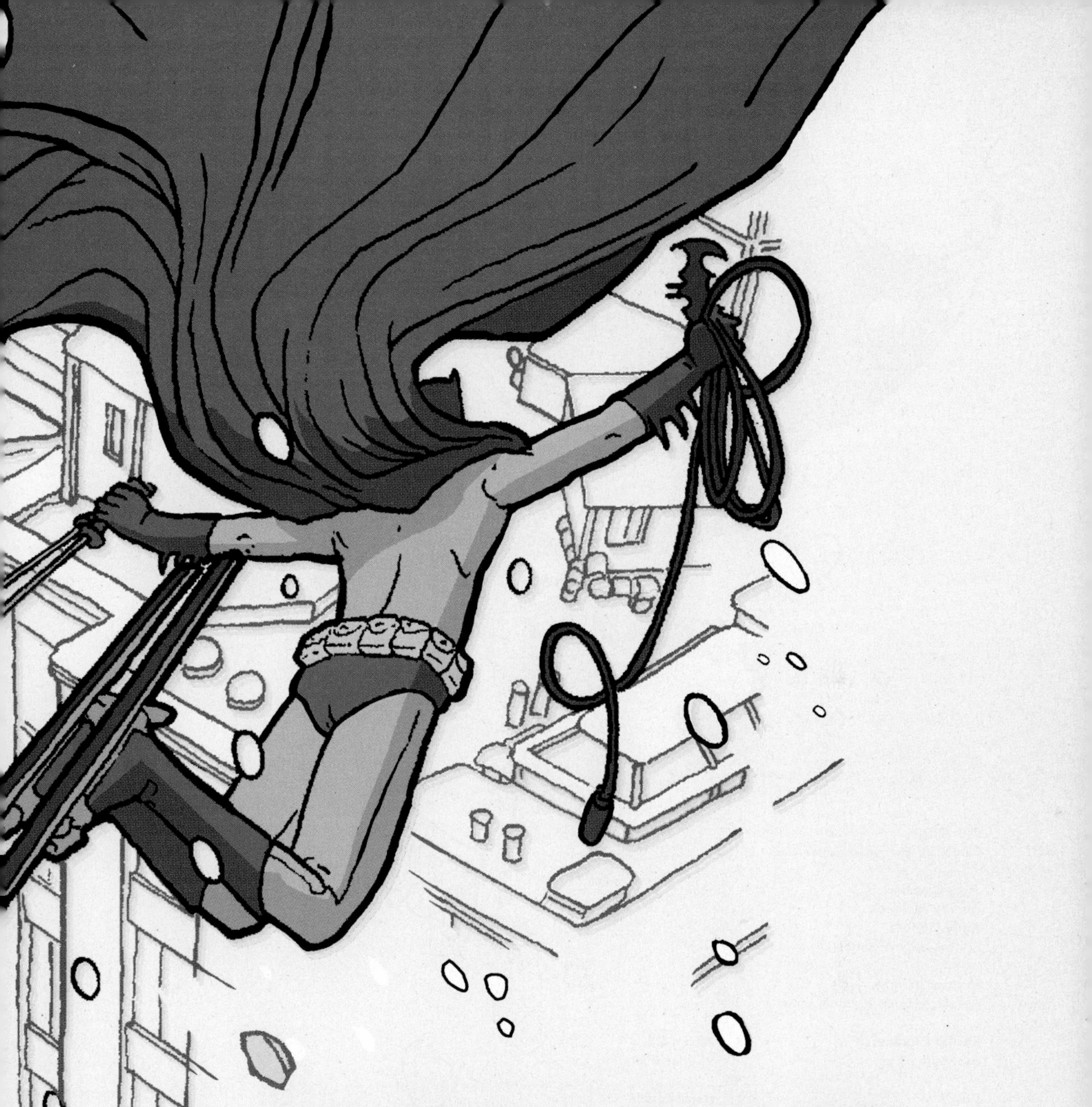

BATMAN SNOW

J.H. WILLIAMS III   DAN CURTIS JOHNSON story

DAN CURTIS JOHNSON script & dialogue

SETH FISHER art and original covers

DAVE STEWART colors

PHIL BALSMAN letterer

Batman created by BOB KANE

Dan DiDio
Senior VP-Executive Editor

Joey Cavalieri
Harvey Richards
Andy Helfer
Editors-original series

Michael Wright
Associate Editor-original series

Rachel Gluckstern
Assistant Editor-original series

Bob Joy
Editor-collected edition

Robbin Brosterman
Senior Art Director

Paul Levitz
President & Publisher

Georg Brewer
VP-Design & DC Direct Creative

Richard Bruning
Senior VP-Creative Director

Patrick Caldon
Executive VP-Finance & Operations

Chris Caramalis
VP-Finance

John Cunningham
VP-Marketing

Terri Cunningham
VP-Managing Editor

Stephanie Fierman
Senior VP-Sales & Marketing

Alison Gill
VP-Manufacturing

Hank Kanalz
VP-General Manager, WildStorm

Jim Lee
Editorial Director-WildStorm

Paula Lowitt
Senior VP-Business & Legal Affairs

MaryEllen McLaughlin
VP-Advertising & Custom Publishing

John Nee
VP-Business Development

Gregory Noveck
Senior VP-Creative Affairs

Cheryl Rubin
Senior VP-Brand Management

Jeff Trojan
VP-Business Development, DC Direct

Bob Wayne
VP-Sales

Cover art by Seth Fisher
Publication design by Amelia Grohman

DC Comics
1700 Broadway New York, NY 10019
A Warner Bros. Entertainment Company

Printed in Canada. First Printing.
ISBN: 1-4012-1265-4
ISBN 13: 978-1-4012-1265-0

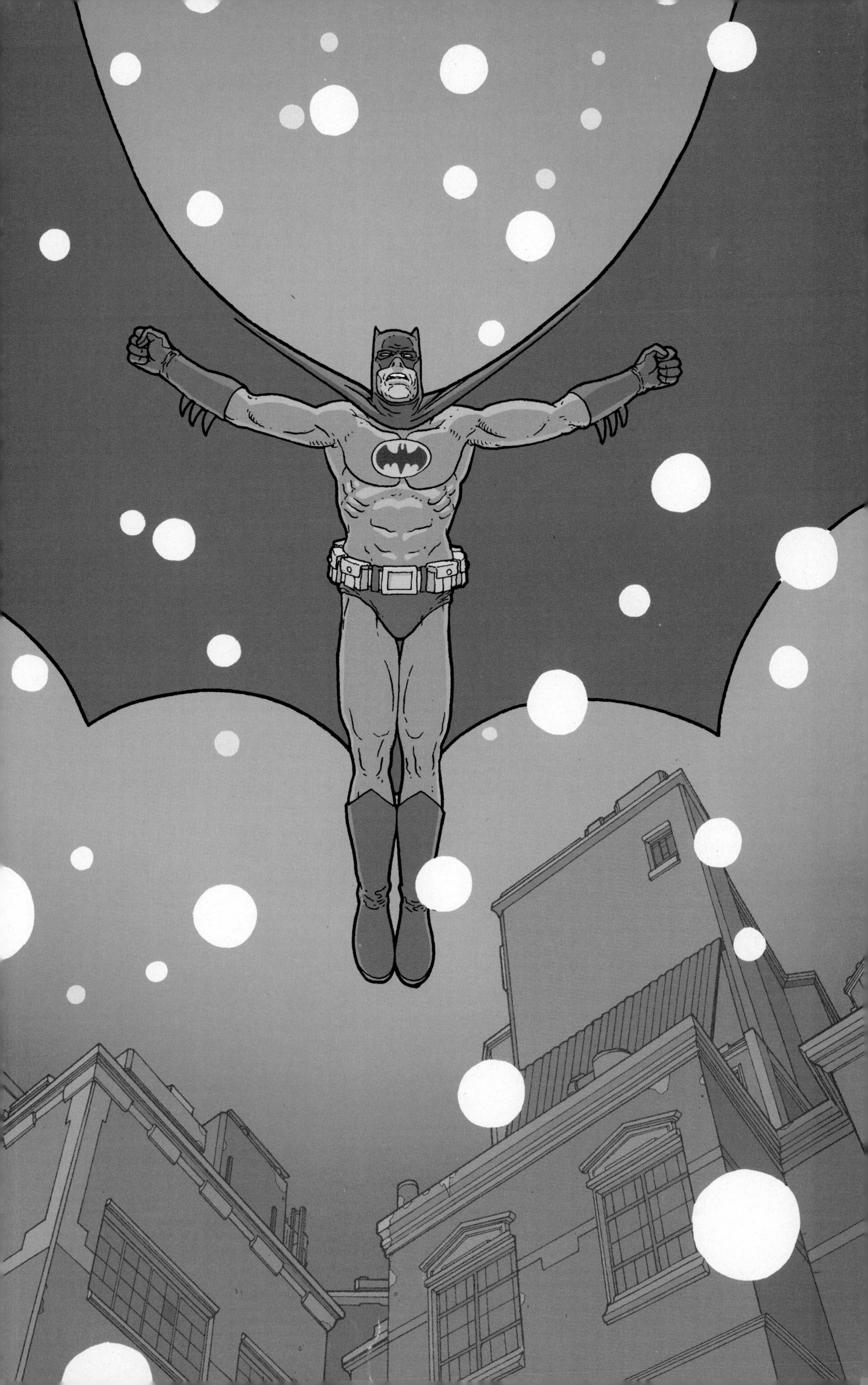

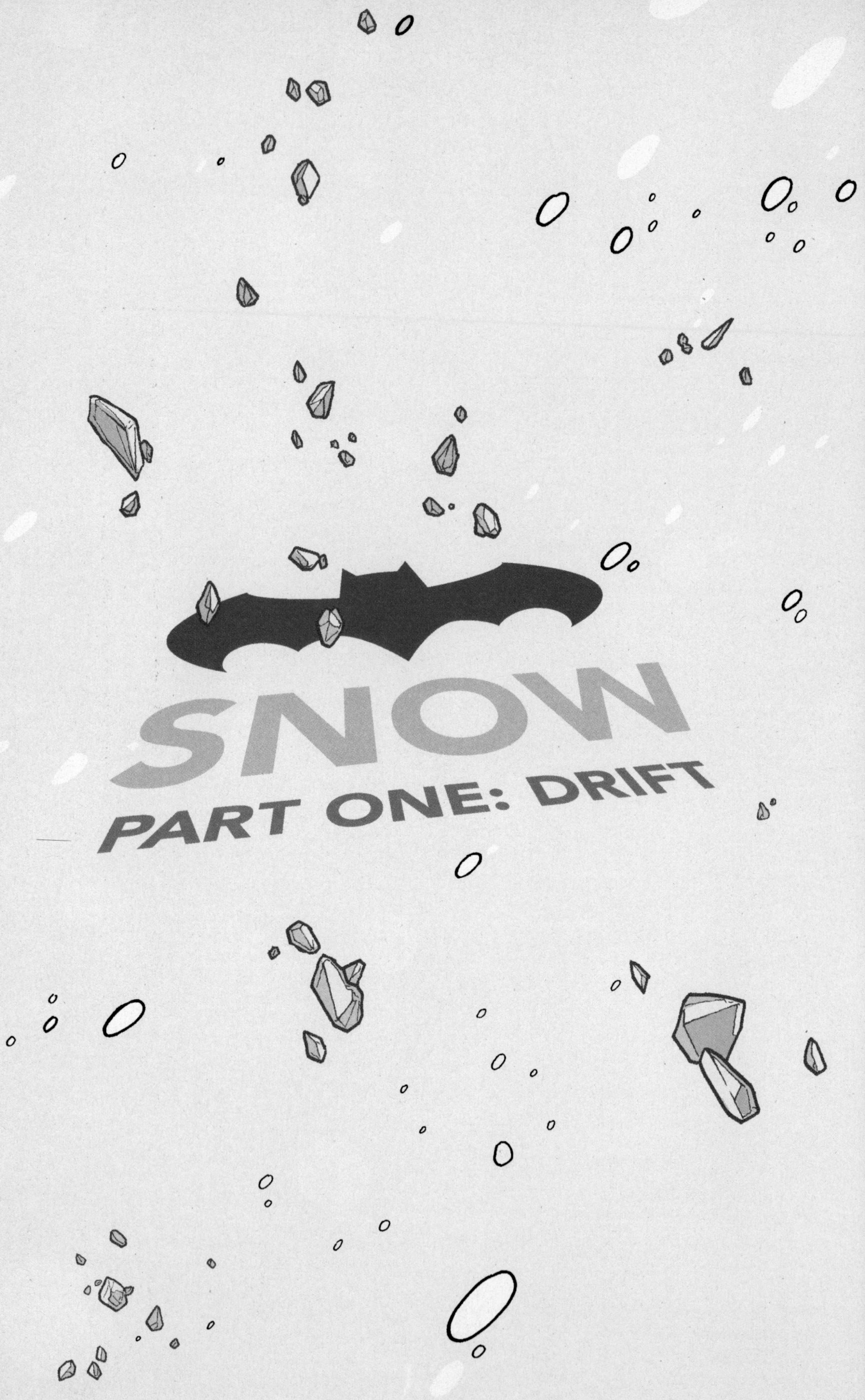
SNOW
PART ONE: DRIFT

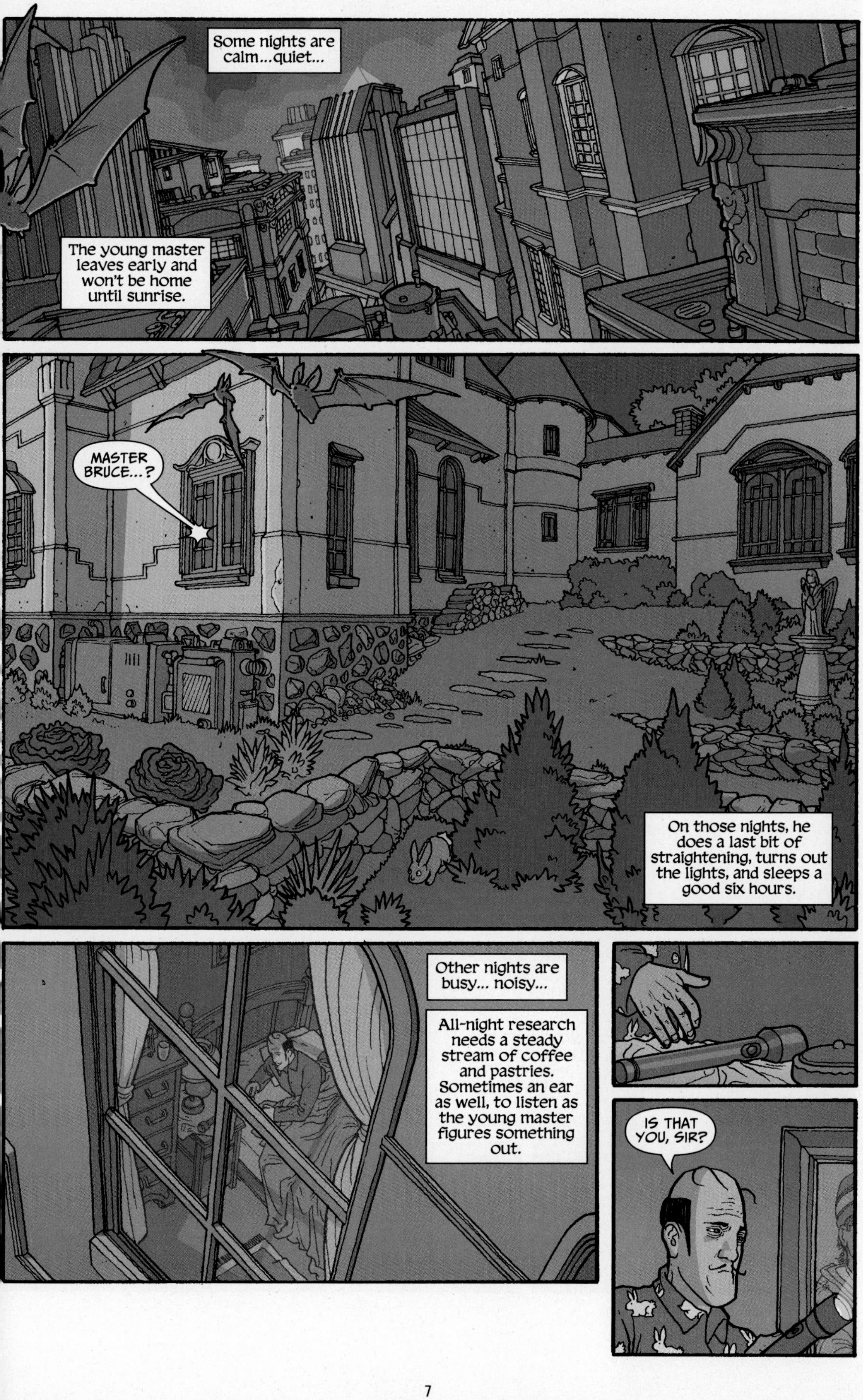

Some nights are calm...quiet...
The young master leaves early and won't be home until sunrise.
MASTER BRUCE...?
On those nights, he does a last bit of straightening, turns out the lights, and sleeps a good six hours.
Other nights are busy... noisy...
All-night research needs a steady stream of coffee and pastries. Sometimes an ear as well, to listen as the young master figures something out.
IS THAT YOU, SIR?

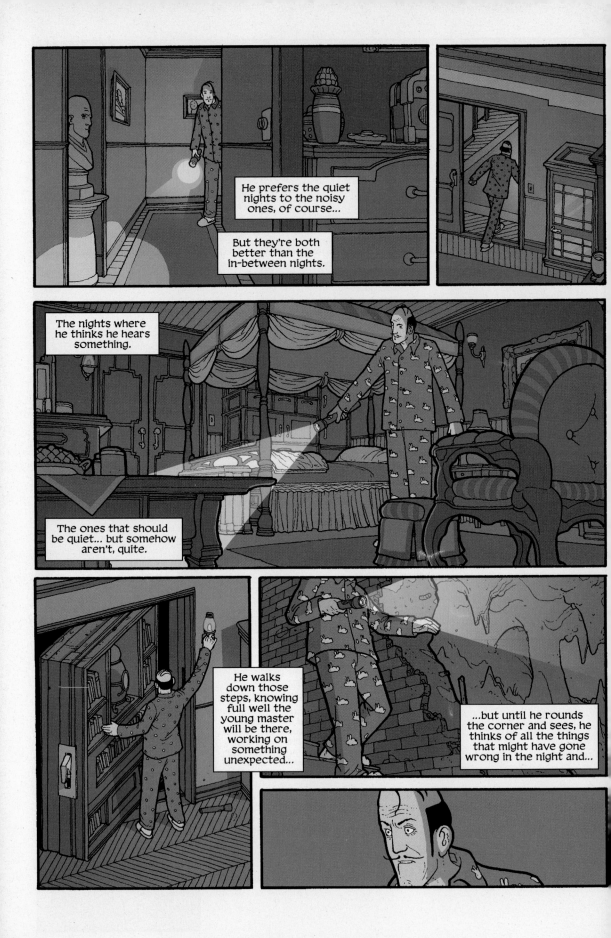

He prefers the quiet nights to the noisy ones, of course...

But they're both better than the in-between nights.

The nights where he thinks he hears something.

The ones that should be quiet... but somehow aren't, quite.

He walks down those steps, knowing full well the young master will be there, working on something unexpected...

...but until he rounds the corner and sees, he thinks of all the things that might have gone wrong in the night and...

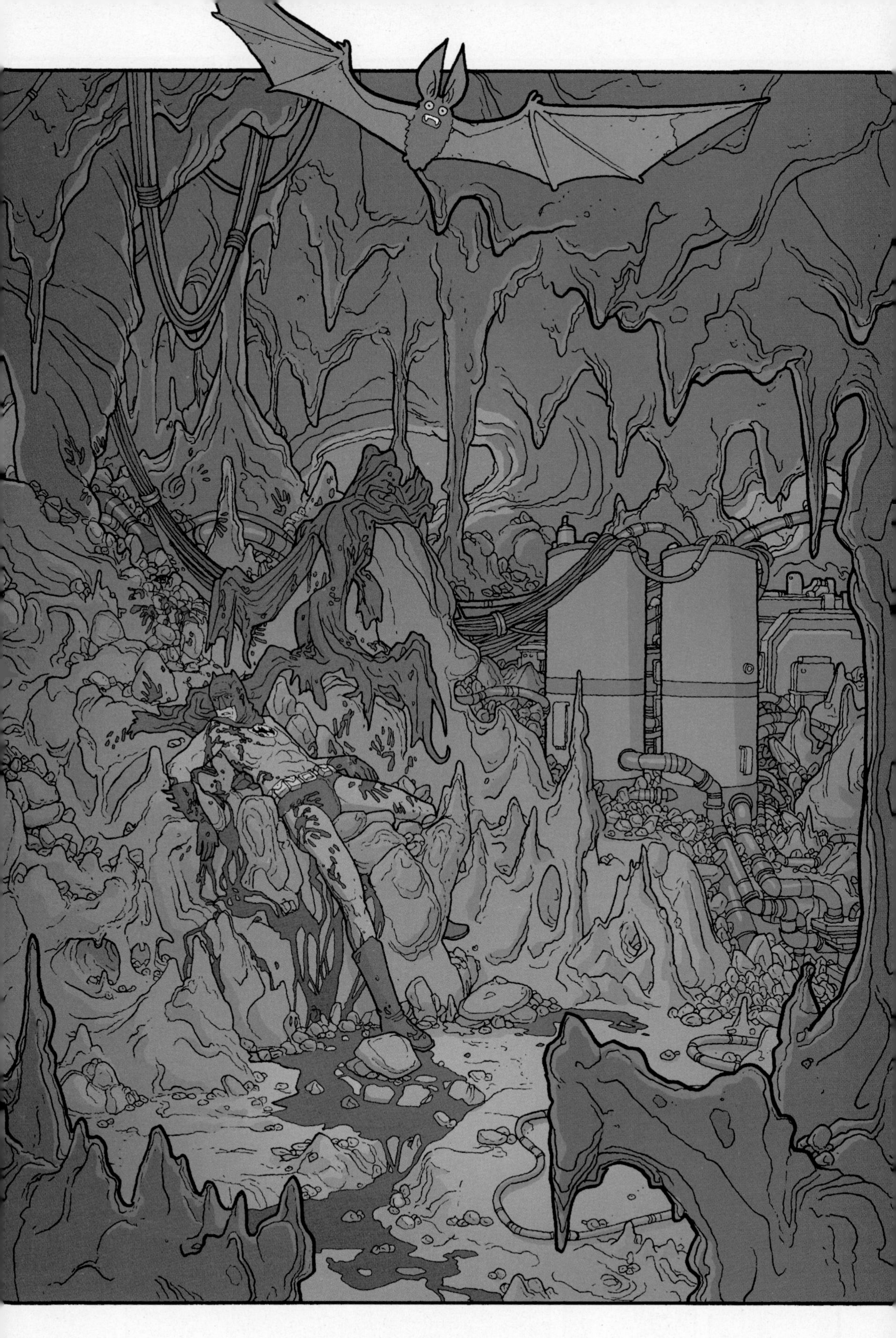

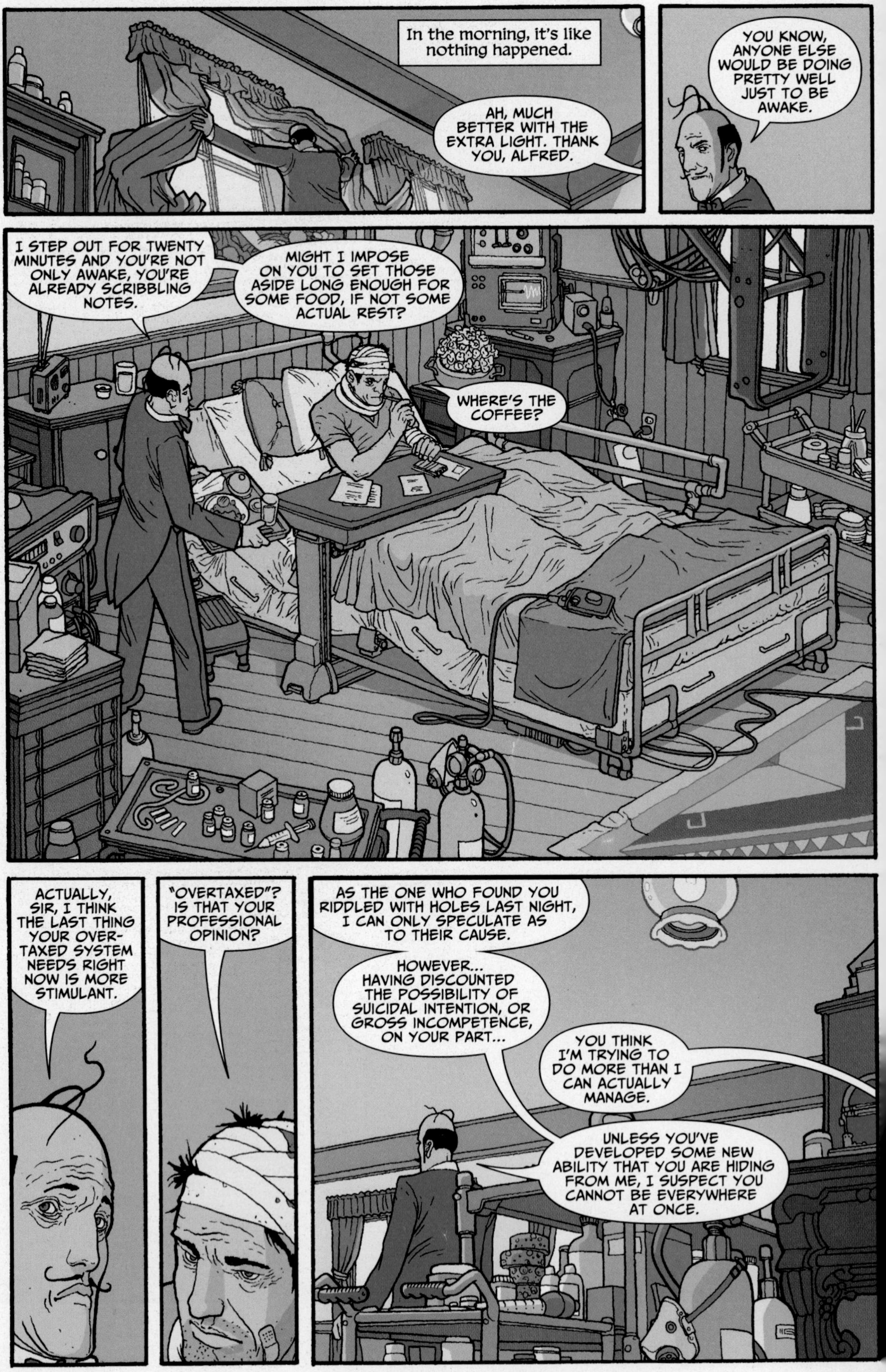
In the morning, it's like nothing happened.
AH, MUCH BETTER WITH THE EXTRA LIGHT. THANK YOU, ALFRED.
YOU KNOW, ANYONE ELSE WOULD BE DOING PRETTY WELL JUST TO BE AWAKE.
I STEP OUT FOR TWENTY MINUTES AND YOU'RE NOT ONLY AWAKE, YOU'RE ALREADY SCRIBBLING NOTES.
MIGHT I IMPOSE ON YOU TO SET THOSE ASIDE LONG ENOUGH FOR SOME FOOD, IF NOT SOME ACTUAL REST?
WHERE'S THE COFFEE?
ACTUALLY, SIR, I THINK THE LAST THING YOUR OVER-TAXED SYSTEM NEEDS RIGHT NOW IS MORE STIMULANT.
"OVERTAXED"? IS THAT YOUR PROFESSIONAL OPINION?
AS THE ONE WHO FOUND YOU RIDDLED WITH HOLES LAST NIGHT, I CAN ONLY SPECULATE AS TO THEIR CAUSE.
HOWEVER... HAVING DISCOUNTED THE POSSIBILITY OF SUICIDAL INTENTION, OR GROSS INCOMPETENCE, ON YOUR PART...
YOU THINK I'M TRYING TO DO MORE THAN I CAN ACTUALLY MANAGE.
UNLESS YOU'VE DEVELOPED SOME NEW ABILITY THAT YOU ARE HIDING FROM ME, I SUSPECT YOU CANNOT BE EVERYWHERE AT ONCE.

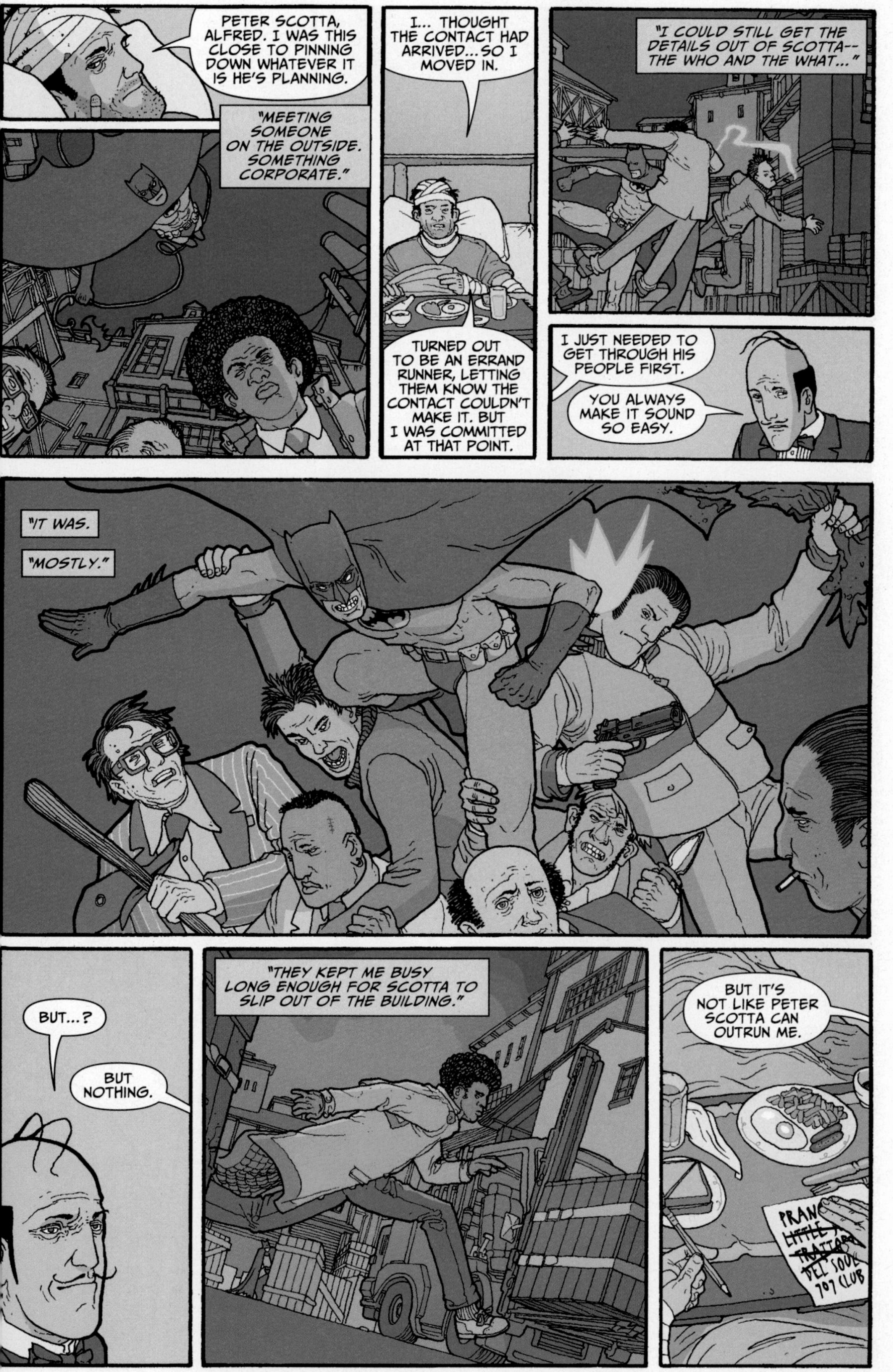
PETER SCOTTA, ALFRED. I WAS THIS CLOSE TO PINNING DOWN WHATEVER IT IS HE'S PLANNING.
"MEETING SOMEONE ON THE OUTSIDE. SOMETHING CORPORATE."
I... THOUGHT THE CONTACT HAD ARRIVED... SO I MOVED IN.
TURNED OUT TO BE AN ERRAND RUNNER, LETTING THEM KNOW THE CONTACT COULDN'T MAKE IT. BUT I WAS COMMITTED AT THAT POINT.
"I COULD STILL GET THE DETAILS OUT OF SCOTTA-- THE WHO AND THE WHAT..."
I JUST NEEDED TO GET THROUGH HIS PEOPLE FIRST.
YOU ALWAYS MAKE IT SOUND SO EASY.
"IT WAS.
"MOSTLY."
BUT...?
BUT NOTHING.
"THEY KEPT ME BUSY LONG ENOUGH FOR SCOTTA TO SLIP OUT OF THE BUILDING."
BUT IT'S NOT LIKE PETER SCOTTA CAN OUTRUN ME.
PRAN
LITTLE
DEL SOUL
707 CLUB

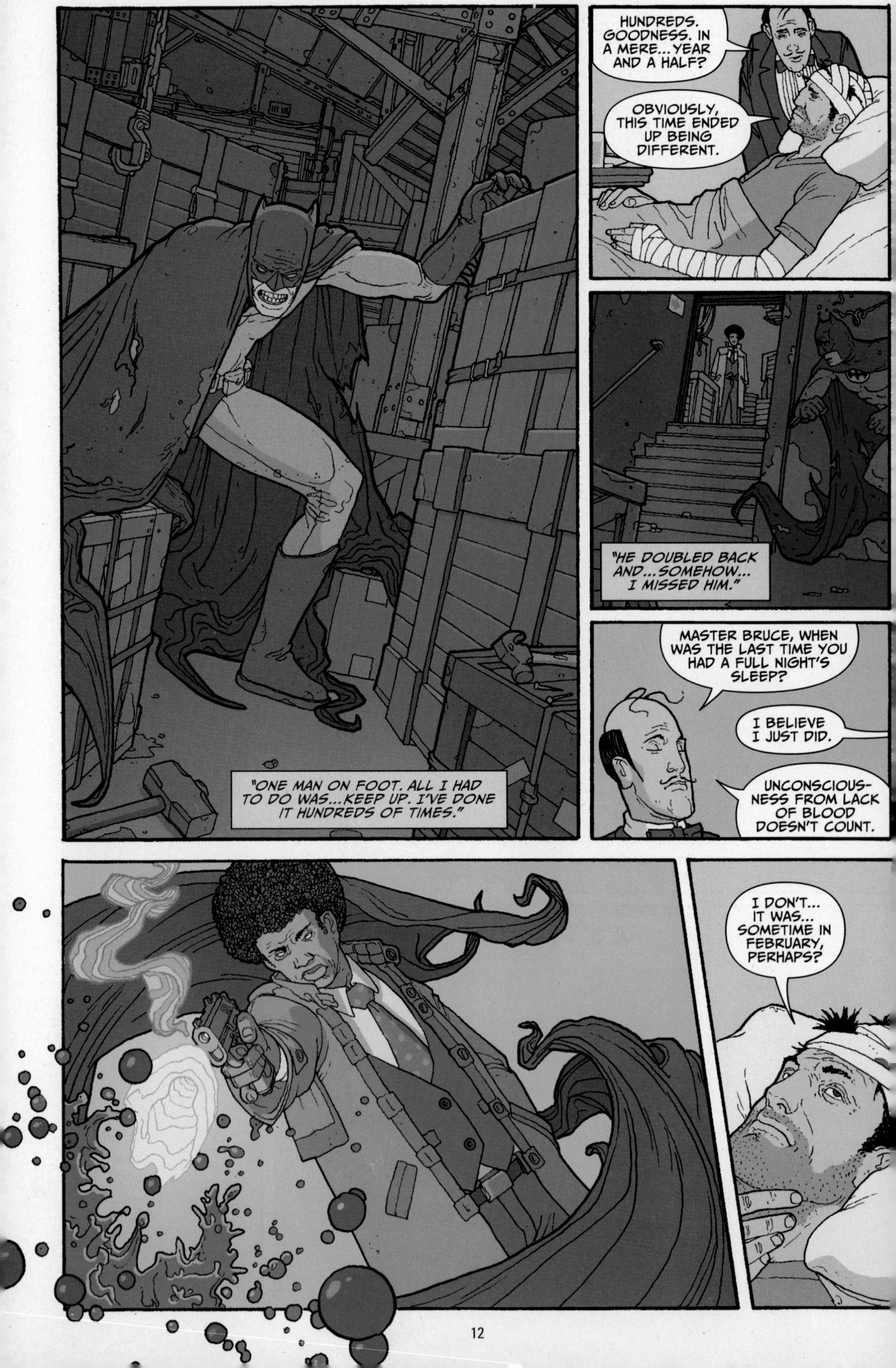
"ONE MAN ON FOOT. ALL I HAD TO DO WAS...KEEP UP. I'VE DONE IT HUNDREDS OF TIMES."
HUNDREDS. GOODNESS. IN A MERE...YEAR AND A HALF?
OBVIOUSLY, THIS TIME ENDED UP BEING DIFFERENT.
"HE DOUBLED BACK AND...SOMEHOW... I MISSED HIM."
MASTER BRUCE, WHEN WAS THE LAST TIME YOU HAD A FULL NIGHT'S SLEEP?
I BELIEVE I JUST DID.
UNCONSCIOUSNESS FROM LACK OF BLOOD DOESN'T COUNT.
I DON'T... IT WAS... SOMETIME IN FEBRUARY, PERHAPS?

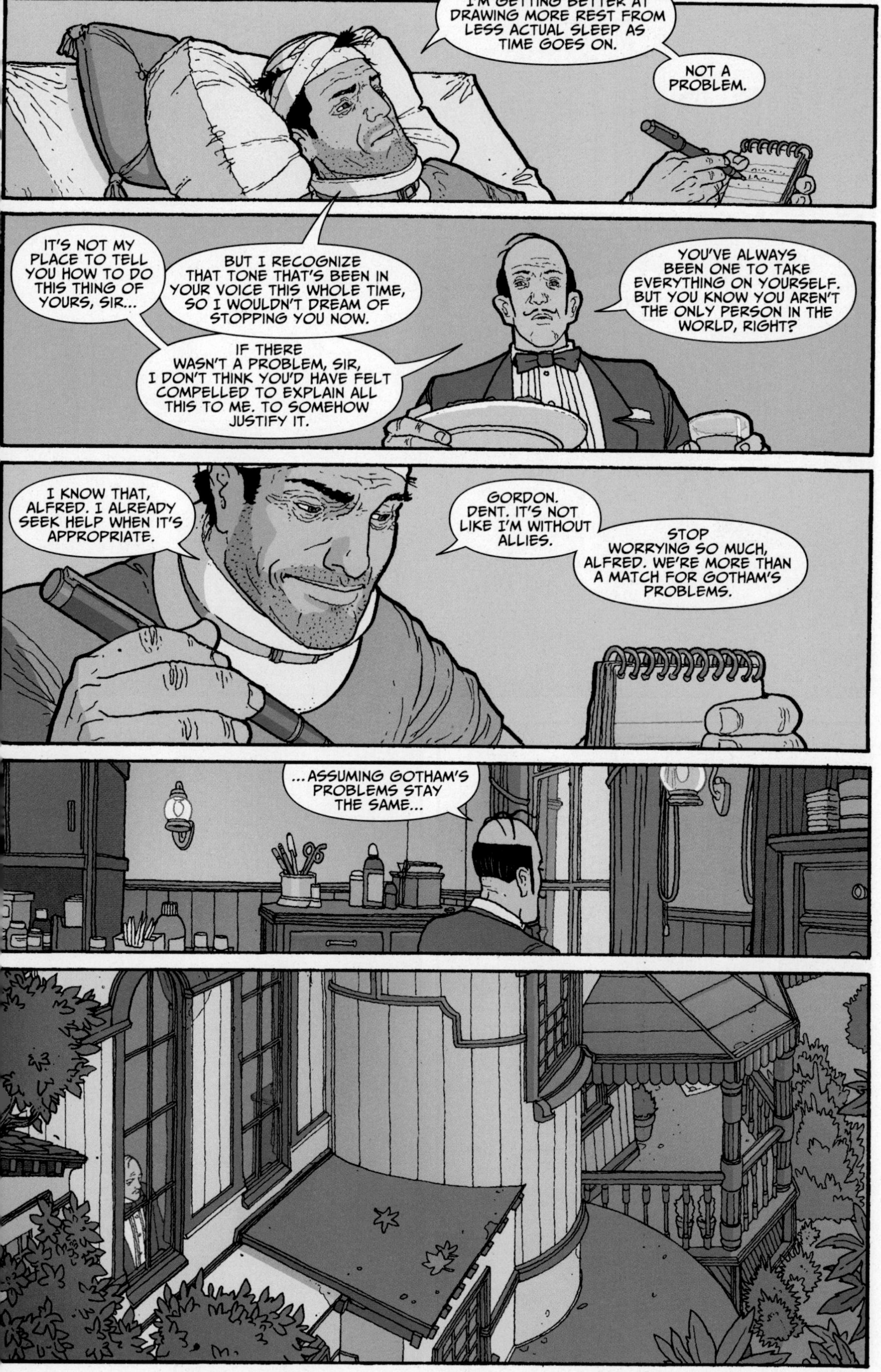
DOESN'T MATTER. I'M GETTING BETTER AT DRAWING MORE REST FROM LESS ACTUAL SLEEP AS TIME GOES ON.
NOT A PROBLEM.
IT'S NOT MY PLACE TO TELL YOU HOW TO DO THIS THING OF YOURS, SIR...
BUT I RECOGNIZE THAT TONE THAT'S BEEN IN YOUR VOICE THIS WHOLE TIME, SO I WOULDN'T DREAM OF STOPPING YOU NOW.
IF THERE WASN'T A PROBLEM, SIR, I DON'T THINK YOU'D HAVE FELT COMPELLED TO EXPLAIN ALL THIS TO ME. TO SOMEHOW JUSTIFY IT.
YOU'VE ALWAYS BEEN ONE TO TAKE EVERYTHING ON YOURSELF. BUT YOU KNOW YOU AREN'T THE ONLY PERSON IN THE WORLD, RIGHT?
I KNOW THAT, ALFRED. I ALREADY SEEK HELP WHEN IT'S APPROPRIATE.
GORDON. DENT. IT'S NOT LIKE I'M WITHOUT ALLIES.
STOP WORRYING SO MUCH, ALFRED. WE'RE MORE THAN A MATCH FOR GOTHAM'S PROBLEMS.
...ASSUMING GOTHAM'S PROBLEMS STAY THE SAME...

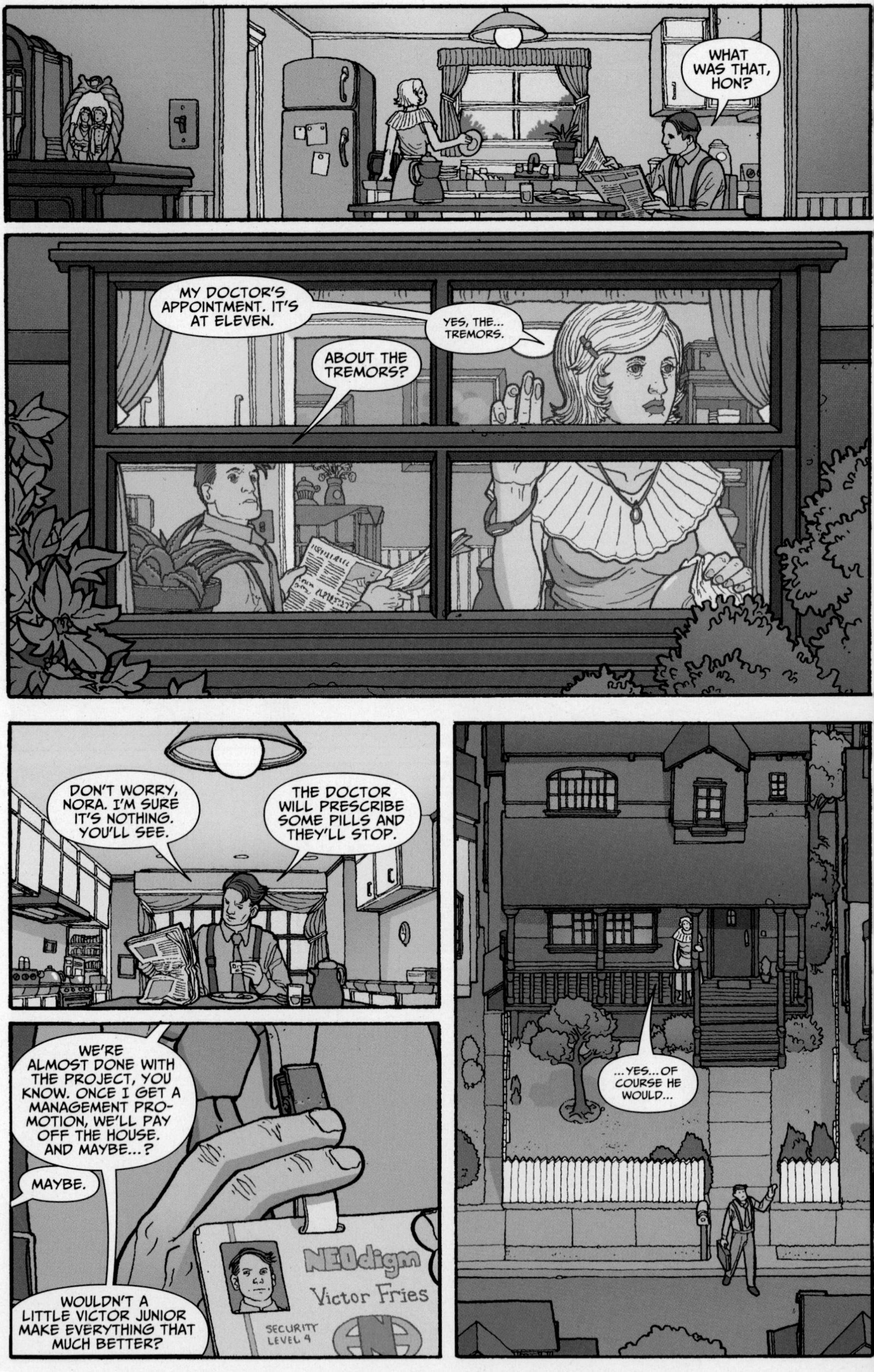
WHAT WAS THAT, HON?
MY DOCTOR'S APPOINTMENT. IT'S AT ELEVEN.
ABOUT THE TREMORS?
YES, THE... TREMORS.
DON'T WORRY, NORA. I'M SURE IT'S NOTHING. YOU'LL SEE.
THE DOCTOR WILL PRESCRIBE SOME PILLS AND THEY'LL STOP.
WE'RE ALMOST DONE WITH THE PROJECT, YOU KNOW. ONCE I GET A MANAGEMENT PROMOTION, WE'LL PAY OFF THE HOUSE. AND MAYBE...?
MAYBE.
WOULDN'T A LITTLE VICTOR JUNIOR MAKE EVERYTHING THAT MUCH BETTER?
NEOdigm
Victor Fries
SECURITY LEVEL 4
...YES... OF COURSE HE WOULD...

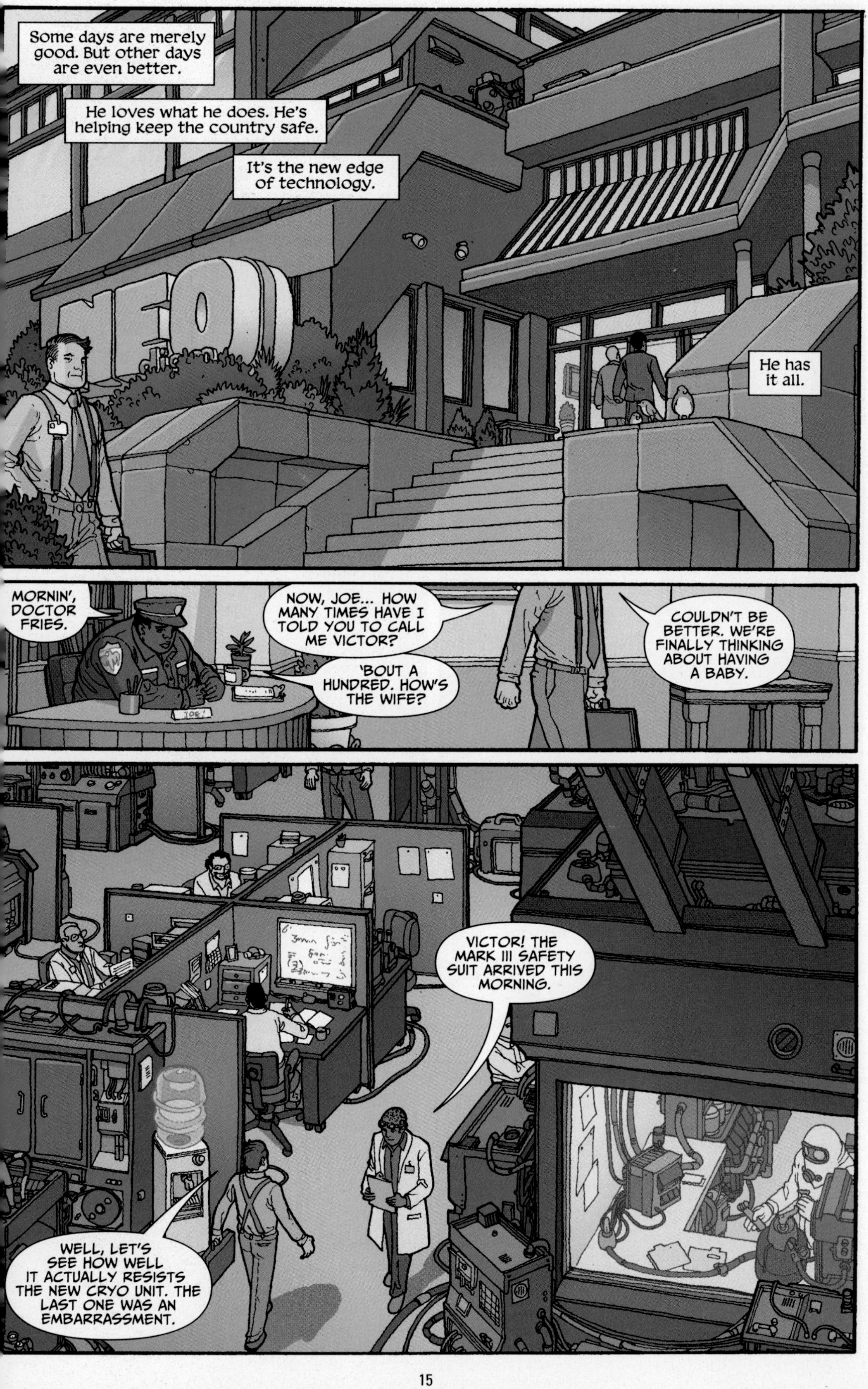
Some days are merely good. But other days are even better.
He loves what he does. He's helping keep the country safe.
It's the new edge of technology.
He has it all.
MORNIN', DOCTOR FRIES.
NOW, JOE... HOW MANY TIMES HAVE I TOLD YOU TO CALL ME VICTOR?
'BOUT A HUNDRED. HOW'S THE WIFE?
COULDN'T BE BETTER. WE'RE FINALLY THINKING ABOUT HAVING A BABY.
VICTOR! THE MARK III SAFETY SUIT ARRIVED THIS MORNING.
WELL, LET'S SEE HOW WELL IT ACTUALLY RESISTS THE NEW CRYO UNIT. THE LAST ONE WAS AN EMBARRASSMENT.

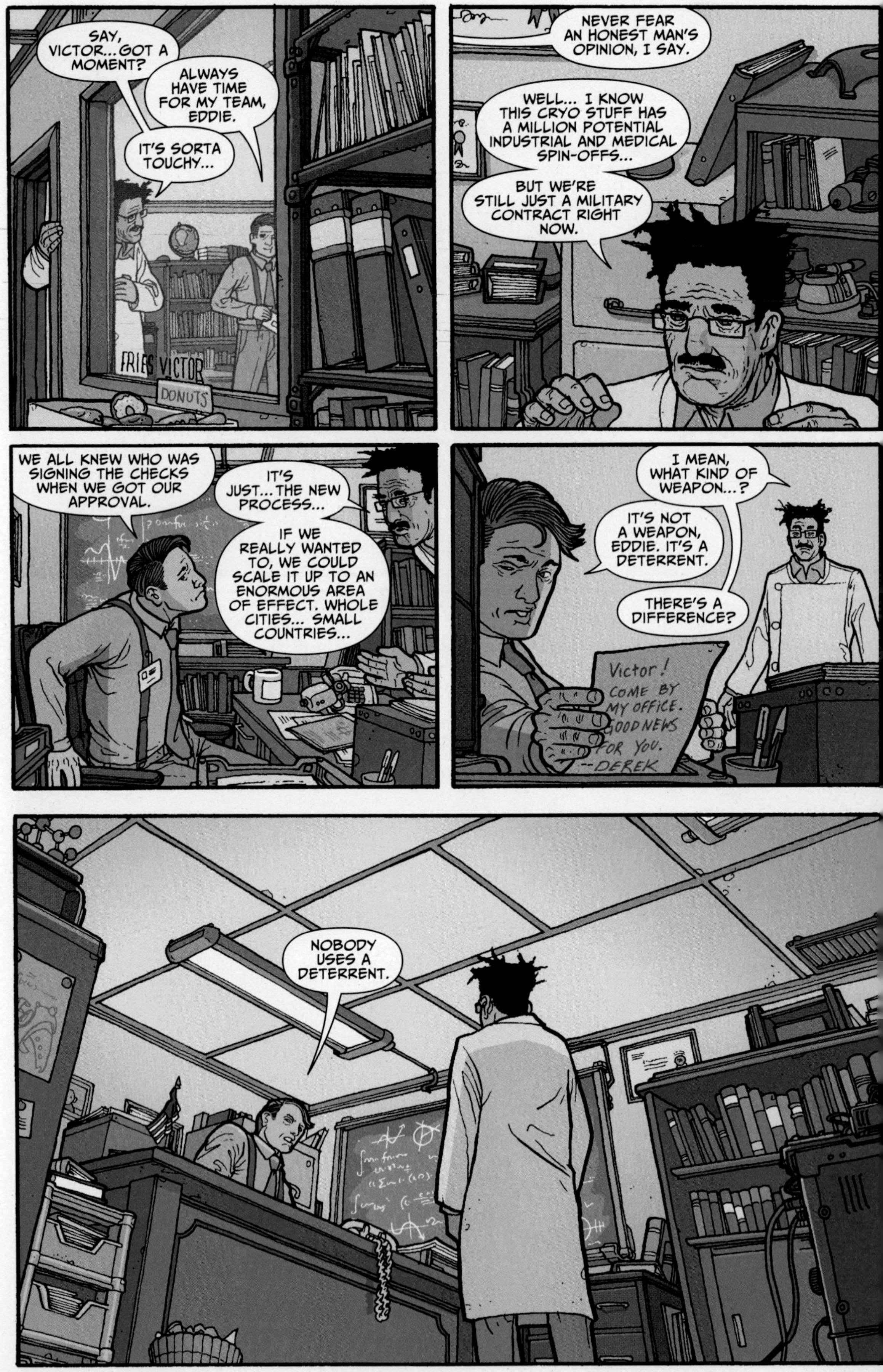
SAY, VICTOR... GOT A MOMENT?
ALWAYS HAVE TIME FOR MY TEAM, EDDIE.
IT'S SORTA TOUCHY...
FRIES VICTOR
DONUTS
NEVER FEAR AN HONEST MAN'S OPINION, I SAY.
WELL... I KNOW THIS CRYO STUFF HAS A MILLION POTENTIAL INDUSTRIAL AND MEDICAL SPIN-OFFS...
BUT WE'RE STILL JUST A MILITARY CONTRACT RIGHT NOW.
WE ALL KNEW WHO WAS SIGNING THE CHECKS WHEN WE GOT OUR APPROVAL.
IT'S JUST... THE NEW PROCESS...
IF WE REALLY WANTED TO, WE COULD SCALE IT UP TO AN ENORMOUS AREA OF EFFECT. WHOLE CITIES... SMALL COUNTRIES...
I MEAN, WHAT KIND OF WEAPON...?
IT'S NOT A WEAPON, EDDIE. IT'S A DETERRENT.
THERE'S A DIFFERENCE?
Victor! COME BY MY OFFICE. GOOD NEWS FOR YOU. --DEREK
NOBODY USES A DETERRENT.

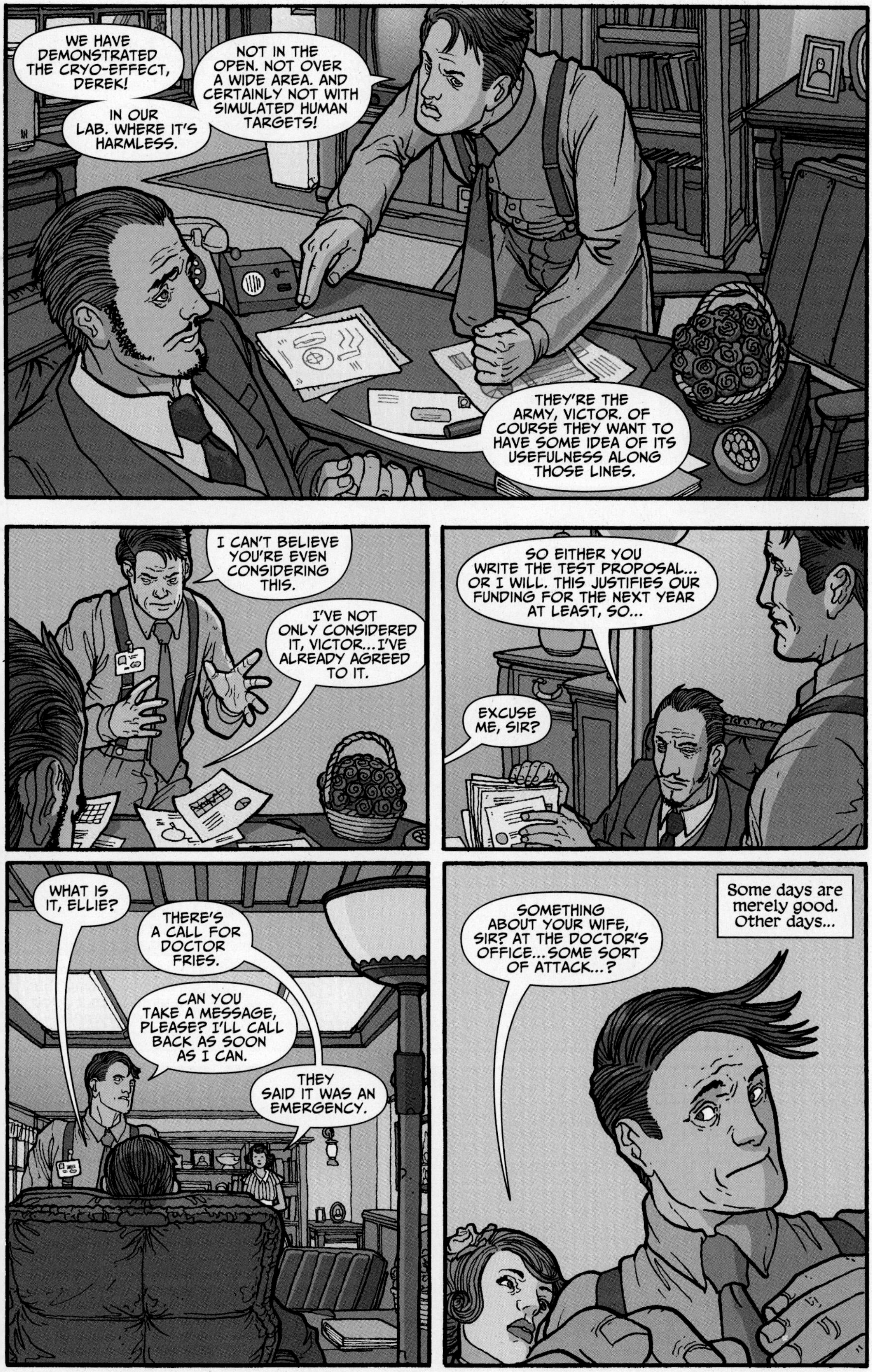
WE HAVE DEMONSTRATED THE CRYO-EFFECT, DEREK!
IN OUR LAB. WHERE IT'S HARMLESS.
NOT IN THE OPEN. NOT OVER A WIDE AREA. AND CERTAINLY NOT WITH SIMULATED HUMAN TARGETS!
THEY'RE THE ARMY, VICTOR. OF COURSE THEY WANT TO HAVE SOME IDEA OF ITS USEFULNESS ALONG THOSE LINES.
I CAN'T BELIEVE YOU'RE EVEN CONSIDERING THIS.
I'VE NOT ONLY CONSIDERED IT, VICTOR...I'VE ALREADY AGREED TO IT.
SO EITHER YOU WRITE THE TEST PROPOSAL... OR I WILL. THIS JUSTIFIES OUR FUNDING FOR THE NEXT YEAR AT LEAST, SO...
EXCUSE ME, SIR?
WHAT IS IT, ELLIE?
THERE'S A CALL FOR DOCTOR FRIES.
CAN YOU TAKE A MESSAGE, PLEASE? I'LL CALL BACK AS SOON AS I CAN.
THEY SAID IT WAS AN EMERGENCY.
Some days are merely good. Other days...
SOMETHING ABOUT YOUR WIFE, SIR? AT THE DOCTOR'S OFFICE... SOME SORT OF ATTACK...?

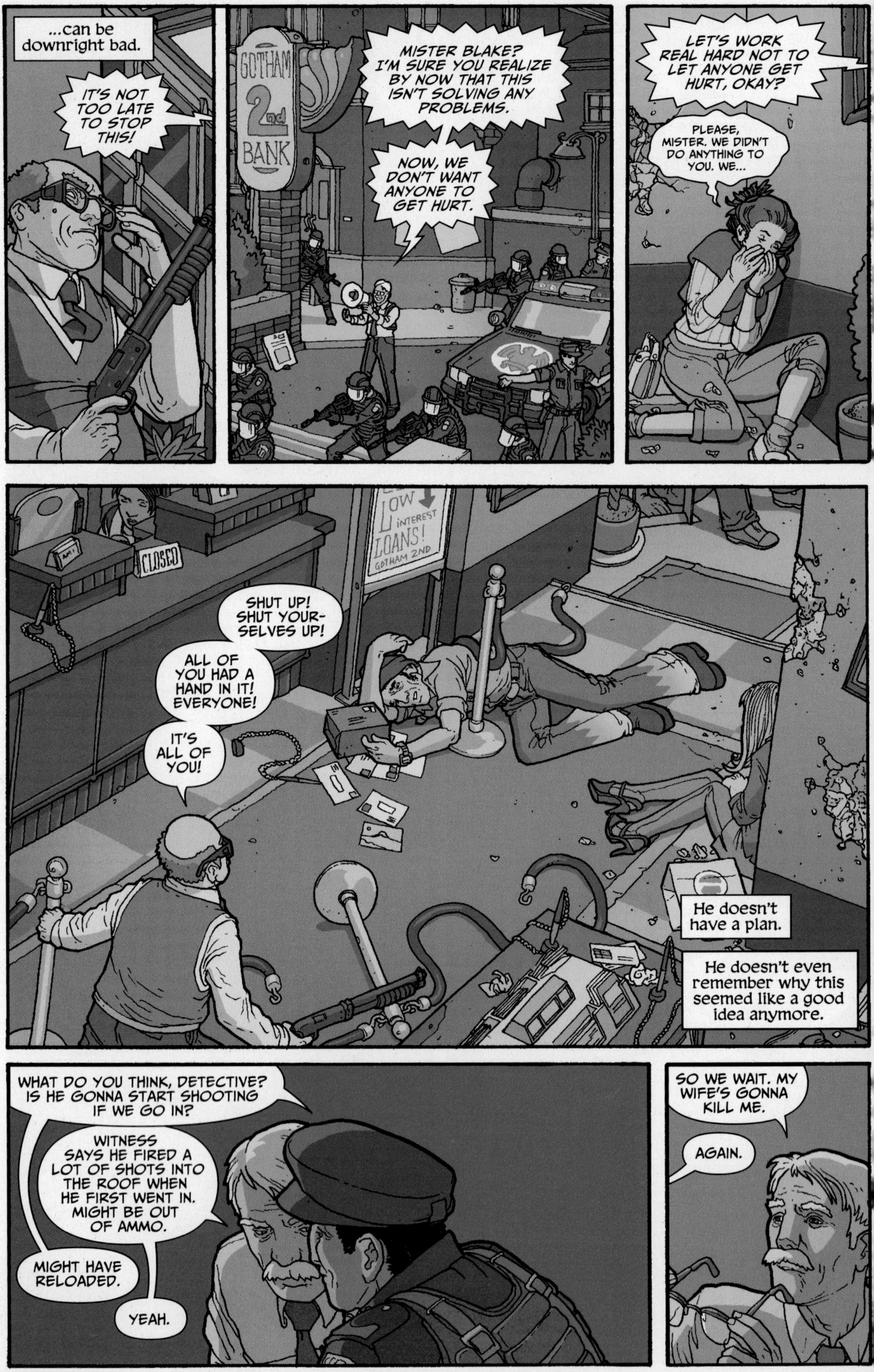
...can be downright bad.
IT'S NOT TOO LATE TO STOP THIS!
GOTHAM 2nd BANK
MISTER BLAKE? I'M SURE YOU REALIZE BY NOW THAT THIS ISN'T SOLVING ANY PROBLEMS.
NOW, WE DON'T WANT ANYONE TO GET HURT.
LET'S WORK REAL HARD NOT TO LET ANYONE GET HURT, OKAY?
PLEASE, MISTER. WE DIDN'T DO ANYTHING TO YOU. WE...
LOW INTEREST LOANS! GOTHAM 2ND
CLOSED
SHUT UP! SHUT YOURSELVES UP!
ALL OF YOU HAD A HAND IN IT! EVERYONE!
IT'S ALL OF YOU!
He doesn't have a plan.
He doesn't even remember why this seemed like a good idea anymore.
WHAT DO YOU THINK, DETECTIVE? IS HE GONNA START SHOOTING IF WE GO IN?
WITNESS SAYS HE FIRED A LOT OF SHOTS INTO THE ROOF WHEN HE FIRST WENT IN. MIGHT BE OUT OF AMMO.
MIGHT HAVE RELOADED.
YEAH.
SO WE WAIT. MY WIFE'S GONNA KILL ME.
AGAIN.

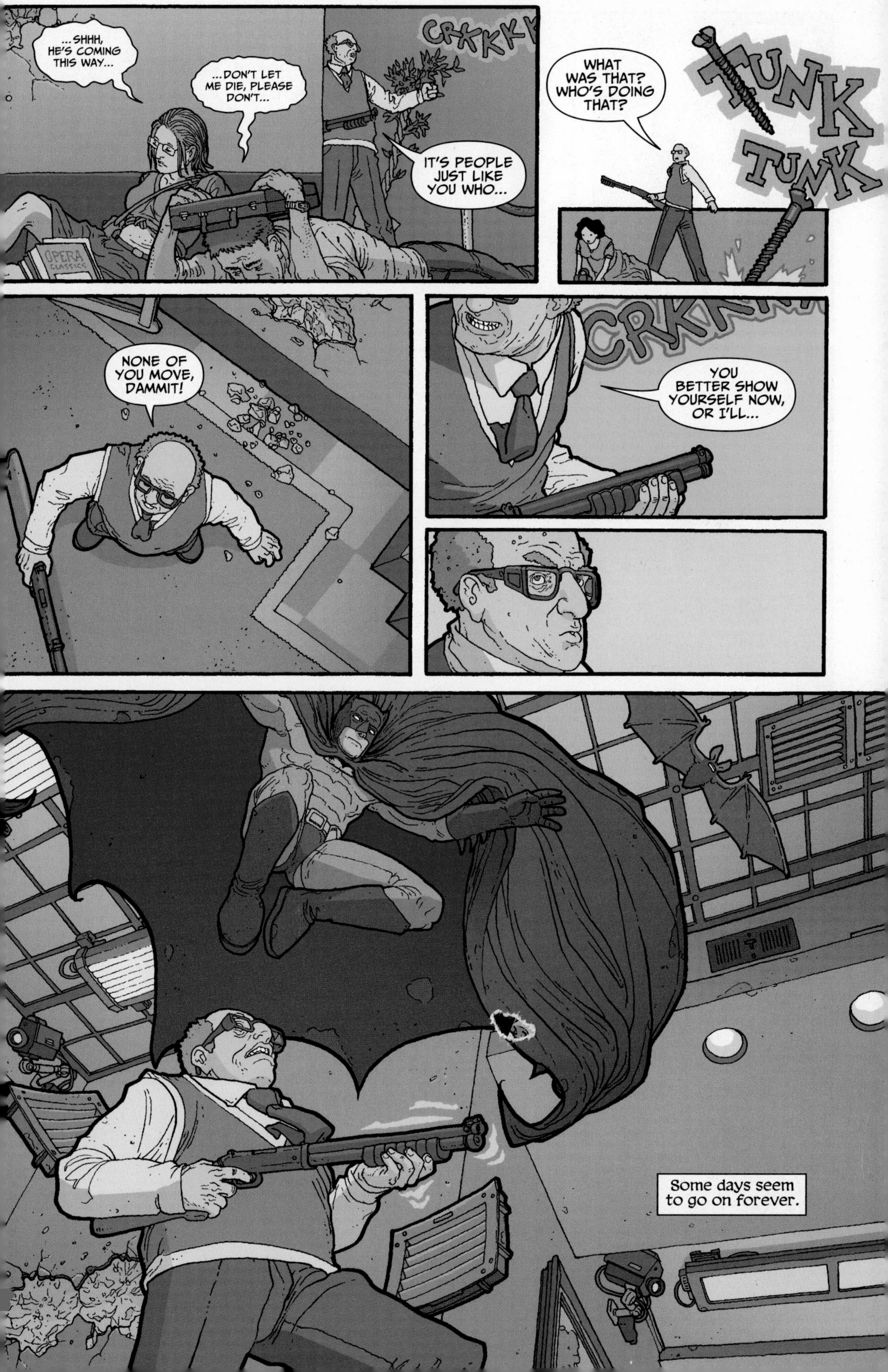
...SHHH, HE'S COMING THIS WAY...
...DON'T LET ME DIE, PLEASE DON'T...
OPERA CLASSICS
CRKKKK
IT'S PEOPLE JUST LIKE YOU WHO...
WHAT WAS THAT? WHO'S DOING THAT?
TUNK
TUNK
NONE OF YOU MOVE, DAMMIT!
CRKKKK
YOU BETTER SHOW YOURSELF NOW, OR I'LL...
Some days seem to go on forever.

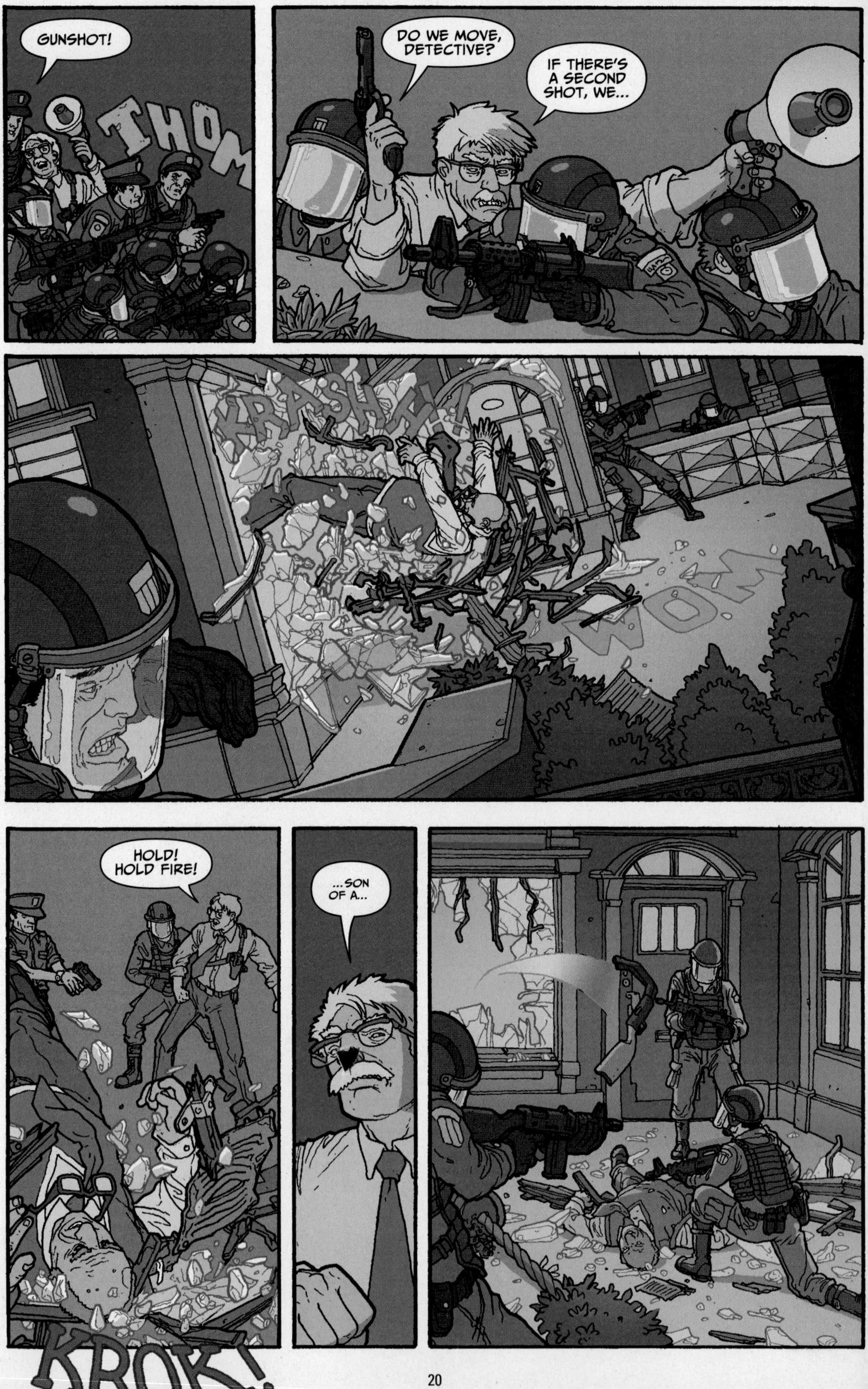
GUNSHOT!
THOM
DO WE MOVE, DETECTIVE?
IF THERE'S A SECOND SHOT, WE...
KRASHH!
WOM
HOLD! HOLD FIRE!
KROK!
...SON OF A...

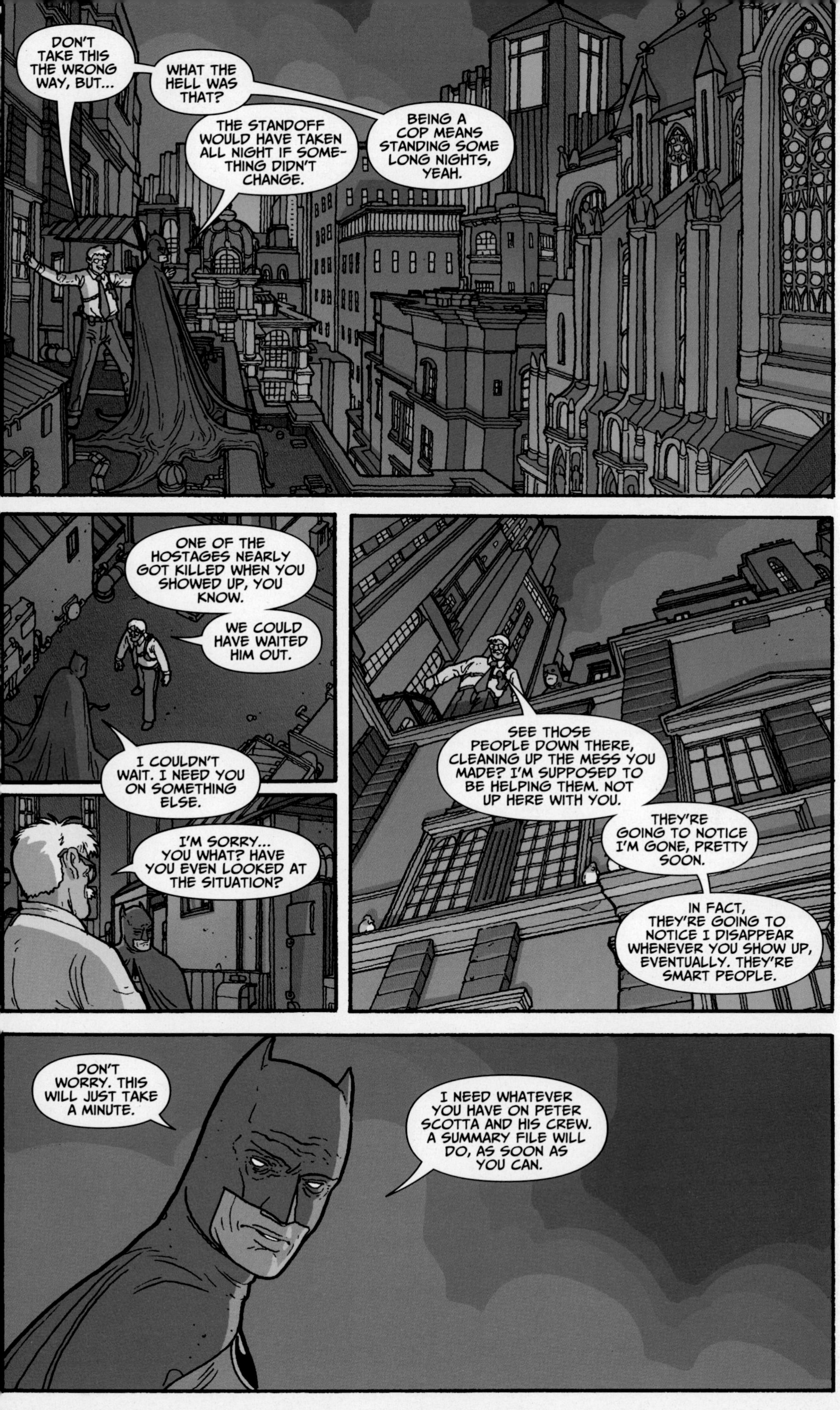
DON'T TAKE THIS THE WRONG WAY, BUT...
WHAT THE HELL WAS THAT?
THE STANDOFF WOULD HAVE TAKEN ALL NIGHT IF SOMETHING DIDN'T CHANGE.
BEING A COP MEANS STANDING SOME LONG NIGHTS, YEAH.
ONE OF THE HOSTAGES NEARLY GOT KILLED WHEN YOU SHOWED UP, YOU KNOW.
WE COULD HAVE WAITED HIM OUT.
I COULDN'T WAIT. I NEED YOU ON SOMETHING ELSE.
I'M SORRY... YOU WHAT? HAVE YOU EVEN LOOKED AT THE SITUATION?
SEE THOSE PEOPLE DOWN THERE, CLEANING UP THE MESS YOU MADE? I'M SUPPOSED TO BE HELPING THEM. NOT UP HERE WITH YOU.
THEY'RE GOING TO NOTICE I'M GONE, PRETTY SOON.
IN FACT, THEY'RE GOING TO NOTICE I DISAPPEAR WHENEVER YOU SHOW UP, EVENTUALLY. THEY'RE SMART PEOPLE.
DON'T WORRY. THIS WILL JUST TAKE A MINUTE.
I NEED WHATEVER YOU HAVE ON PETER SCOTTA AND HIS CREW. A SUMMARY FILE WILL DO, AS SOON AS YOU CAN.

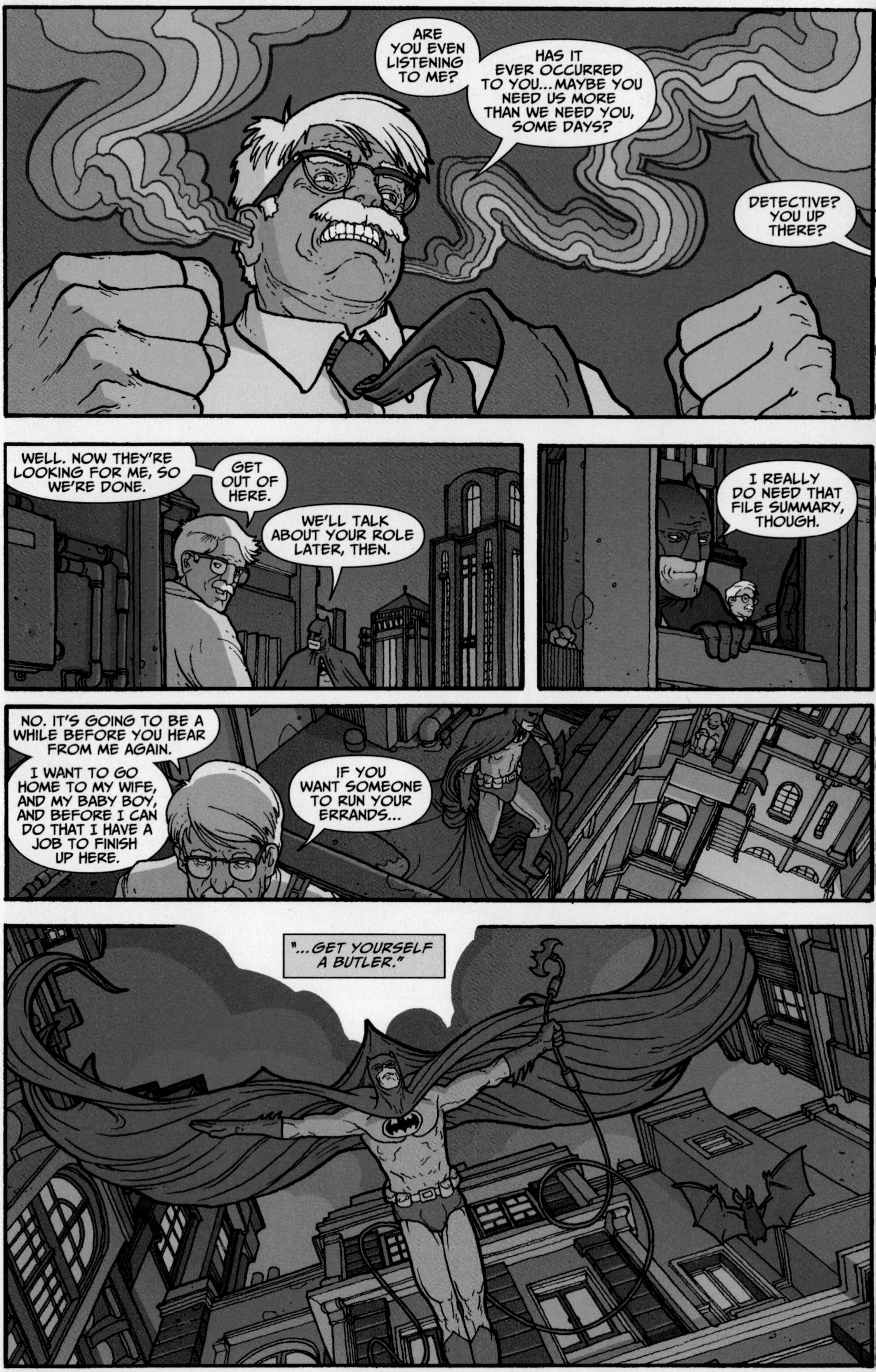
ARE YOU EVEN LISTENING TO ME?
HAS IT EVER OCCURRED TO YOU...MAYBE YOU NEED US MORE THAN WE NEED YOU, SOME DAYS?
DETECTIVE? YOU UP THERE?
WELL. NOW THEY'RE LOOKING FOR ME, SO WE'RE DONE.
GET OUT OF HERE.
WE'LL TALK ABOUT YOUR ROLE LATER, THEN.
I REALLY DO NEED THAT FILE SUMMARY, THOUGH.
NO. IT'S GOING TO BE A WHILE BEFORE YOU HEAR FROM ME AGAIN.
I WANT TO GO HOME TO MY WIFE, AND MY BABY BOY, AND BEFORE I CAN DO THAT I HAVE A JOB TO FINISH UP HERE.
IF YOU WANT SOMEONE TO RUN YOUR ERRANDS...
"...GET YOURSELF A BUTLER."

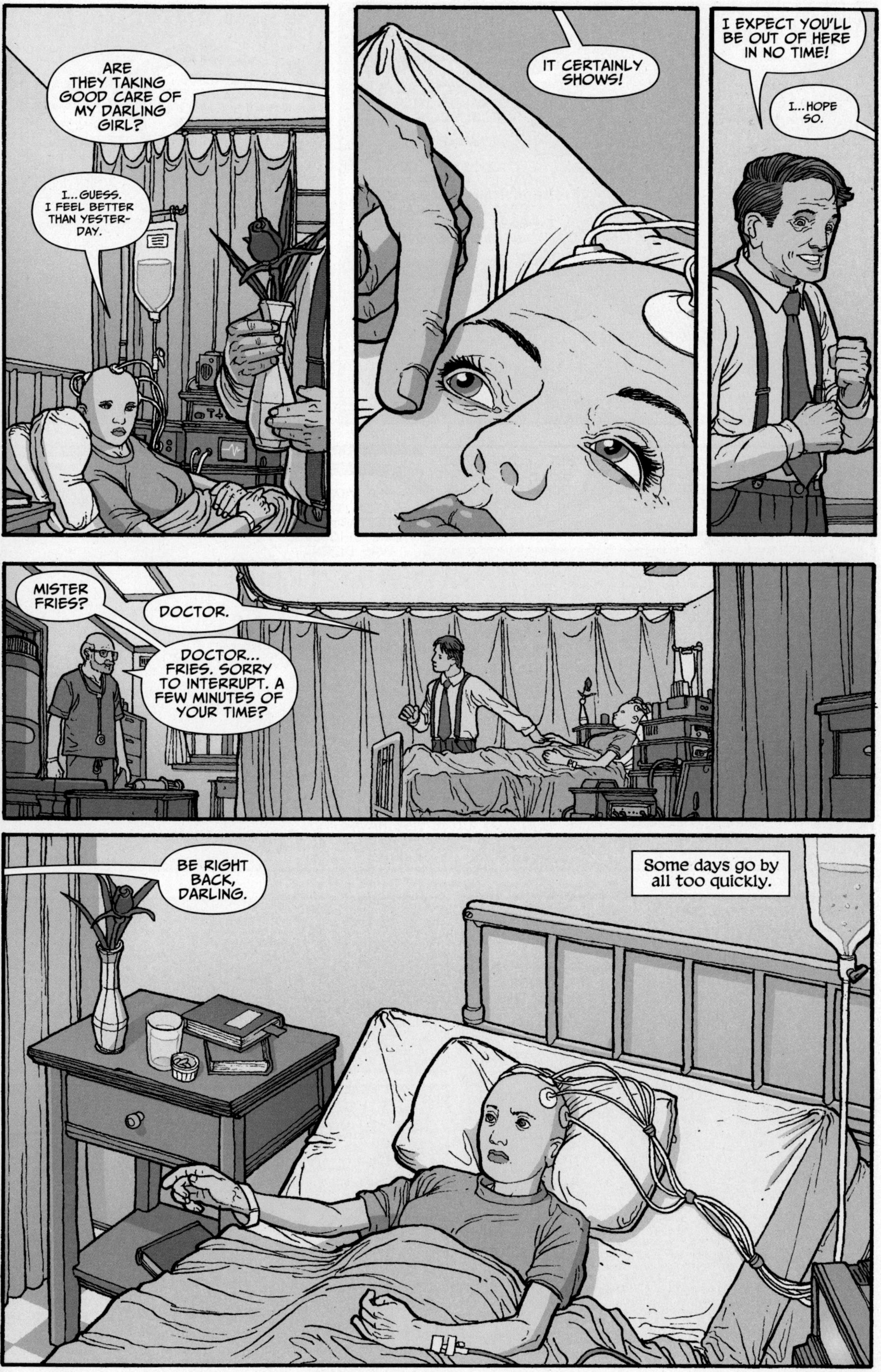
ARE THEY TAKING GOOD CARE OF MY DARLING GIRL?
I...GUESS. I FEEL BETTER THAN YESTER-DAY.
IT CERTAINLY SHOWS!
I EXPECT YOU'LL BE OUT OF HERE IN NO TIME!
I...HOPE SO.
MISTER FRIES?
DOCTOR.
DOCTOR... FRIES. SORRY TO INTERRUPT. A FEW MINUTES OF YOUR TIME?
BE RIGHT BACK, DARLING.
Some days go by all too quickly.

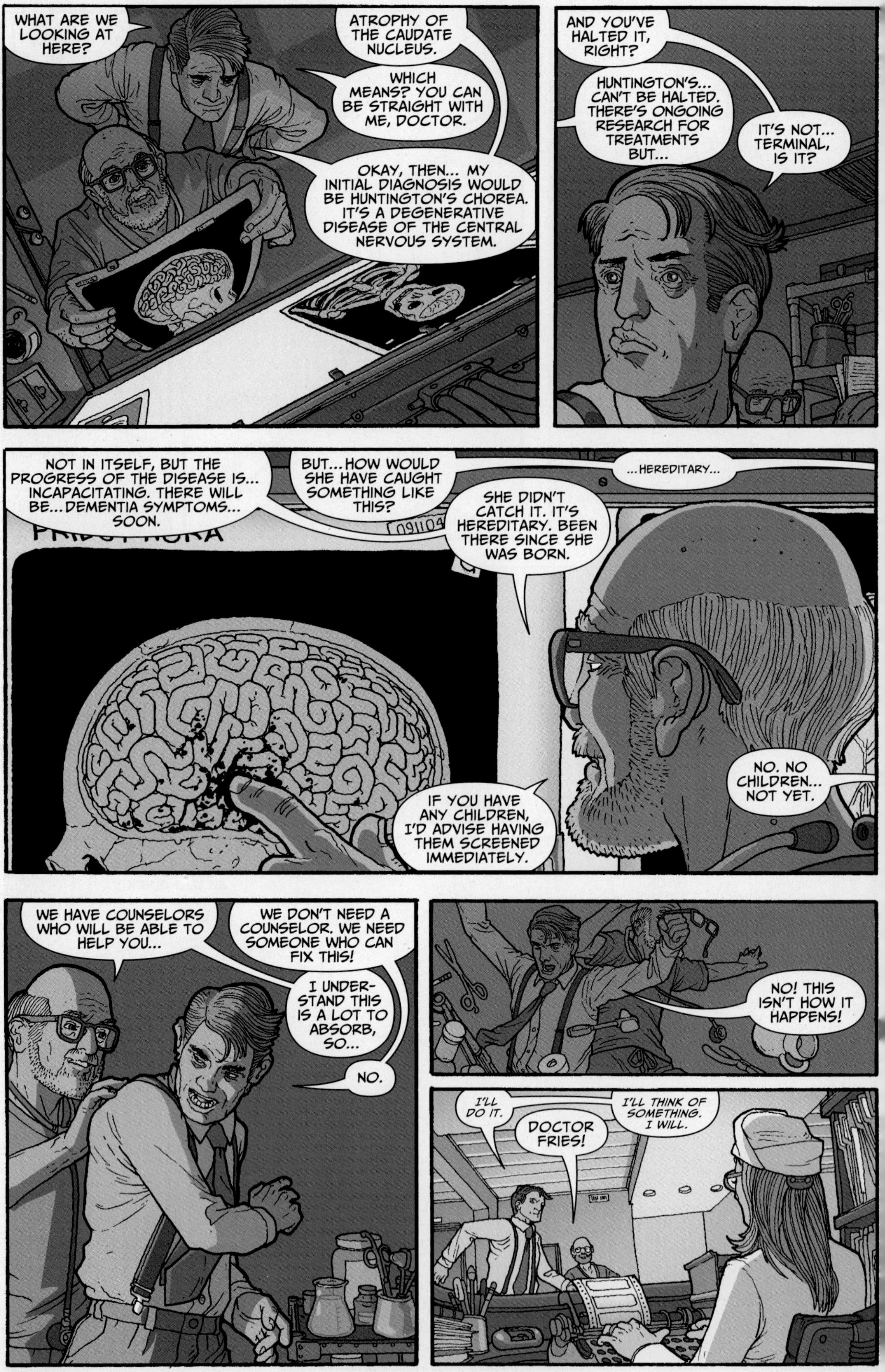
WHAT ARE WE LOOKING AT HERE?
ATROPHY OF THE CAUDATE NUCLEUS.
WHICH MEANS? YOU CAN BE STRAIGHT WITH ME, DOCTOR.
OKAY, THEN... MY INITIAL DIAGNOSIS WOULD BE HUNTINGTON'S CHOREA. IT'S A DEGENERATIVE DISEASE OF THE CENTRAL NERVOUS SYSTEM.
AND YOU'VE HALTED IT, RIGHT?
HUNTINGTON'S... CAN'T BE HALTED. THERE'S ONGOING RESEARCH FOR TREATMENTS BUT...
IT'S NOT... TERMINAL, IS IT?
NOT IN ITSELF, BUT THE PROGRESS OF THE DISEASE IS... INCAPACITATING. THERE WILL BE... DEMENTIA SYMPTOMS... SOON.
BUT... HOW WOULD SHE HAVE CAUGHT SOMETHING LIKE THIS?
SHE DIDN'T CATCH IT. IT'S HEREDITARY. BEEN THERE SINCE SHE WAS BORN.
...HEREDITARY...
IF YOU HAVE ANY CHILDREN, I'D ADVISE HAVING THEM SCREENED IMMEDIATELY.
NO. NO CHILDREN... NOT YET.
WE HAVE COUNSELORS WHO WILL BE ABLE TO HELP YOU...
WE DON'T NEED A COUNSELOR. WE NEED SOMEONE WHO CAN FIX THIS!
I UNDERSTAND THIS IS A LOT TO ABSORB, SO...
NO.
NO! THIS ISN'T HOW IT HAPPENS!
I'LL DO IT.
DOCTOR FRIES!
I'LL THINK OF SOMETHING. I WILL.

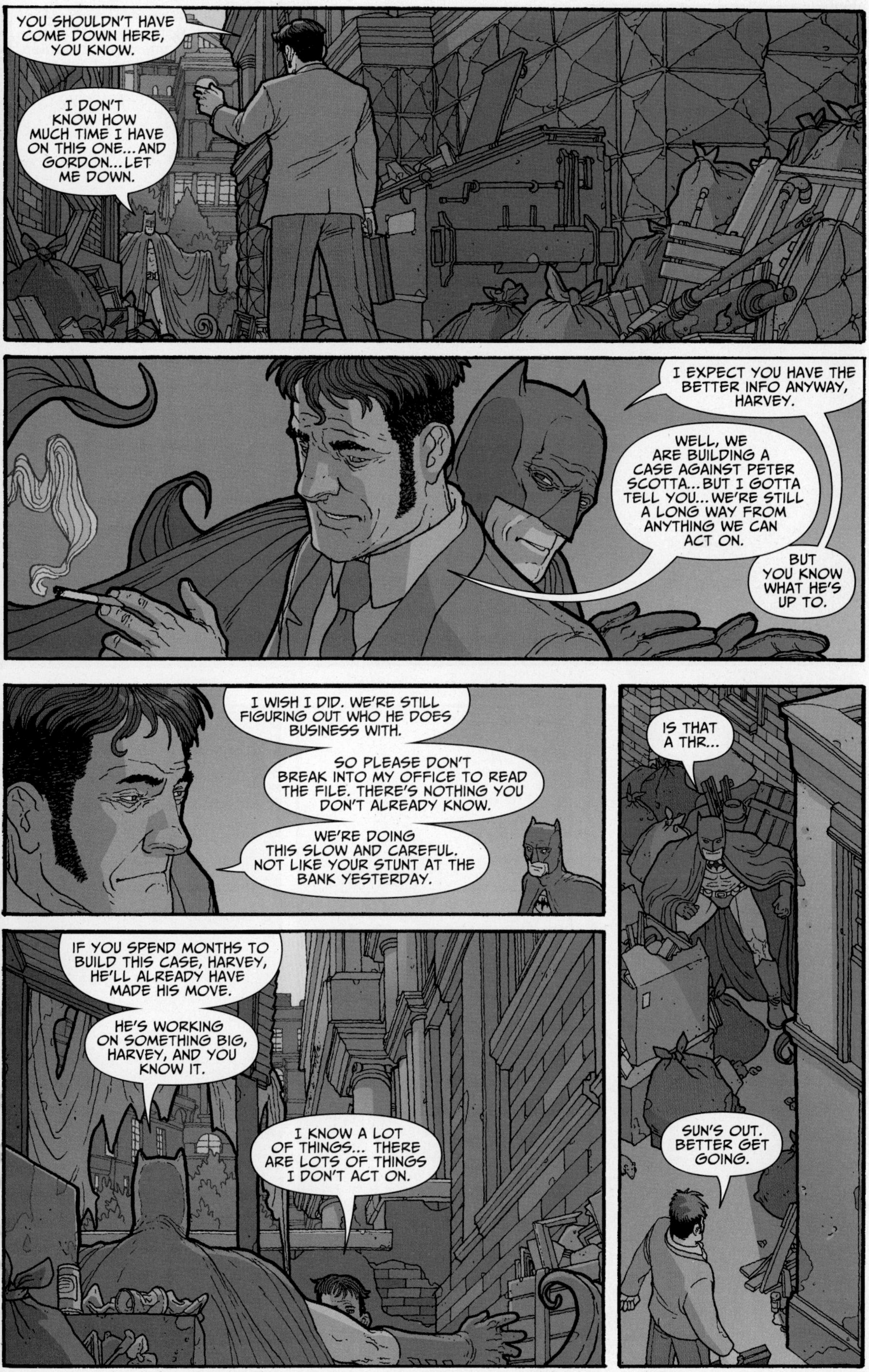
YOU SHOULDN'T HAVE COME DOWN HERE, YOU KNOW.
I DON'T KNOW HOW MUCH TIME I HAVE ON THIS ONE... AND GORDON... LET ME DOWN.
I EXPECT YOU HAVE THE BETTER INFO ANYWAY, HARVEY.
WELL, WE ARE BUILDING A CASE AGAINST PETER SCOTTA... BUT I GOTTA TELL YOU... WE'RE STILL A LONG WAY FROM ANYTHING WE CAN ACT ON.
BUT YOU KNOW WHAT HE'S UP TO.
I WISH I DID. WE'RE STILL FIGURING OUT WHO HE DOES BUSINESS WITH.
SO PLEASE DON'T BREAK INTO MY OFFICE TO READ THE FILE. THERE'S NOTHING YOU DON'T ALREADY KNOW.
WE'RE DOING THIS SLOW AND CAREFUL. NOT LIKE YOUR STUNT AT THE BANK YESTERDAY.
IF YOU SPEND MONTHS TO BUILD THIS CASE, HARVEY, HE'LL ALREADY HAVE MADE HIS MOVE.
HE'S WORKING ON SOMETHING BIG, HARVEY, AND YOU KNOW IT.
I KNOW A LOT OF THINGS... THERE ARE LOTS OF THINGS I DON'T ACT ON.
IS THAT A THR...
SUN'S OUT. BETTER GET GOING.

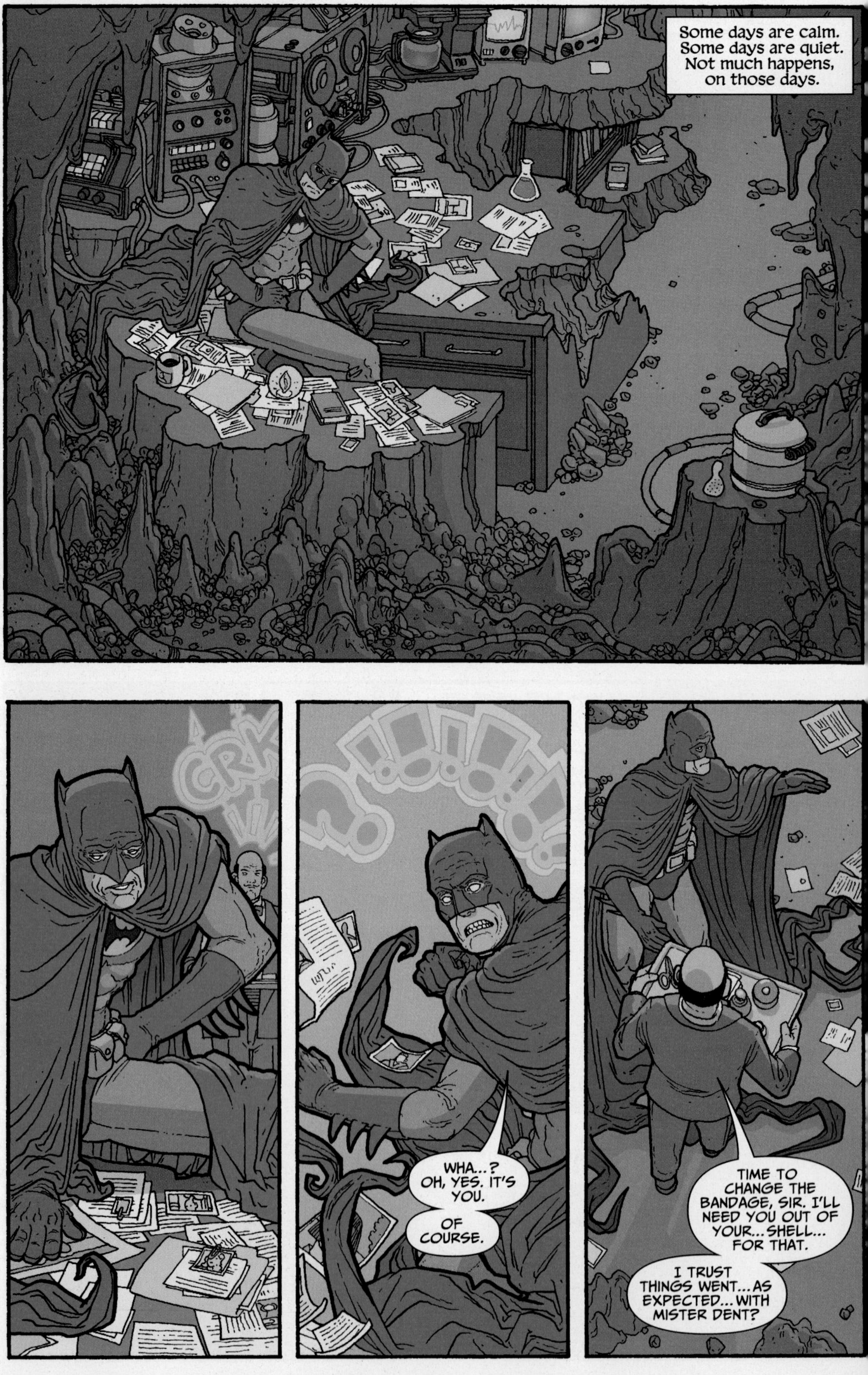
Some days are calm. Some days are quiet. Not much happens, on those days.
WHA...? OH, YES. IT'S YOU.
OF COURSE.
TIME TO CHANGE THE BANDAGE, SIR. I'LL NEED YOU OUT OF YOUR...SHELL... FOR THAT.
I TRUST THINGS WENT...AS EXPECTED...WITH MISTER DENT?

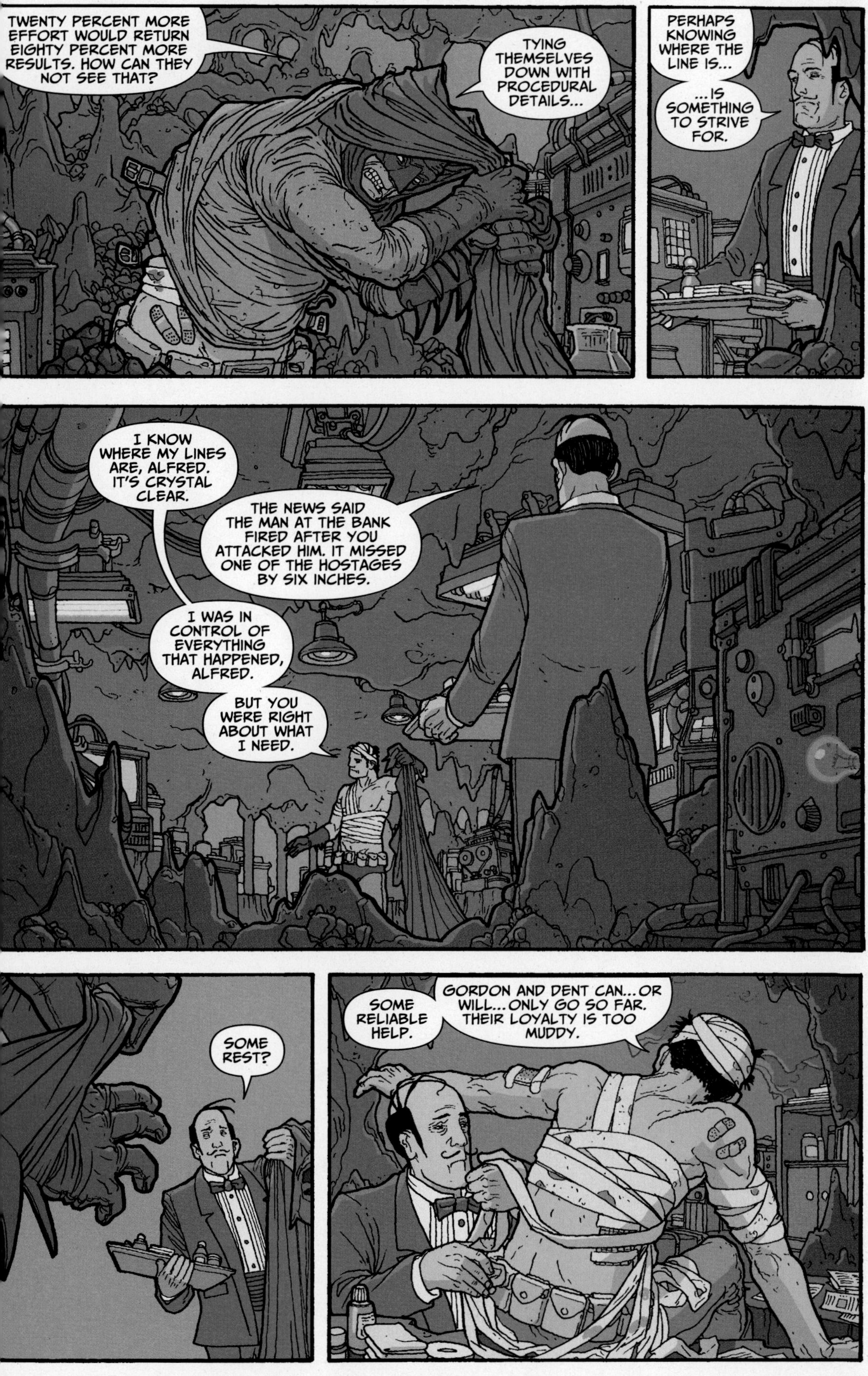
TWENTY PERCENT MORE EFFORT WOULD RETURN EIGHTY PERCENT MORE RESULTS. HOW CAN THEY NOT SEE THAT?
TYING THEMSELVES DOWN WITH PROCEDURAL DETAILS...
PERHAPS KNOWING WHERE THE LINE IS...
...IS SOMETHING TO STRIVE FOR.
I KNOW WHERE MY LINES ARE, ALFRED. IT'S CRYSTAL CLEAR.
THE NEWS SAID THE MAN AT THE BANK FIRED AFTER YOU ATTACKED HIM. IT MISSED ONE OF THE HOSTAGES BY SIX INCHES.
I WAS IN CONTROL OF EVERYTHING THAT HAPPENED, ALFRED.
BUT YOU WERE RIGHT ABOUT WHAT I NEED.
SOME REST?
SOME RELIABLE HELP.
GORDON AND DENT CAN...OR WILL...ONLY GO SO FAR. THEIR LOYALTY IS TOO MUDDY.

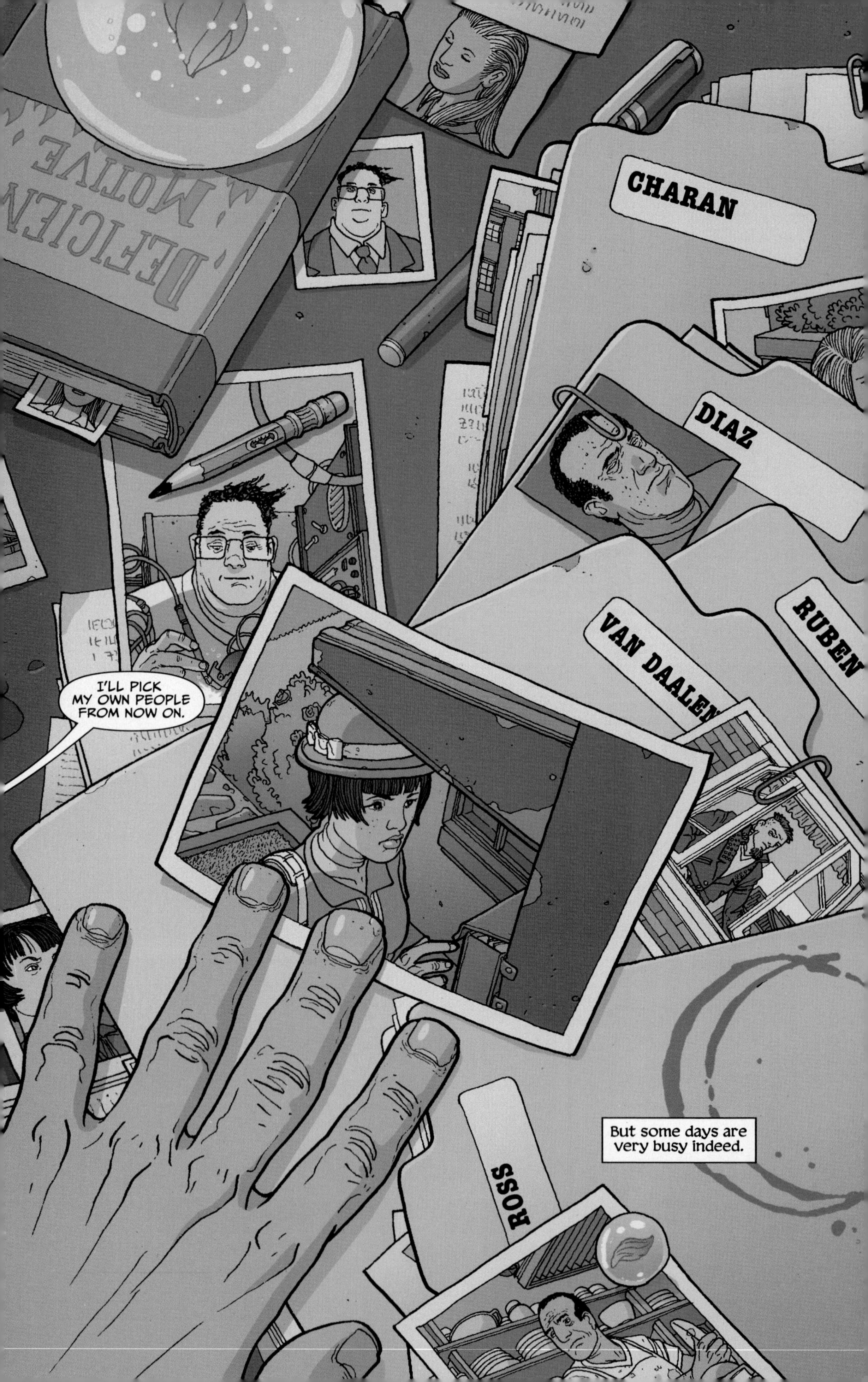
DEFICIEN MOTIVE
CHARAN
DIAZ
VAN DAALEN
RUBEN
I'LL PICK MY OWN PEOPLE FROM NOW ON.
But some days are very busy indeed.
ROSS

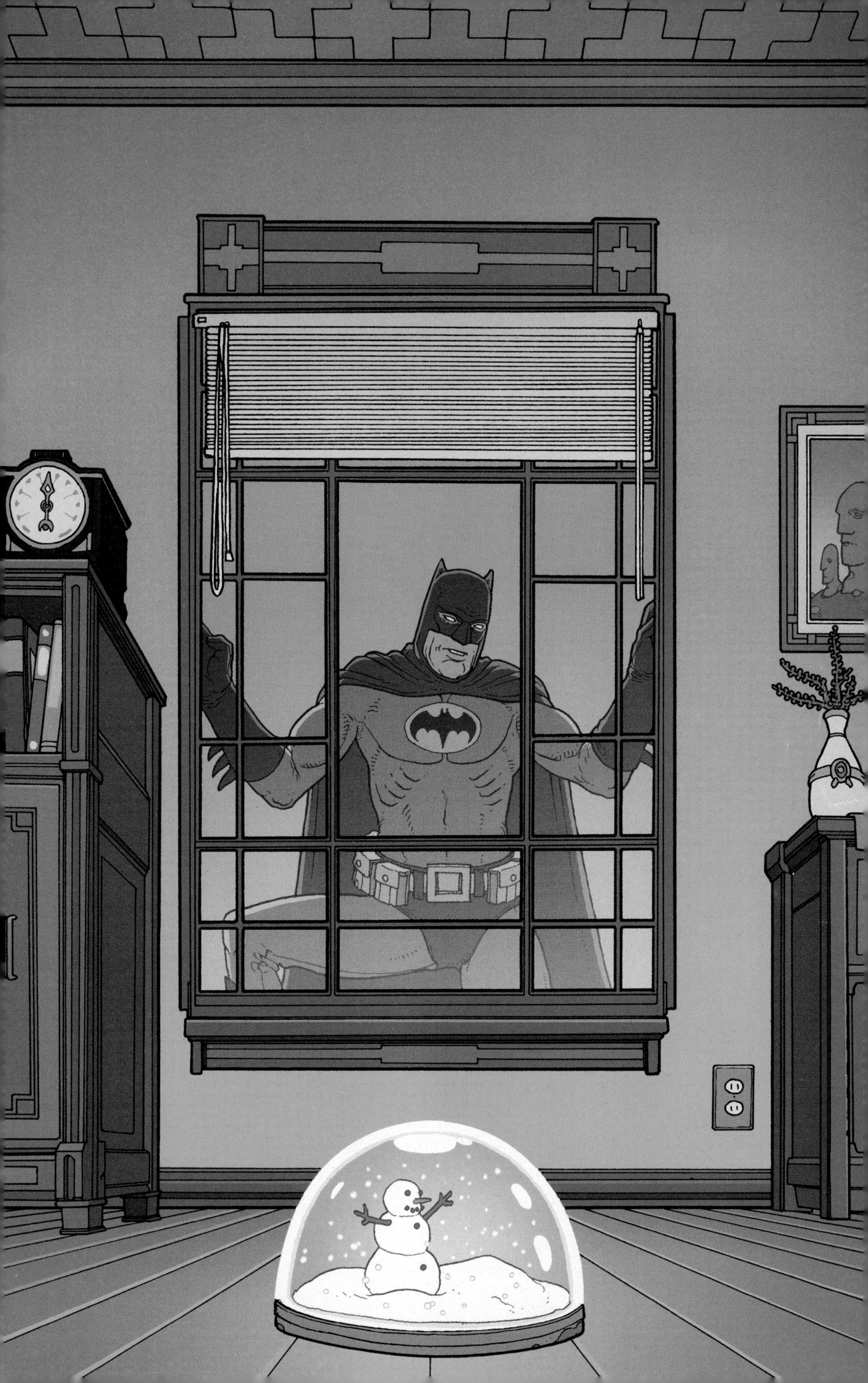

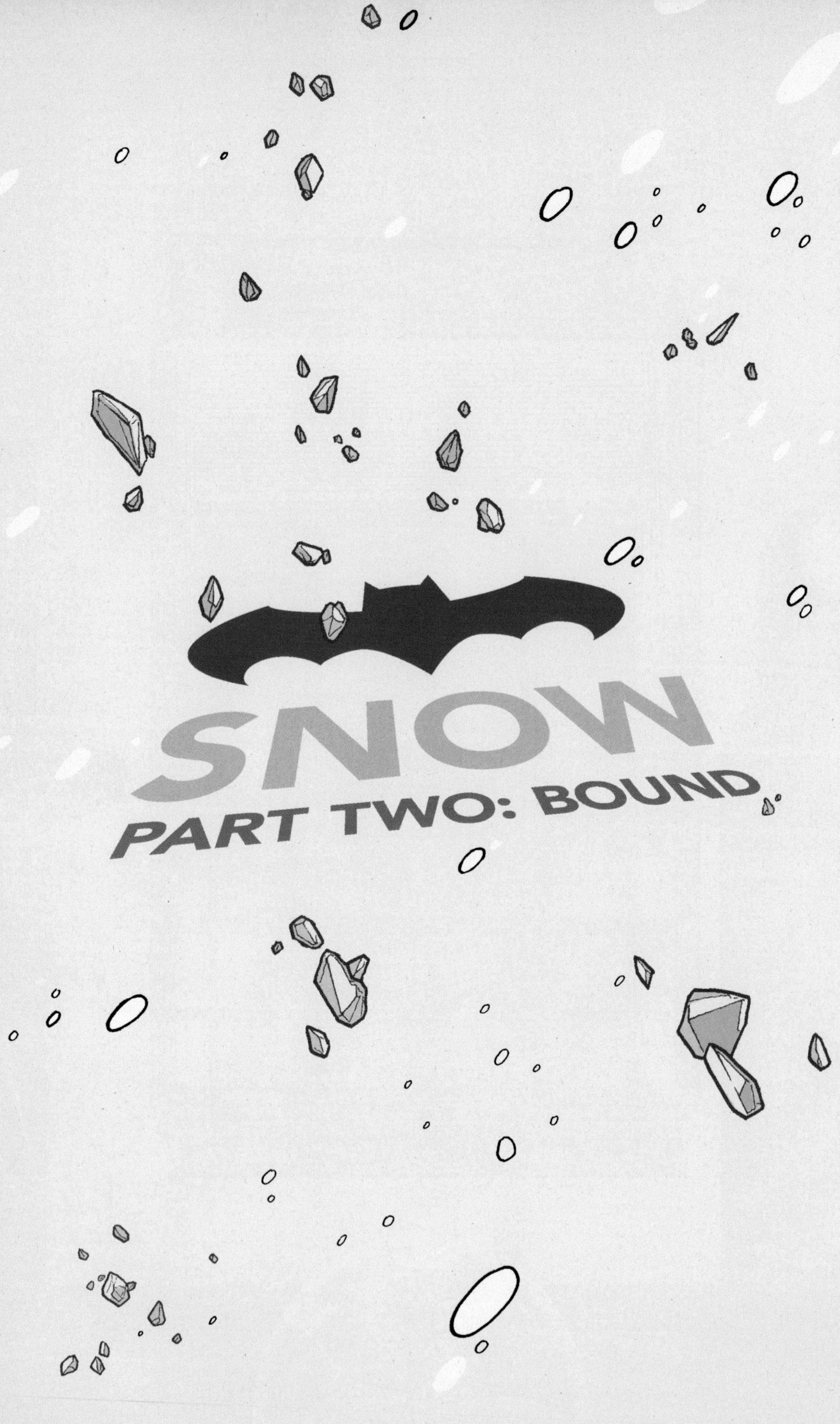
SNOW
PART TWO: BOUND

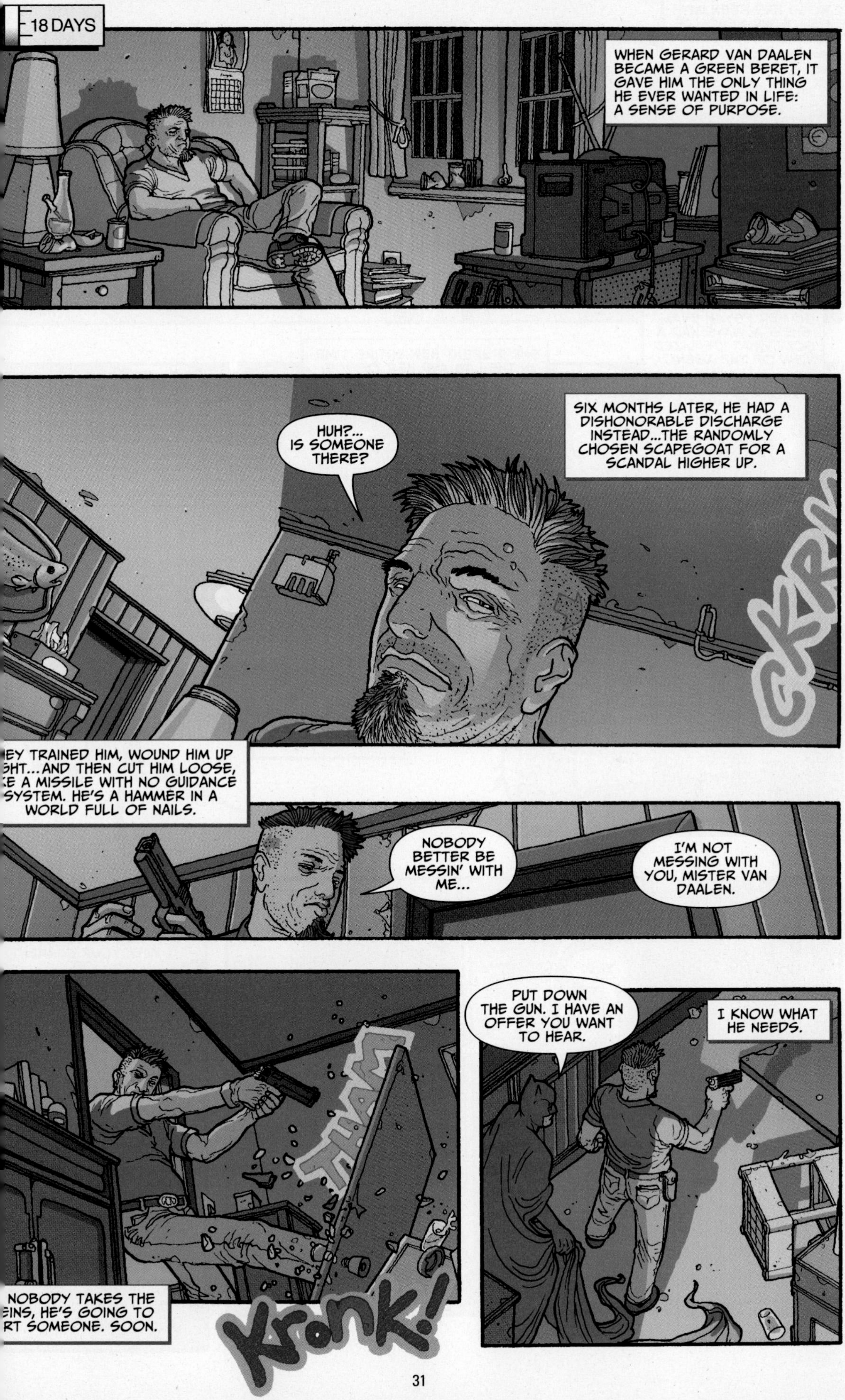

18 DAYS
WHEN GERARD VAN DAALEN BECAME A GREEN BERET, IT GAVE HIM THE ONLY THING HE EVER WANTED IN LIFE: A SENSE OF PURPOSE.
SIX MONTHS LATER, HE HAD A DISHONORABLE DISCHARGE INSTEAD...THE RANDOMLY CHOSEN SCAPEGOAT FOR A SCANDAL HIGHER UP.
HUH?... IS SOMEONE THERE?
EY TRAINED HIM, WOUND HIM UP GHT... AND THEN CUT HIM LOOSE, E A MISSILE WITH NO GUIDANCE SYSTEM. HE'S A HAMMER IN A WORLD FULL OF NAILS.
NOBODY BETTER BE MESSIN' WITH ME...
I'M NOT MESSING WITH YOU, MISTER VAN DAALEN.
THWAM
NOBODY TAKES THE EINS, HE'S GOING TO RT SOMEONE. SOON.
Kronk!
PUT DOWN THE GUN. I HAVE AN OFFER YOU WANT TO HEAR.
I KNOW WHAT HE NEEDS.

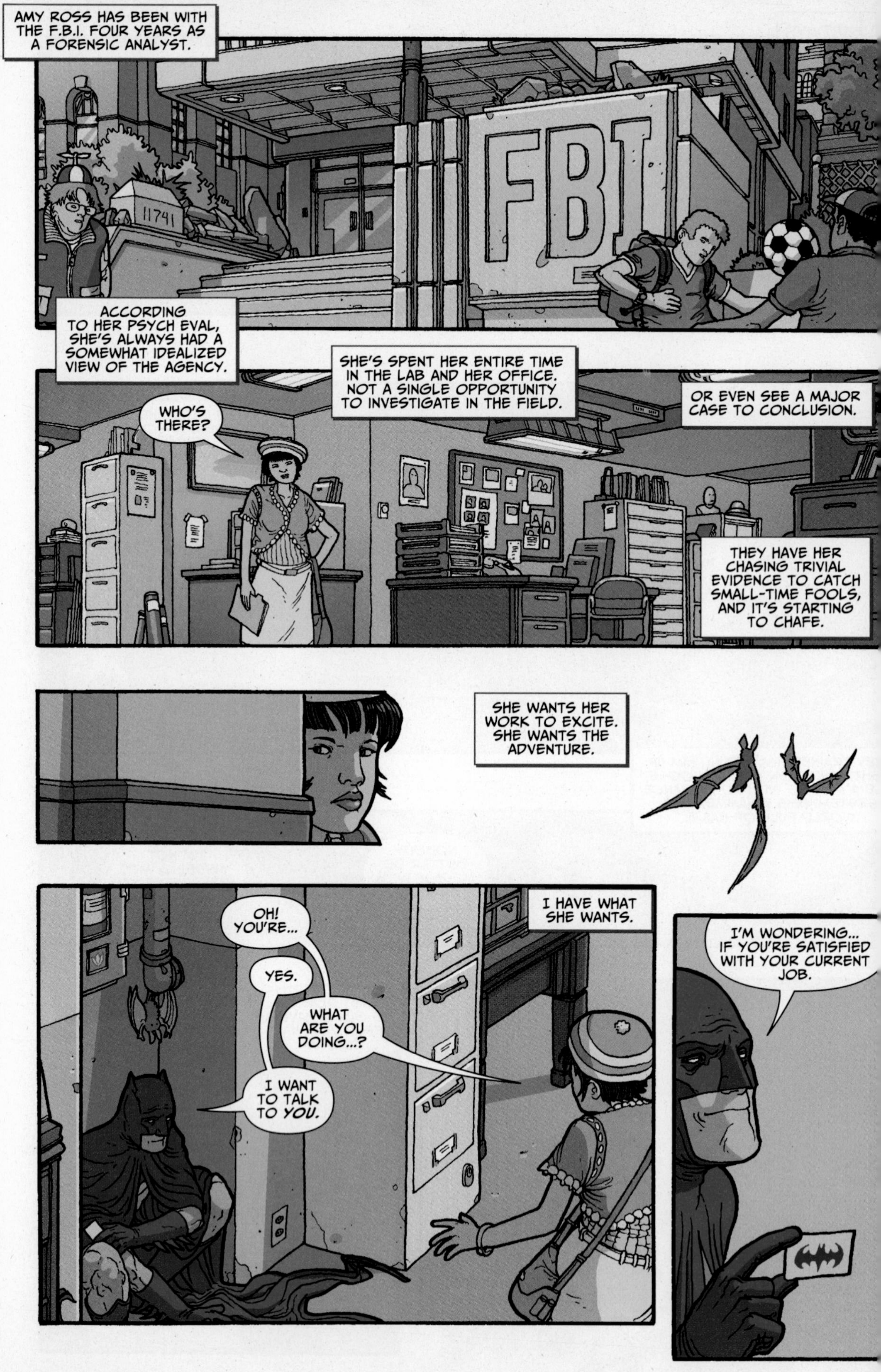
AMY ROSS HAS BEEN WITH THE F.B.I. FOUR YEARS AS A FORENSIC ANALYST.
11741
FBI
ACCORDING TO HER PSYCH EVAL, SHE'S ALWAYS HAD A SOMEWHAT IDEALIZED VIEW OF THE AGENCY.
WHO'S THERE?
SHE'S SPENT HER ENTIRE TIME IN THE LAB AND HER OFFICE. NOT A SINGLE OPPORTUNITY TO INVESTIGATE IN THE FIELD.
OR EVEN SEE A MAJOR CASE TO CONCLUSION.
THEY HAVE HER CHASING TRIVIAL EVIDENCE TO CATCH SMALL-TIME FOOLS, AND IT'S STARTING TO CHAFE.
SHE WANTS HER WORK TO EXCITE. SHE WANTS THE ADVENTURE.
OH! YOU'RE...
YES.
WHAT ARE YOU DOING...?
I WANT TO TALK TO *YOU*.
I HAVE WHAT SHE WANTS.
I'M WONDERING... IF YOU'RE SATISFIED WITH YOUR CURRENT JOB.

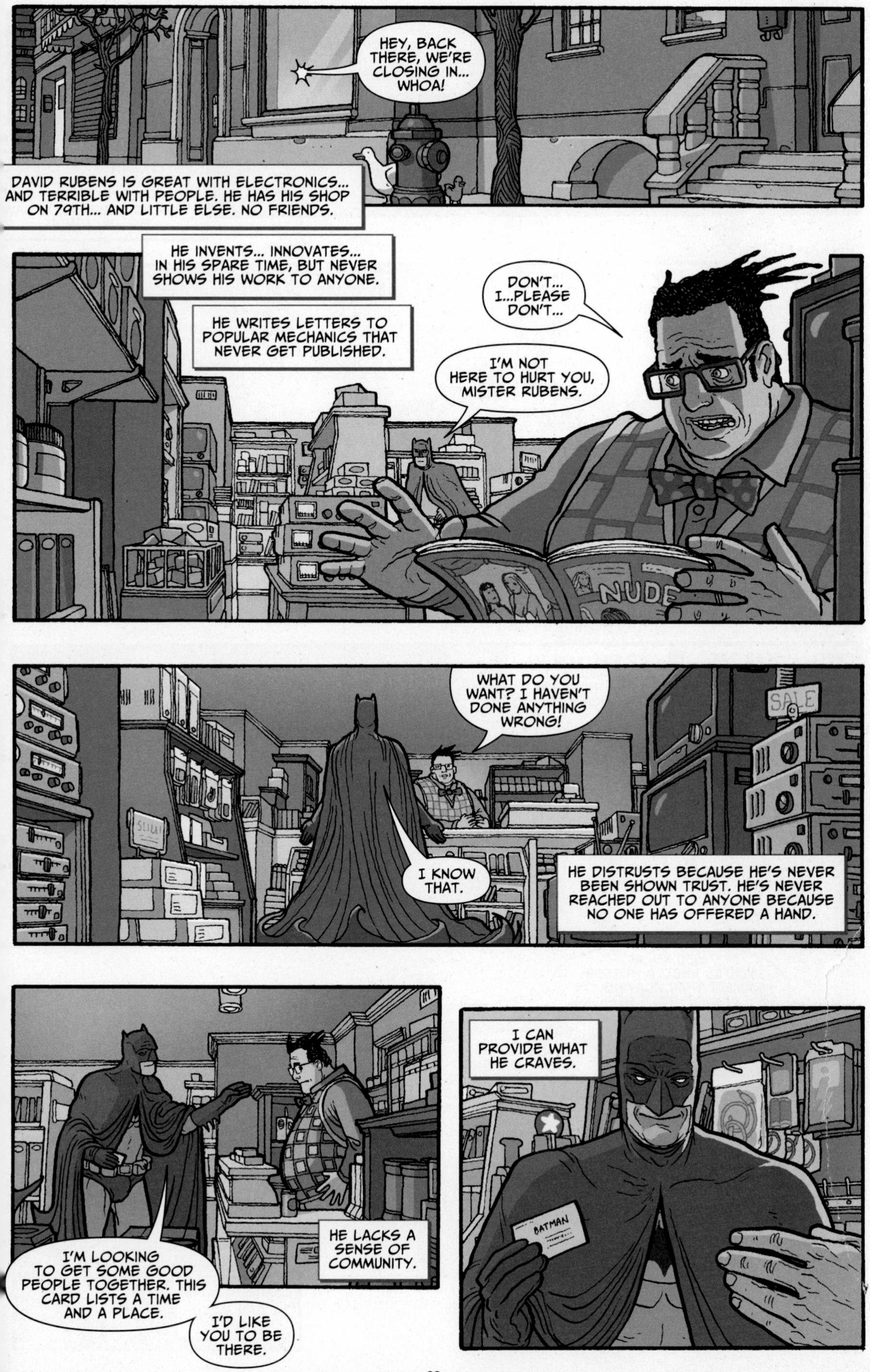
HEY, BACK THERE, WE'RE CLOSING IN... WHOA!
DAVID RUBENS IS GREAT WITH ELECTRONICS... AND TERRIBLE WITH PEOPLE. HE HAS HIS SHOP ON 79TH... AND LITTLE ELSE. NO FRIENDS.
HE INVENTS... INNOVATES... IN HIS SPARE TIME, BUT NEVER SHOWS HIS WORK TO ANYONE.
HE WRITES LETTERS TO POPULAR MECHANICS THAT NEVER GET PUBLISHED.
DON'T... I...PLEASE DON'T...
I'M NOT HERE TO HURT YOU, MISTER RUBENS.
NUDE
WHAT DO YOU WANT? I HAVEN'T DONE ANYTHING WRONG!
SALE
I KNOW THAT.
HE DISTRUSTS BECAUSE HE'S NEVER BEEN SHOWN TRUST. HE'S NEVER REACHED OUT TO ANYONE BECAUSE NO ONE HAS OFFERED A HAND.
HE LACKS A SENSE OF COMMUNITY.
I'M LOOKING TO GET SOME GOOD PEOPLE TOGETHER. THIS CARD LISTS A TIME AND A PLACE.
I'D LIKE YOU TO BE THERE.
I CAN PROVIDE WHAT HE CRAVES.
BATMAN

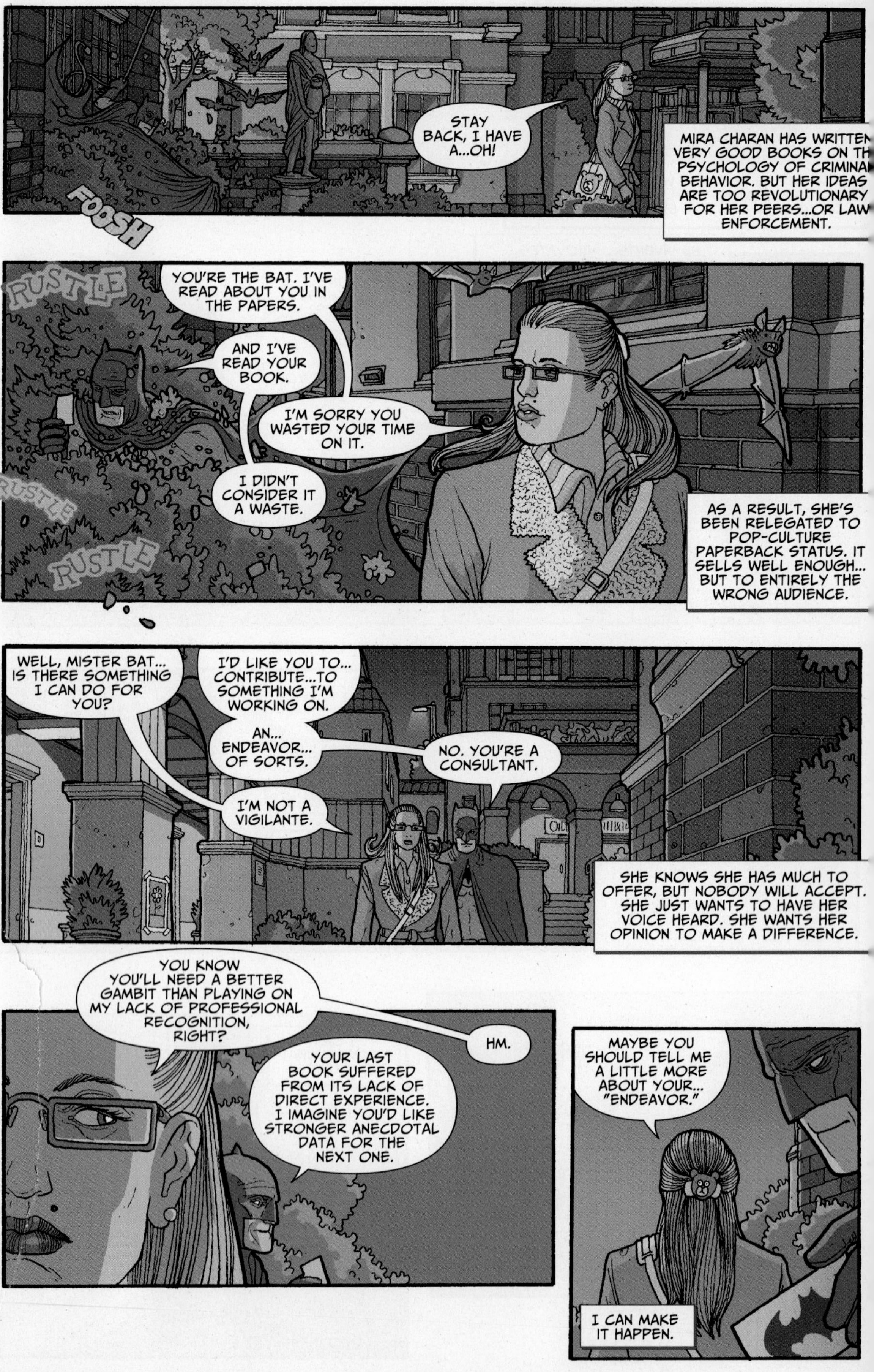
STAY BACK, I HAVE A...OH!
MIRA CHARAN HAS WRITTEN VERY GOOD BOOKS ON TH PSYCHOLOGY OF CRIMINA BEHAVIOR. BUT HER IDEAS ARE TOO REVOLUTIONARY FOR HER PEERS...OR LAW ENFORCEMENT.
FOOSH
RUSTLE
YOU'RE THE BAT. I'VE READ ABOUT YOU IN THE PAPERS.
AND I'VE READ YOUR BOOK.
I'M SORRY YOU WASTED YOUR TIME ON IT.
I DIDN'T CONSIDER IT A WASTE.
RUSTLE
RUSTLE
AS A RESULT, SHE'S BEEN RELEGATED TO POP-CULTURE PAPERBACK STATUS. IT SELLS WELL ENOUGH... BUT TO ENTIRELY THE WRONG AUDIENCE.
WELL, MISTER BAT... IS THERE SOMETHING I CAN DO FOR YOU?
I'D LIKE YOU TO... CONTRIBUTE...TO SOMETHING I'M WORKING ON.
AN... ENDEAVOR... OF SORTS.
NO. YOU'RE A CONSULTANT.
I'M NOT A VIGILANTE.
SHE KNOWS SHE HAS MUCH TO OFFER, BUT NOBODY WILL ACCEPT. SHE JUST WANTS TO HAVE HER VOICE HEARD. SHE WANTS HER OPINION TO MAKE A DIFFERENCE.
YOU KNOW YOU'LL NEED A BETTER GAMBIT THAN PLAYING ON MY LACK OF PROFESSIONAL RECOGNITION, RIGHT?
HM.
YOUR LAST BOOK SUFFERED FROM ITS LACK OF DIRECT EXPERIENCE. I IMAGINE YOU'D LIKE STRONGER ANECDOTAL DATA FOR THE NEXT ONE.
MAYBE YOU SHOULD TELL ME A LITTLE MORE ABOUT YOUR... "ENDEAVOR."
I CAN MAKE IT HAPPEN.

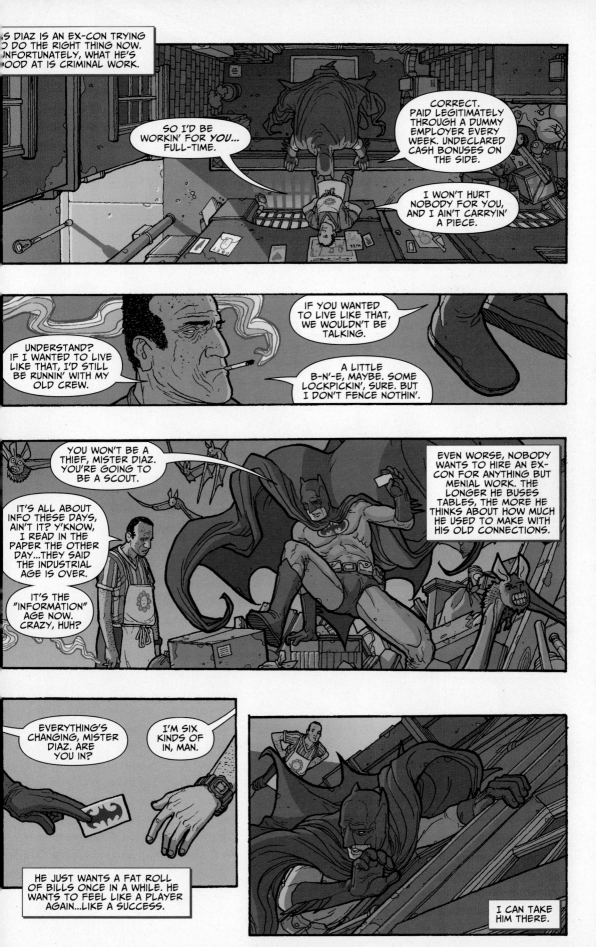

...S DIAZ IS AN EX-CON TRYING TO DO THE RIGHT THING NOW. UNFORTUNATELY, WHAT HE'S GOOD AT IS CRIMINAL WORK.

SO I'D BE WORKIN' FOR *YOU*... FULL-TIME.

CORRECT. PAID LEGITIMATELY THROUGH A DUMMY EMPLOYER EVERY WEEK. UNDECLARED CASH BONUSES ON THE SIDE.

I WON'T HURT NOBODY FOR YOU, AND I AIN'T CARRYIN' A PIECE.

IF YOU WANTED TO LIVE LIKE THAT, WE WOULDN'T BE TALKING.

UNDERSTAND? IF I WANTED TO LIVE LIKE THAT, I'D STILL BE RUNNIN' WITH MY OLD CREW.

A LITTLE B-N'-E, MAYBE. SOME LOCKPICKIN', SURE. BUT I DON'T FENCE NOTHIN'.

YOU WON'T BE A THIEF, MISTER DIAZ. YOU'RE GOING TO BE A SCOUT.

IT'S ALL ABOUT INFO THESE DAYS, AIN'T IT? Y'KNOW, I READ IN THE PAPER THE OTHER DAY...THEY SAID THE INDUSTRIAL AGE IS OVER.

IT'S THE "INFORMATION" AGE NOW. CRAZY, HUH?

EVEN WORSE, NOBODY WANTS TO HIRE AN EX-CON FOR ANYTHING BUT MENIAL WORK. THE LONGER HE BUSES TABLES, THE MORE HE THINKS ABOUT HOW MUCH HE USED TO MAKE WITH HIS OLD CONNECTIONS.

EVERYTHING'S CHANGING, MISTER DIAZ. ARE YOU IN?

I'M SIX KINDS OF IN, MAN.

HE JUST WANTS A FAT ROLL OF BILLS ONCE IN A WHILE. HE WANTS TO FEEL LIKE A PLAYER AGAIN...LIKE A SUCCESS.

I CAN TAKE HIM THERE.

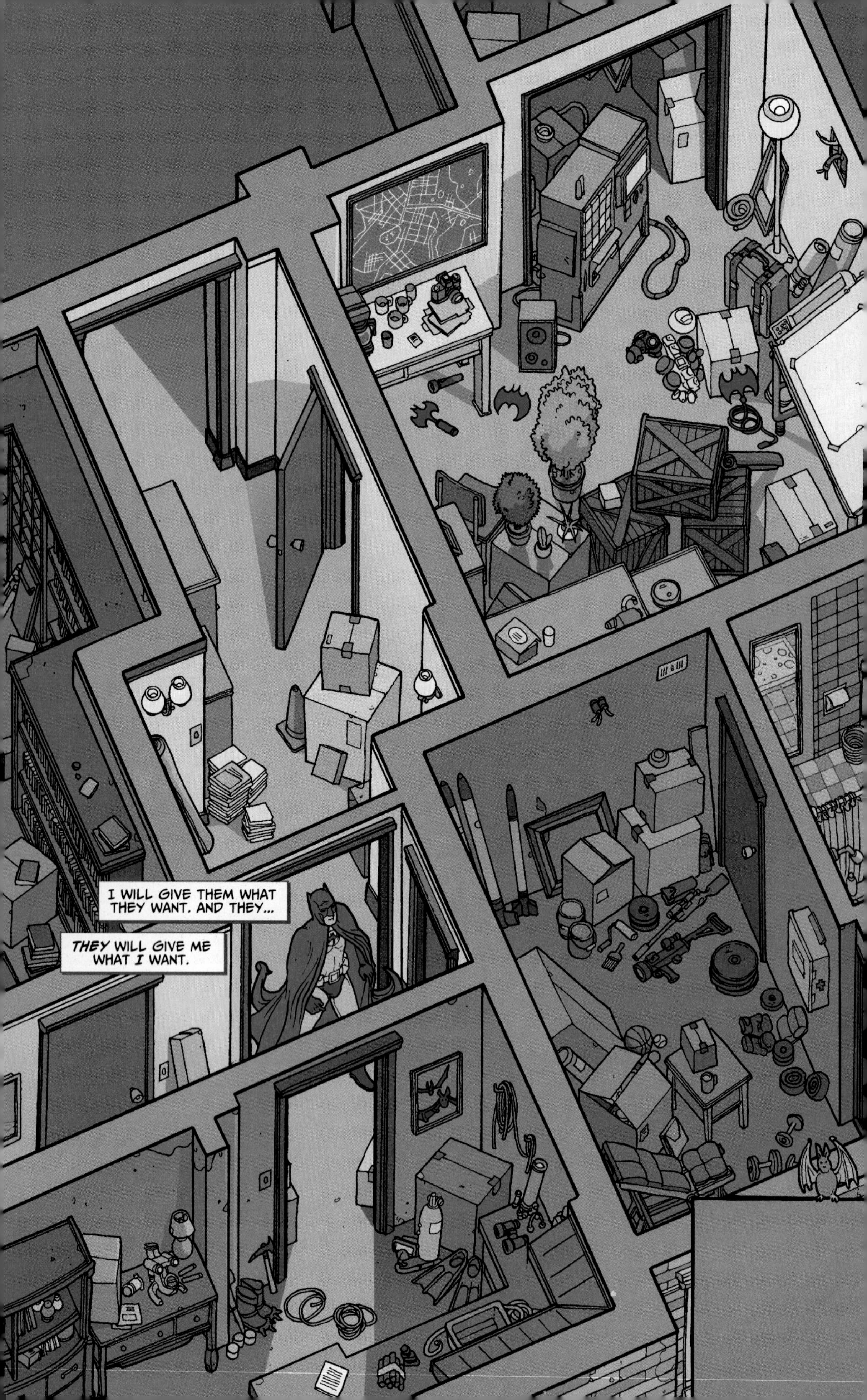
I WILL GIVE THEM WHAT THEY WANT. AND THEY...
THEY WILL GIVE ME WHAT *I* WANT.

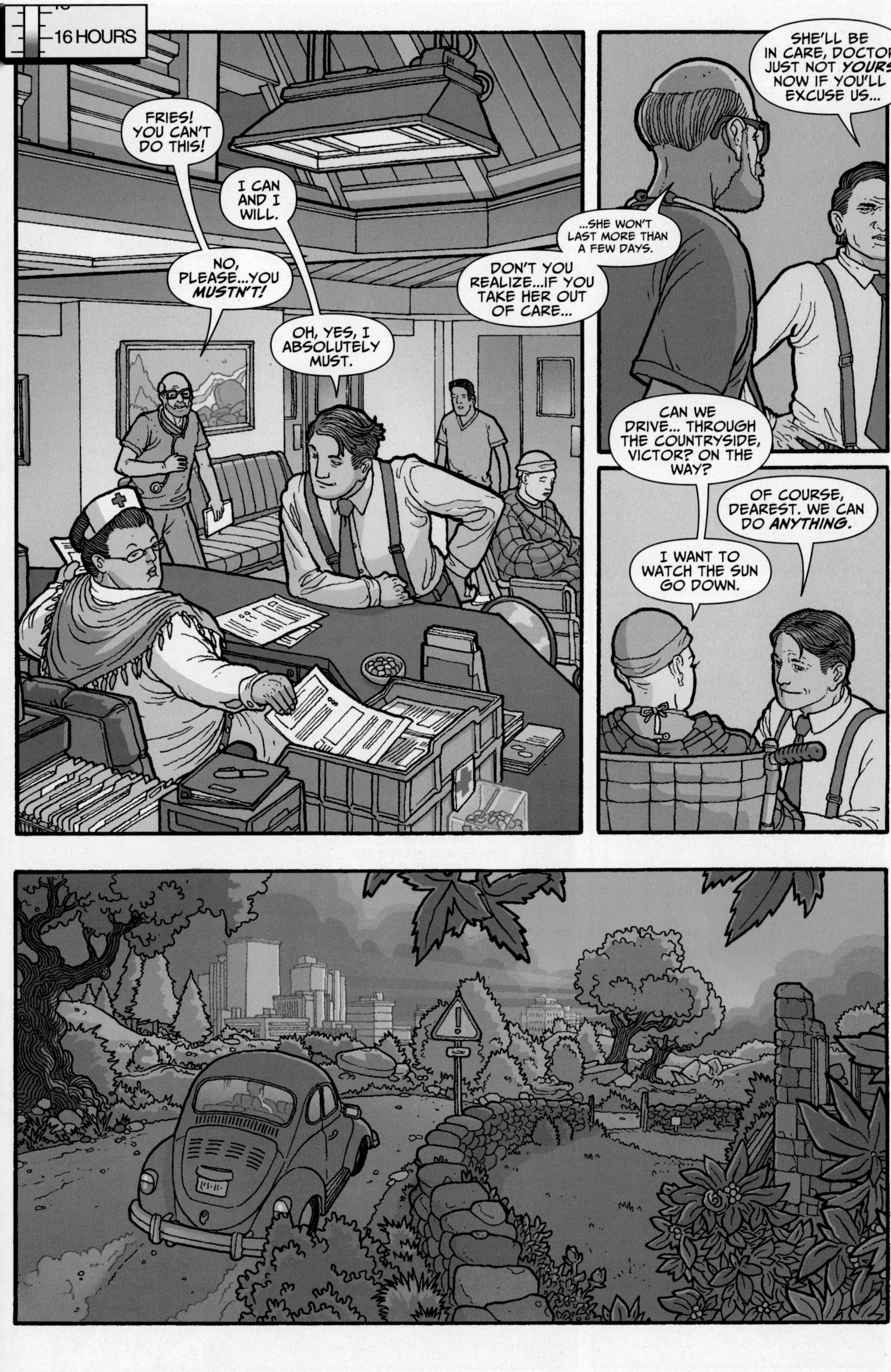
16 HOURS
FRIES! YOU CAN'T DO THIS!
I CAN AND I WILL.
NO, PLEASE...YOU *MUSTN'T!*
OH, YES, I ABSOLUTELY MUST.
DON'T YOU REALIZE...IF YOU TAKE HER OUT OF CARE...
...SHE WON'T LAST MORE THAN A FEW DAYS.
SHE'LL BE IN CARE, DOCTOR. JUST NOT *YOURS.* NOW IF YOU'LL EXCUSE US...
CAN WE DRIVE... THROUGH THE COUNTRYSIDE, VICTOR? ON THE WAY?
I WANT TO WATCH THE SUN GO DOWN.
OF COURSE, DEAREST. WE CAN DO *ANYTHING.*

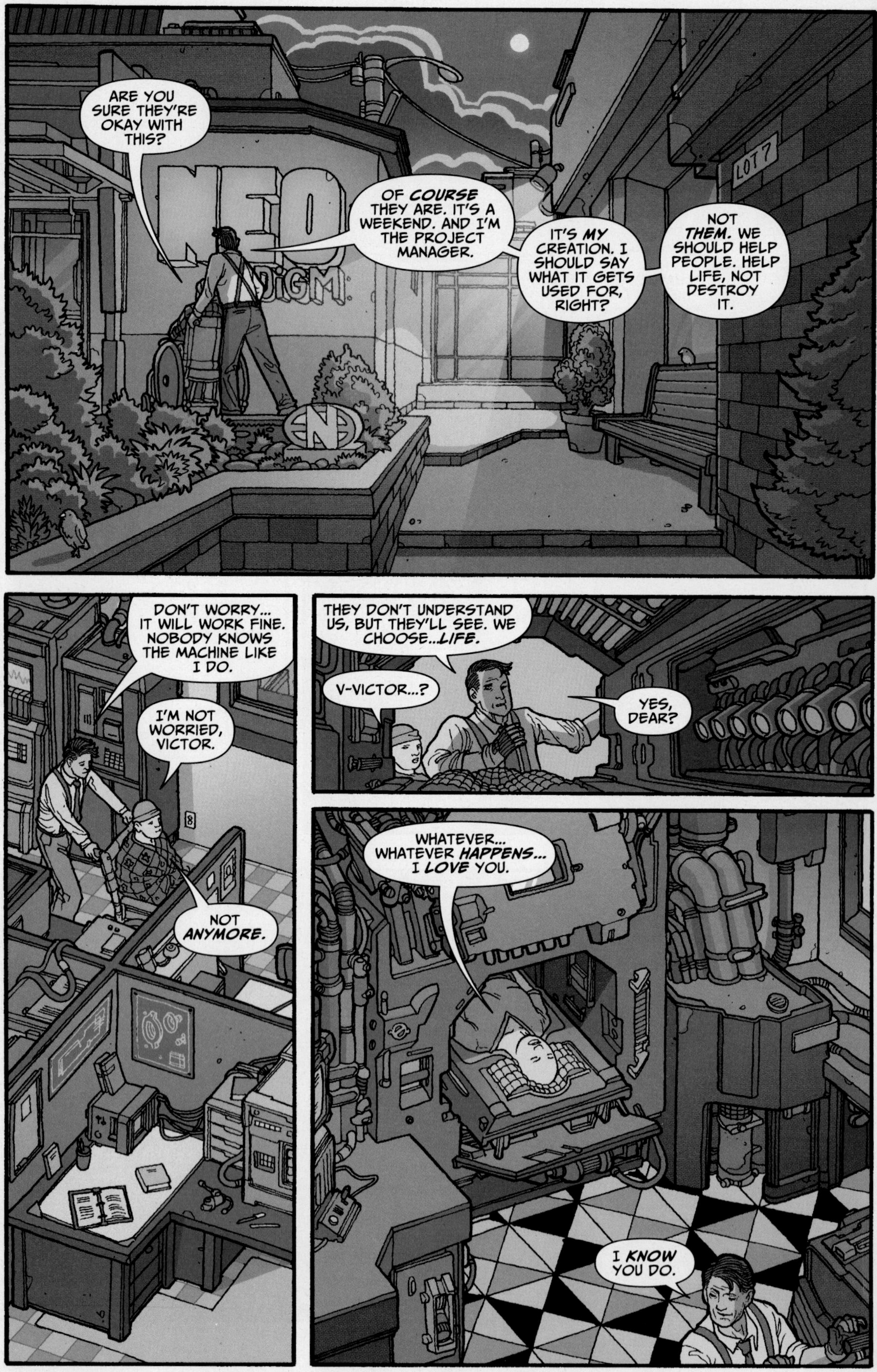
ARE YOU SURE THEY'RE OKAY WITH THIS?
NEO
OF COURSE THEY ARE. IT'S A WEEKEND. AND I'M THE PROJECT MANAGER.
IT'S MY CREATION. I SHOULD SAY WHAT IT GETS USED FOR, RIGHT?
NOT THEM. WE SHOULD HELP PEOPLE. HELP LIFE, NOT DESTROY IT.
LOT 7
DON'T WORRY... IT WILL WORK FINE. NOBODY KNOWS THE MACHINE LIKE I DO.
I'M NOT WORRIED, VICTOR.
NOT ANYMORE.
THEY DON'T UNDERSTAND US, BUT THEY'LL SEE. WE CHOOSE...LIFE.
V-VICTOR...?
YES, DEAR?
WHATEVER... WHATEVER HAPPENS... I LOVE YOU.
I KNOW YOU DO.

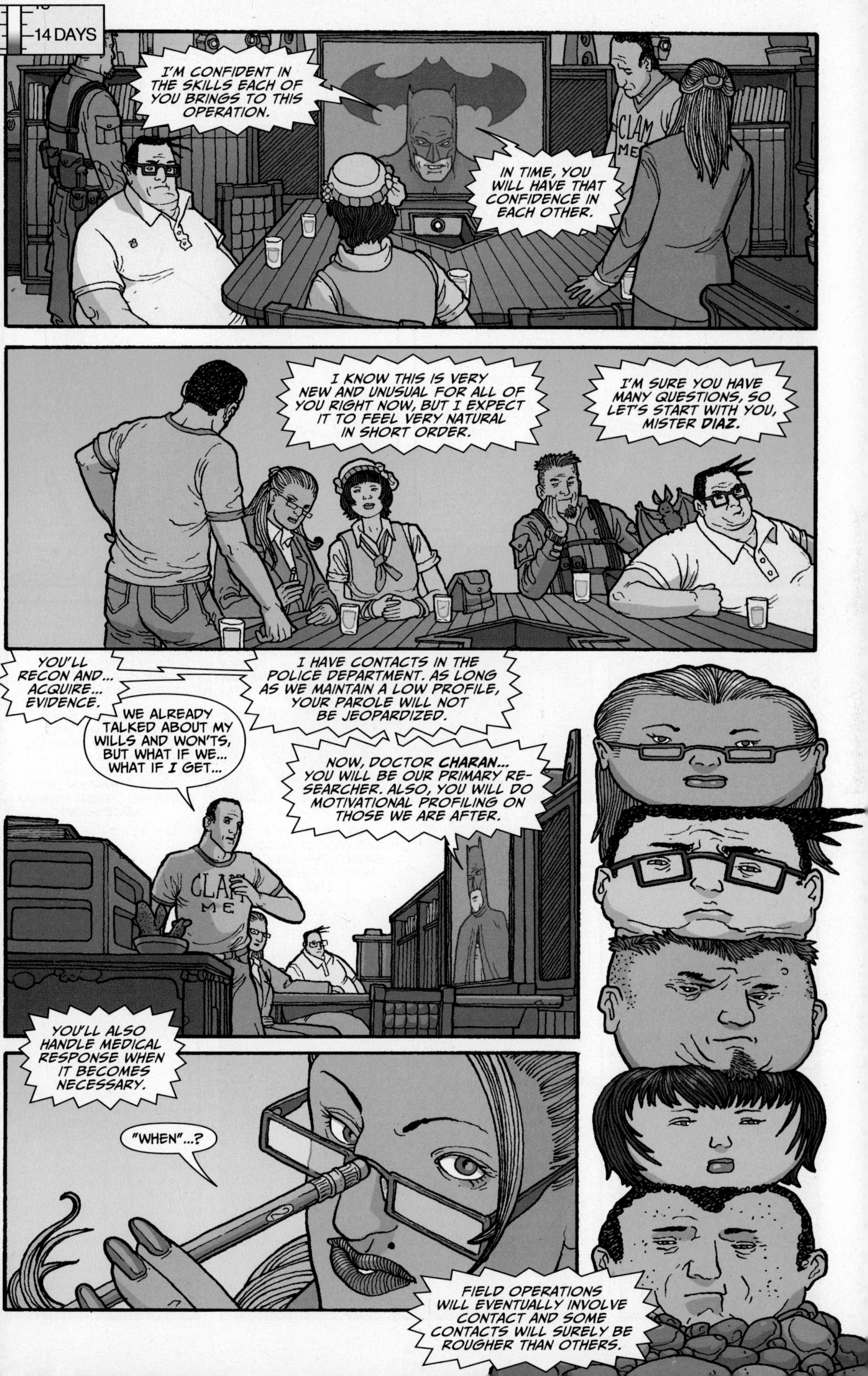
14 DAYS
I'M CONFIDENT IN THE SKILLS EACH OF YOU BRINGS TO THIS OPERATION.
IN TIME, YOU WILL HAVE THAT CONFIDENCE IN EACH OTHER.
I KNOW THIS IS VERY NEW AND UNUSUAL FOR ALL OF YOU RIGHT NOW, BUT I EXPECT IT TO FEEL VERY NATURAL IN SHORT ORDER.
I'M SURE YOU HAVE MANY QUESTIONS, SO LET'S START WITH YOU, MISTER **DIAZ**.
YOU'LL RECON AND... ACQUIRE... EVIDENCE.
WE ALREADY TALKED ABOUT MY WILLS AND WON'TS, BUT WHAT IF WE... WHAT IF *I* GET...
I HAVE CONTACTS IN THE POLICE DEPARTMENT. AS LONG AS WE MAINTAIN A LOW PROFILE, YOUR PAROLE WILL NOT BE JEOPARDIZED.
NOW, DOCTOR **CHARAN**... YOU WILL BE OUR PRIMARY RESEARCHER. ALSO, YOU WILL DO MOTIVATIONAL PROFILING ON THOSE WE ARE AFTER.
YOU'LL ALSO HANDLE MEDICAL RESPONSE WHEN IT BECOMES NECESSARY.
"WHEN"...?
FIELD OPERATIONS WILL EVENTUALLY INVOLVE CONTACT AND SOME CONTACTS WILL SURELY BE ROUGHER THAN OTHERS.

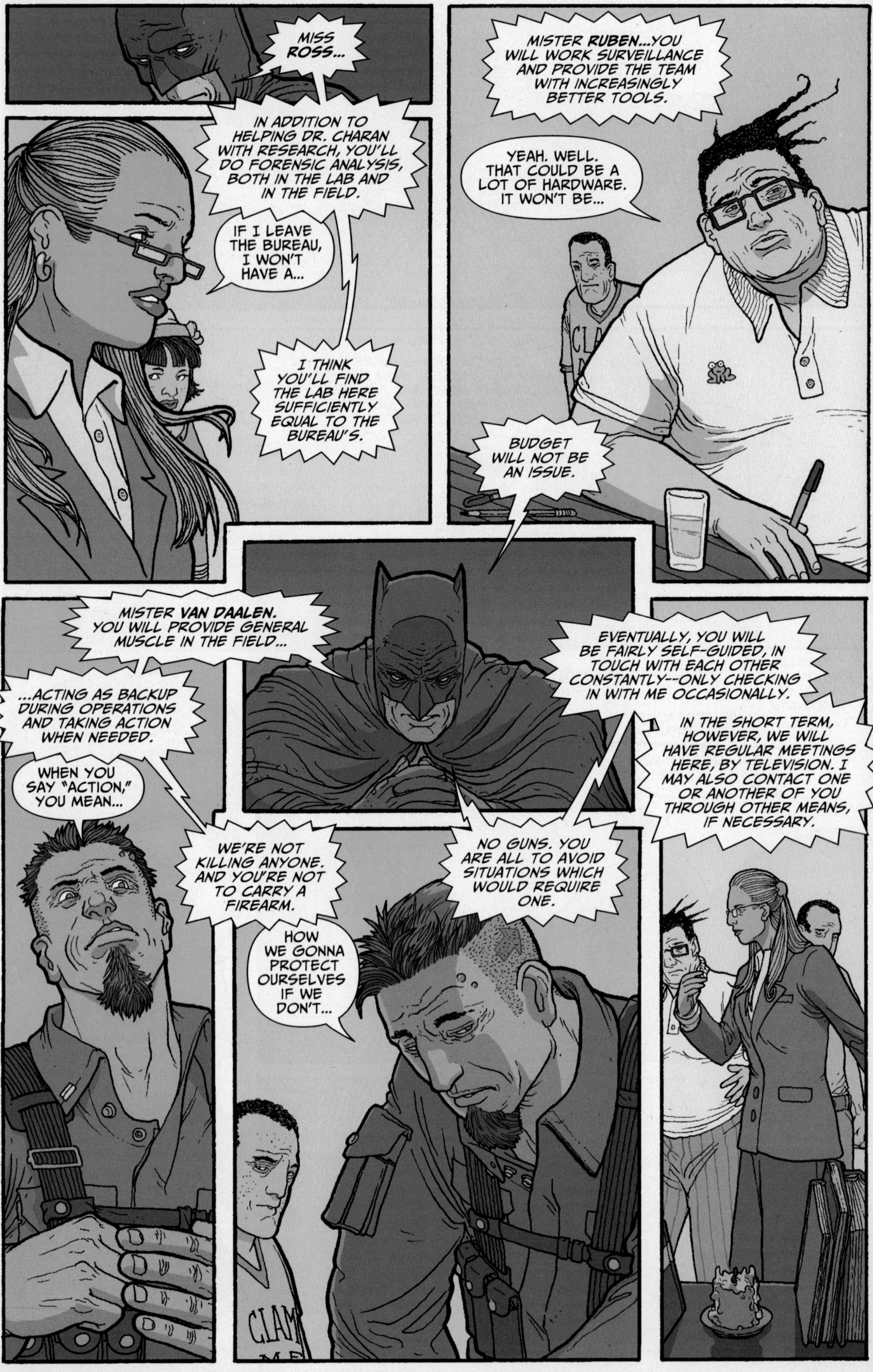
MISS ROSS...
IN ADDITION TO HELPING DR. CHARAN WITH RESEARCH, YOU'LL DO FORENSIC ANALYSIS, BOTH IN THE LAB AND IN THE FIELD.
IF I LEAVE THE BUREAU, I WON'T HAVE A...
I THINK YOU'LL FIND THE LAB HERE SUFFICIENTLY EQUAL TO THE BUREAU'S.
MISTER RUBEN...YOU WILL WORK SURVEILLANCE AND PROVIDE THE TEAM WITH INCREASINGLY BETTER TOOLS.
YEAH. WELL. THAT COULD BE A LOT OF HARDWARE. IT WON'T BE...
BUDGET WILL NOT BE AN ISSUE.
MISTER VAN DAALEN. YOU WILL PROVIDE GENERAL MUSCLE IN THE FIELD...
...ACTING AS BACKUP DURING OPERATIONS AND TAKING ACTION WHEN NEEDED.
WHEN YOU SAY "ACTION," YOU MEAN...
WE'RE NOT KILLING ANYONE. AND YOU'RE NOT TO CARRY A FIREARM.
HOW WE GONNA PROTECT OURSELVES IF WE DON'T...
NO GUNS. YOU ARE ALL TO AVOID SITUATIONS WHICH WOULD REQUIRE ONE.
EVENTUALLY, YOU WILL BE FAIRLY SELF-GUIDED, IN TOUCH WITH EACH OTHER CONSTANTLY--ONLY CHECKING IN WITH ME OCCASIONALLY.
IN THE SHORT TERM, HOWEVER, WE WILL HAVE REGULAR MEETINGS HERE, BY TELEVISION. I MAY ALSO CONTACT ONE OR ANOTHER OF YOU THROUGH OTHER MEANS, IF NECESSARY.

UNDER YOUR SEATS, YOU WILL EACH FIND A DOCUMENT PACK OUTLINING, IN MORE DETAIL, WHAT I FEEL YOUR CONTRIBUTIONS TO THE GROUP SHOULD BE.

IT ALSO CONTAINS DOSSIER INFORMATION ON THE ORGANIZATION AND INDIVIDUALS I INTEND AS OUR FIRST TARGET OF INVESTIGATION.

YOU CAN, AND SHOULD, COMPARE NOTES. REVIEW THE INFORMATION AS A *TEAM.*

WE'LL TALK HERE, EVERY NIGHT AT THE SAME TIME, UNTIL YOU'RE READY TO GO.

THEN WE'LL START IN *EARNEST.*

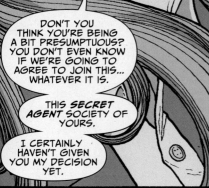

DON'T YOU THINK YOU'RE BEING A BIT PRESUMPTUOUS? YOU DON'T EVEN KNOW IF WE'RE GOING TO AGREE TO JOIN THIS... WHATEVER IT IS.

THIS *SECRET AGENT* SOCIETY OF YOURS.

I CERTAINLY HAVEN'T GIVEN YOU MY DECISION YET.

NO, BUT YOU'VE ALREADY *MADE* IT.

TOMORROW NIGHT. PLEASE BE ON TIME.

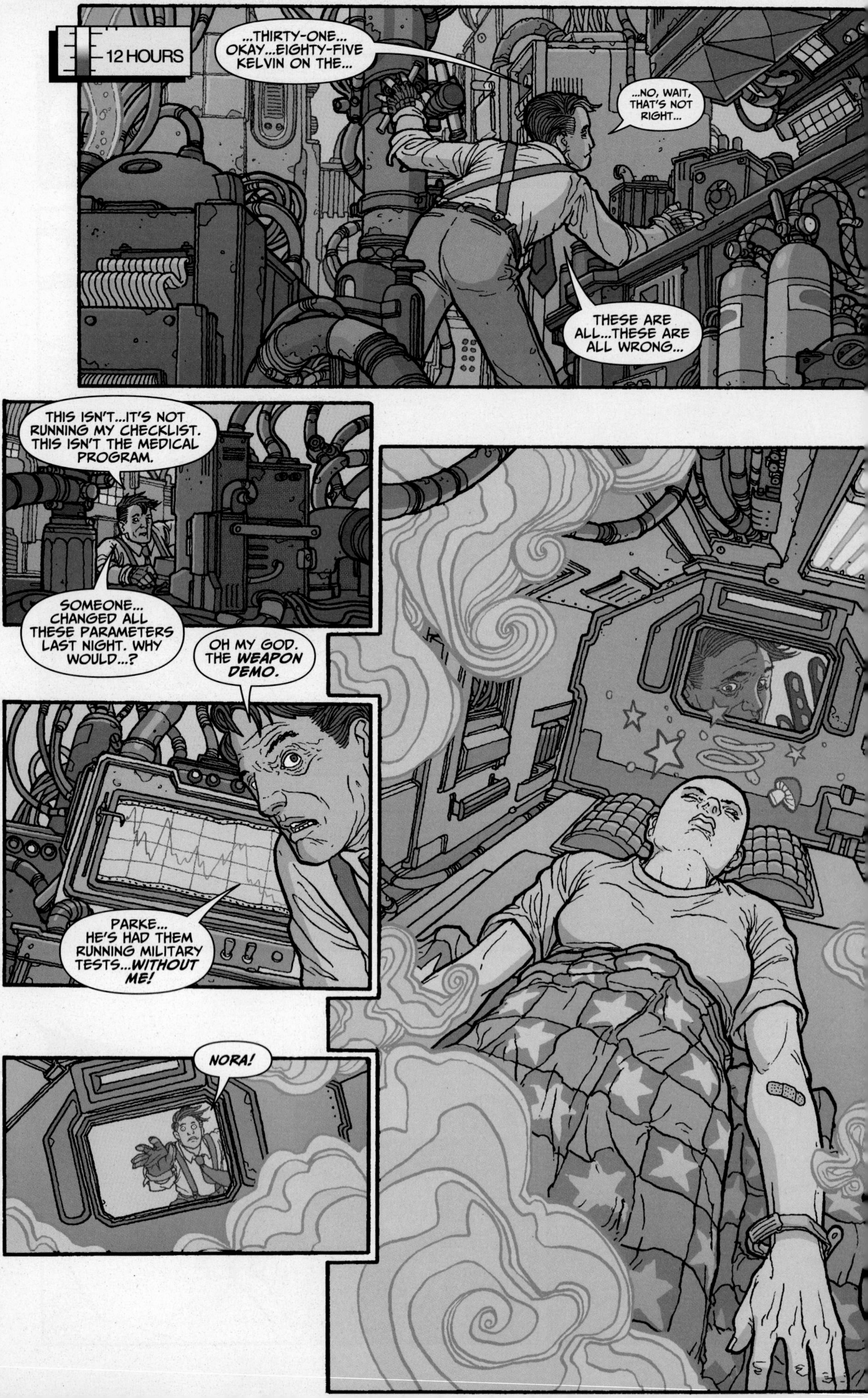
12 HOURS
...THIRTY-ONE... OKAY...EIGHTY-FIVE KELVIN ON THE...
...NO, WAIT, THAT'S NOT RIGHT...
THESE ARE ALL...THESE ARE ALL WRONG...
THIS ISN'T...IT'S NOT RUNNING MY CHECKLIST. THIS ISN'T THE MEDICAL PROGRAM.
SOMEONE... CHANGED ALL THESE PARAMETERS LAST NIGHT. WHY WOULD...?
OH MY GOD. THE *WEAPON DEMO.*
PARKE... HE'S HAD THEM RUNNING MILITARY TESTS...*WITHOUT ME!*
NORA!

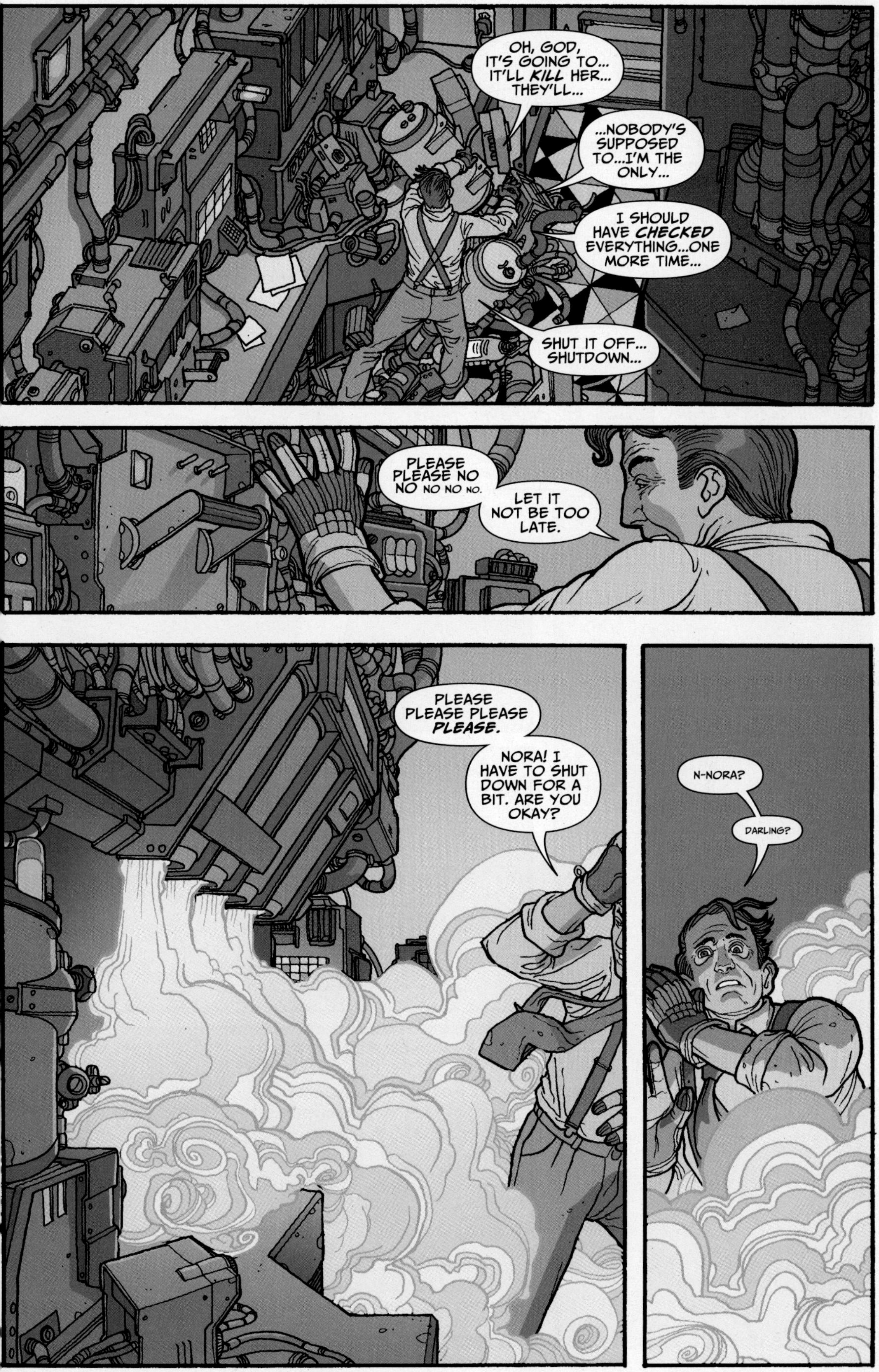
OH, GOD, IT'S GOING TO... IT'LL KILL HER... THEY'LL...
...NOBODY'S SUPPOSED TO...I'M THE ONLY...
I SHOULD HAVE CHECKED EVERYTHING...ONE MORE TIME...
SHUT IT OFF... SHUTDOWN...
PLEASE PLEASE NO NO NO NO NO.
LET IT NOT BE TOO LATE.
PLEASE PLEASE PLEASE PLEASE.
NORA! I HAVE TO SHUT DOWN FOR A BIT. ARE YOU OKAY?
N-NORA?
DARLING?

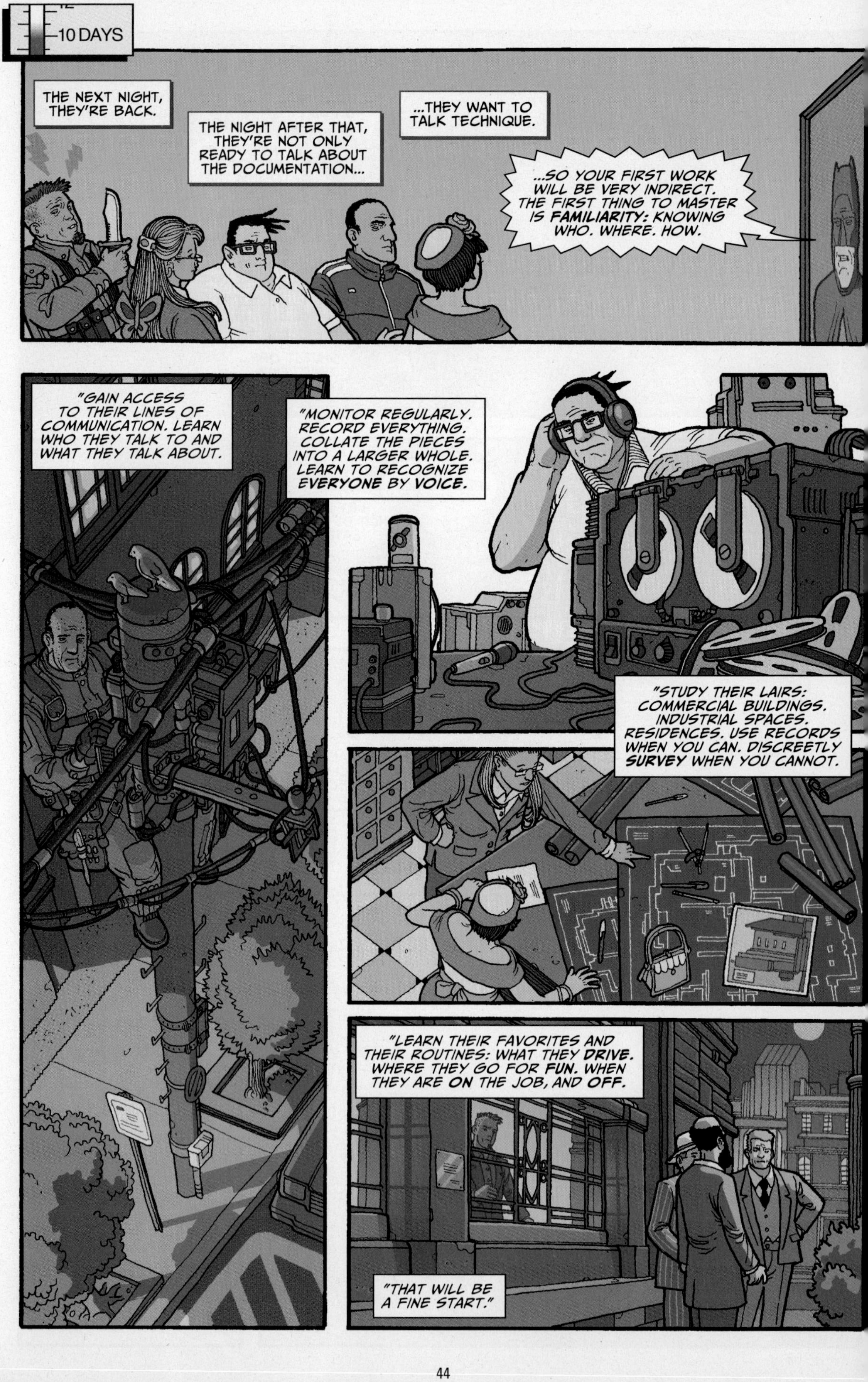
10 DAYS
THE NEXT NIGHT, THEY'RE BACK.
THE NIGHT AFTER THAT, THEY'RE NOT ONLY READY TO TALK ABOUT THE DOCUMENTATION...
...THEY WANT TO TALK TECHNIQUE.
...SO YOUR FIRST WORK WILL BE VERY INDIRECT. THE FIRST THING TO MASTER IS FAMILIARITY: KNOWING WHO. WHERE. HOW.
"GAIN ACCESS TO THEIR LINES OF COMMUNICATION. LEARN WHO THEY TALK TO AND WHAT THEY TALK ABOUT.
"MONITOR REGULARLY. RECORD EVERYTHING. COLLATE THE PIECES INTO A LARGER WHOLE. LEARN TO RECOGNIZE EVERYONE BY VOICE.
"STUDY THEIR LAIRS: COMMERCIAL BUILDINGS. INDUSTRIAL SPACES. RESIDENCES. USE RECORDS WHEN YOU CAN. DISCREETLY SURVEY WHEN YOU CANNOT.
"LEARN THEIR FAVORITES AND THEIR ROUTINES: WHAT THEY DRIVE. WHERE THEY GO FOR FUN. WHEN THEY ARE ON THE JOB, AND OFF.
"THAT WILL BE A FINE START."

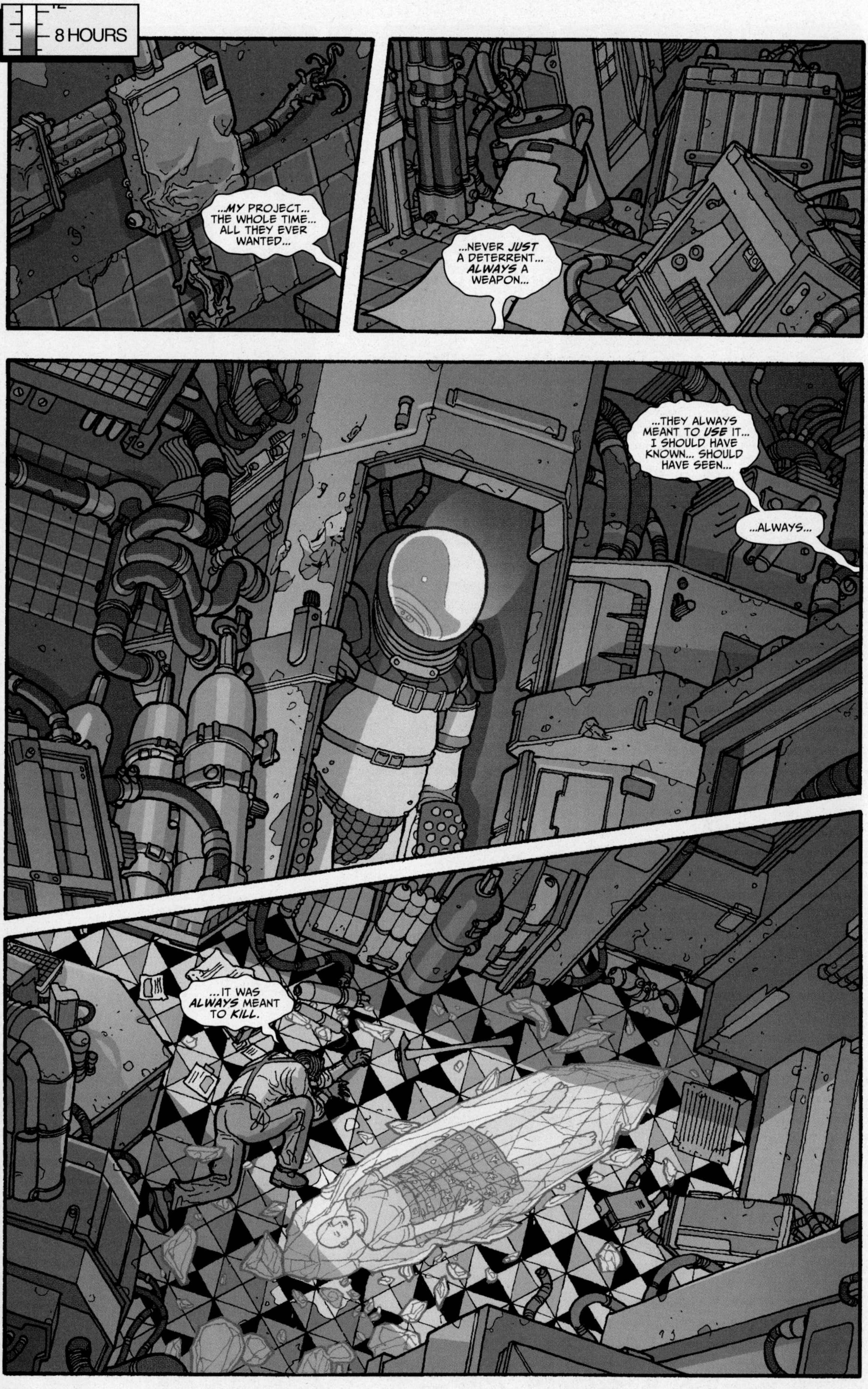

8 HOURS
...MY PROJECT... THE WHOLE TIME... ALL THEY EVER WANTED...
...NEVER JUST A DETERRENT... ALWAYS A WEAPON...
...THEY ALWAYS MEANT TO USE IT... I SHOULD HAVE KNOWN... SHOULD HAVE SEEN...
...ALWAYS...
...IT WAS ALWAYS MEANT TO KILL.

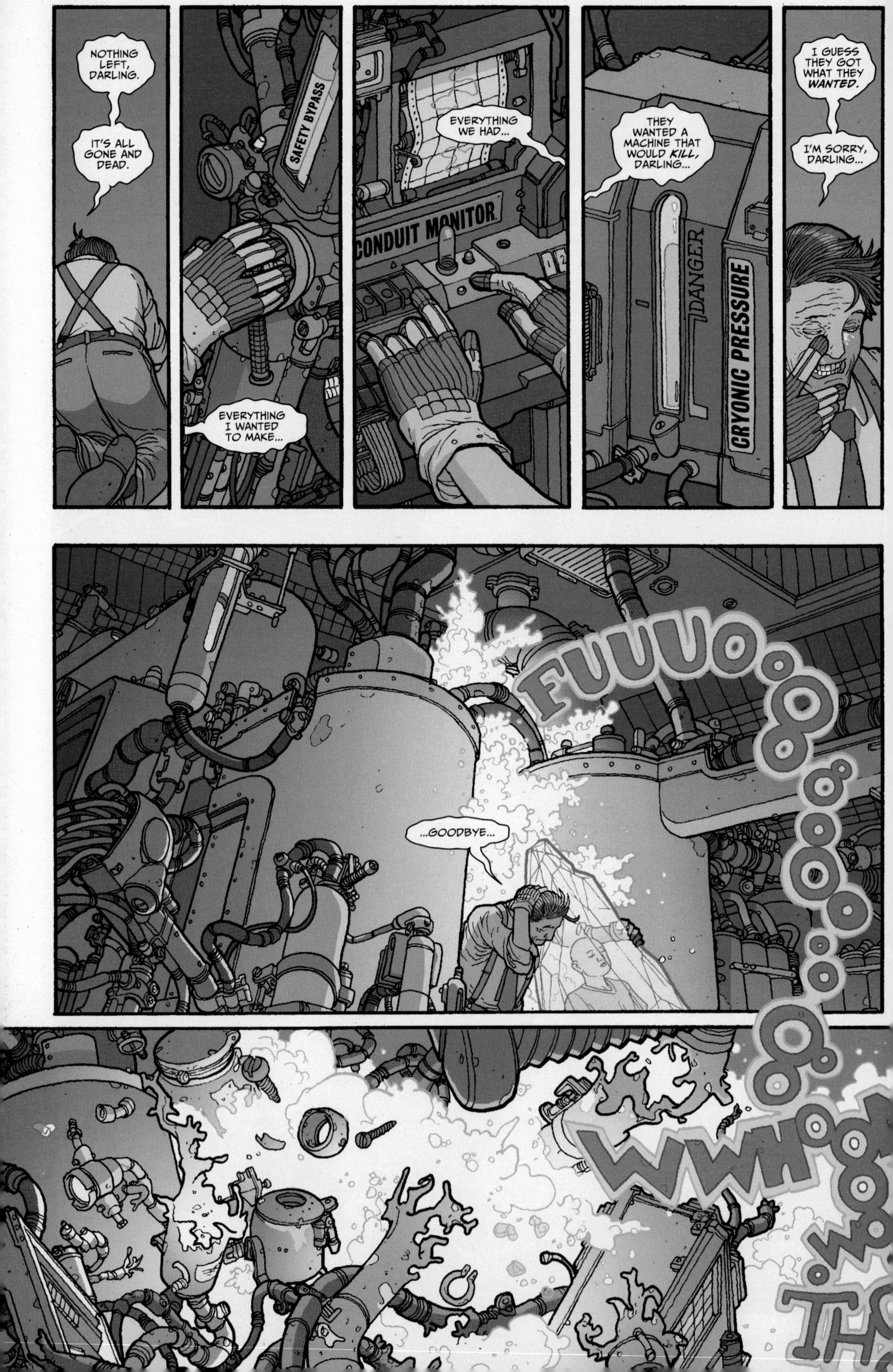

NOTHING LEFT, DARLING.
IT'S ALL GONE AND DEAD.
SAFETY BYPASS
EVERYTHING I WANTED TO MAKE...
EVERYTHING WE HAD...
CONDUIT MONITOR
THEY WANTED A MACHINE THAT WOULD *KILL,* DARLING...
DANGER
CRYONIC PRESSURE
I GUESS THEY GOT WHAT THEY *WANTED.*
I'M SORRY, DARLING...
FUUUO-O-O-O-O-O-O-O-O-O-O
...GOODBYE...
WWHOOOOOOTHO

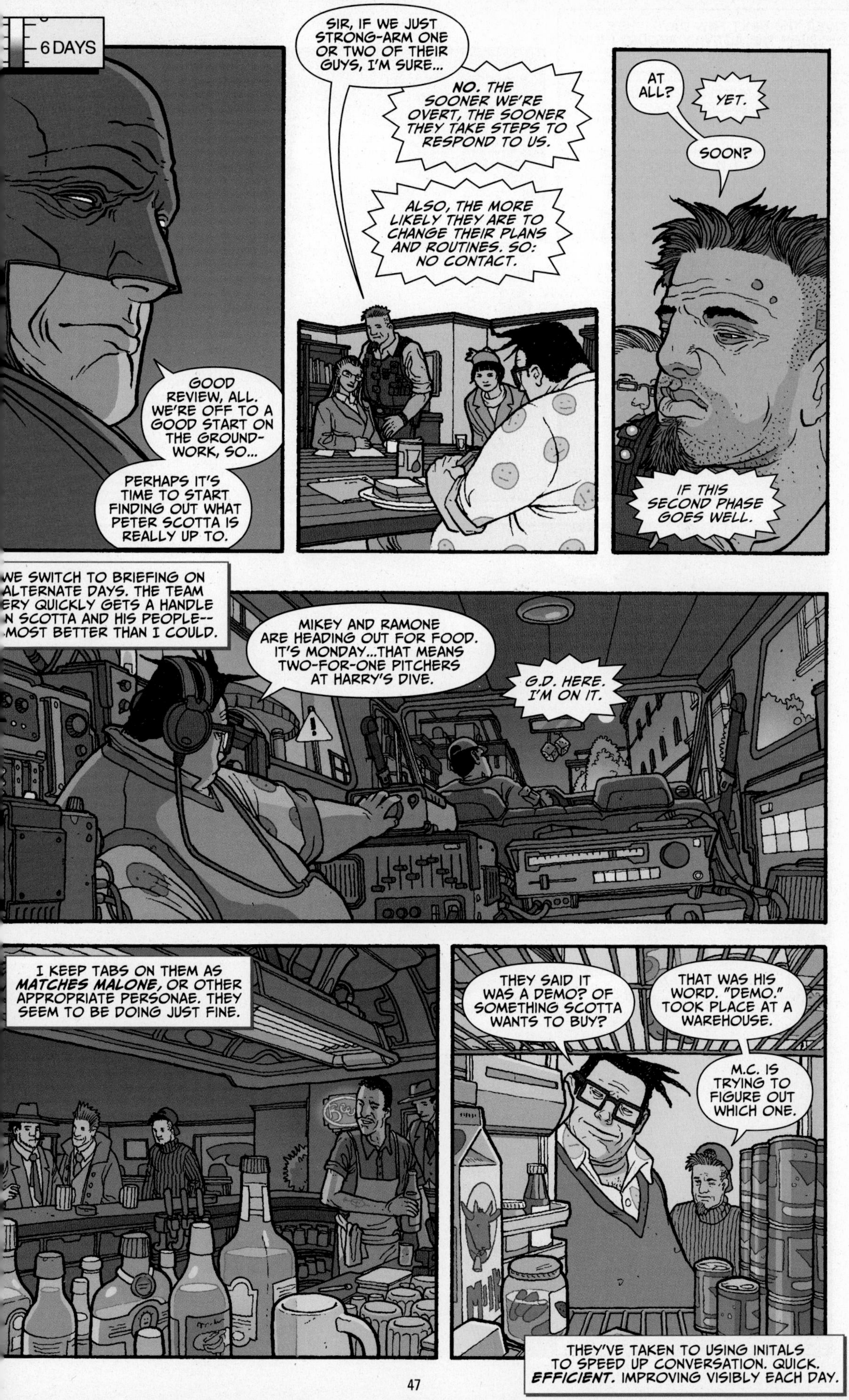
6 DAYS
GOOD REVIEW, ALL. WE'RE OFF TO A GOOD START ON THE GROUND-WORK, SO...
PERHAPS IT'S TIME TO START FINDING OUT WHAT PETER SCOTTA IS REALLY UP TO.
SIR, IF WE JUST STRONG-ARM ONE OR TWO OF THEIR GUYS, I'M SURE...
NO. THE SOONER WE'RE OVERT, THE SOONER THEY TAKE STEPS TO RESPOND TO US.
ALSO, THE MORE LIKELY THEY ARE TO CHANGE THEIR PLANS AND ROUTINES. SO: NO CONTACT.
AT ALL?
YET.
SOON?
IF THIS SECOND PHASE GOES WELL.
WE SWITCH TO BRIEFING ON ALTERNATE DAYS. THE TEAM ERY QUICKLY GETS A HANDLE N SCOTTA AND HIS PEOPLE-- MOST BETTER THAN I COULD.
MIKEY AND RAMONE ARE HEADING OUT FOR FOOD. IT'S MONDAY...THAT MEANS TWO-FOR-ONE PITCHERS AT HARRY'S DIVE.
G.D. HERE. I'M ON IT.
I KEEP TABS ON THEM AS MATCHES MALONE, OR OTHER APPROPRIATE PERSONAE. THEY SEEM TO BE DOING JUST FINE.
THEY SAID IT WAS A DEMO? OF SOMETHING SCOTTA WANTS TO BUY?
THAT WAS HIS WORD. "DEMO." TOOK PLACE AT A WAREHOUSE.
M.C. IS TRYING TO FIGURE OUT WHICH ONE.
THEY'VE TAKEN TO USING INITALS TO SPEED UP CONVERSATION. QUICK. EFFICIENT. IMPROVING VISIBLY EACH DAY.

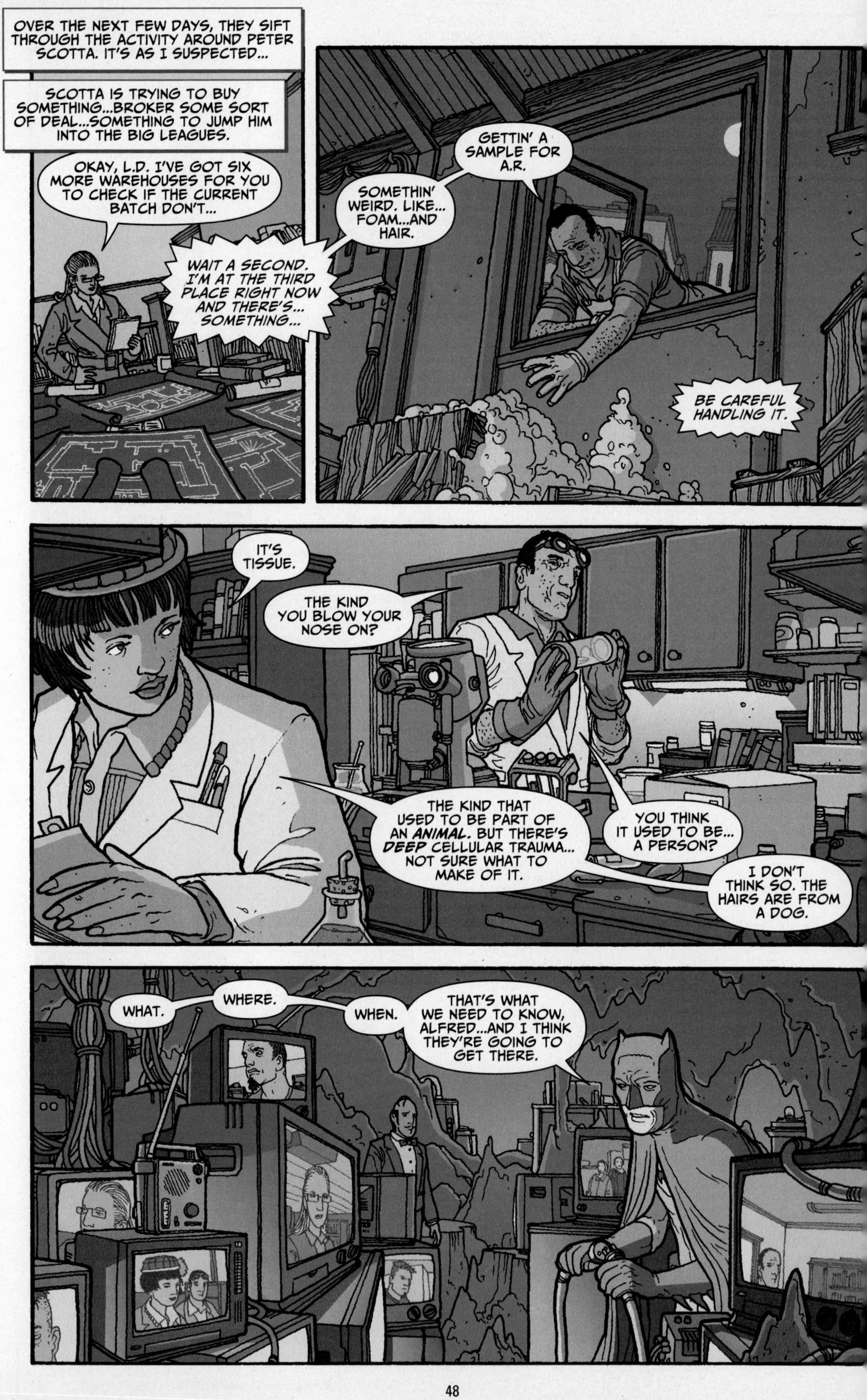
OVER THE NEXT FEW DAYS, THEY SIFT THROUGH THE ACTIVITY AROUND PETER SCOTTA. IT'S AS I SUSPECTED...
SCOTTA IS TRYING TO BUY SOMETHING...BROKER SOME SORT OF DEAL...SOMETHING TO JUMP HIM INTO THE BIG LEAGUES.
OKAY, L.D. I'VE GOT SIX MORE WAREHOUSES FOR YOU TO CHECK IF THE CURRENT BATCH DON'T...
WAIT A SECOND. I'M AT THE THIRD PLACE RIGHT NOW AND THERE'S... SOMETHING...
SOMETHIN' WEIRD. LIKE... FOAM...AND HAIR.
GETTIN' A SAMPLE FOR A.R.
BE CAREFUL HANDLING IT.
IT'S TISSUE.
THE KIND YOU BLOW YOUR NOSE ON?
THE KIND THAT USED TO BE PART OF AN ANIMAL. BUT THERE'S DEEP CELLULAR TRAUMA... NOT SURE WHAT TO MAKE OF IT.
YOU THINK IT USED TO BE... A PERSON?
I DON'T THINK SO. THE HAIRS ARE FROM A DOG.
WHAT.
WHERE.
WHEN.
THAT'S WHAT WE NEED TO KNOW, ALFRED...AND I THINK THEY'RE GOING TO GET THERE.

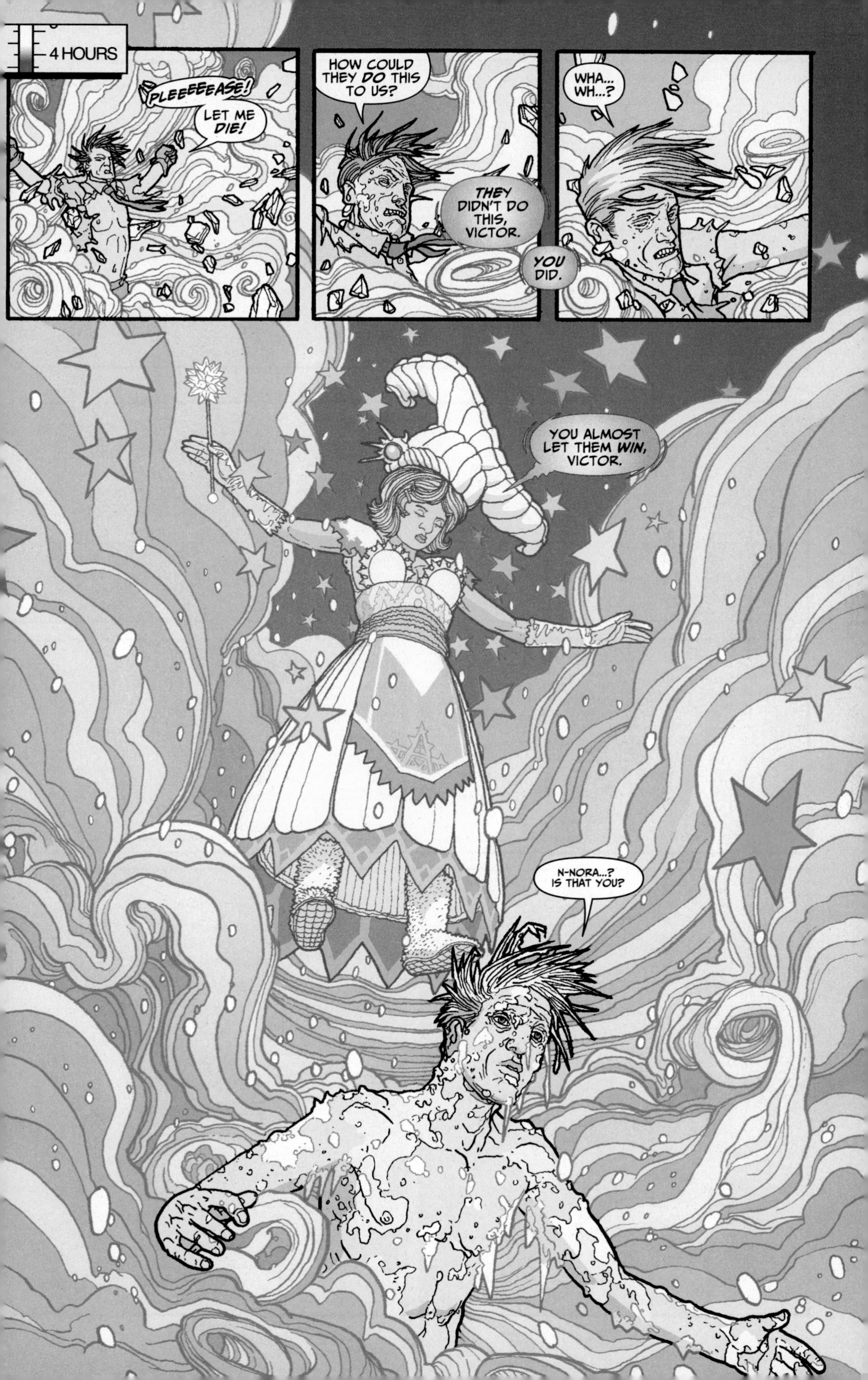
4 HOURS
PLEEEEEEASE!
LET ME DIE!
HOW COULD THEY DO THIS TO US?
THEY DIDN'T DO THIS, VICTOR.
YOU DID.
WHA... WH...?
YOU ALMOST LET THEM WIN, VICTOR.
N-NORA...? IS THAT YOU?

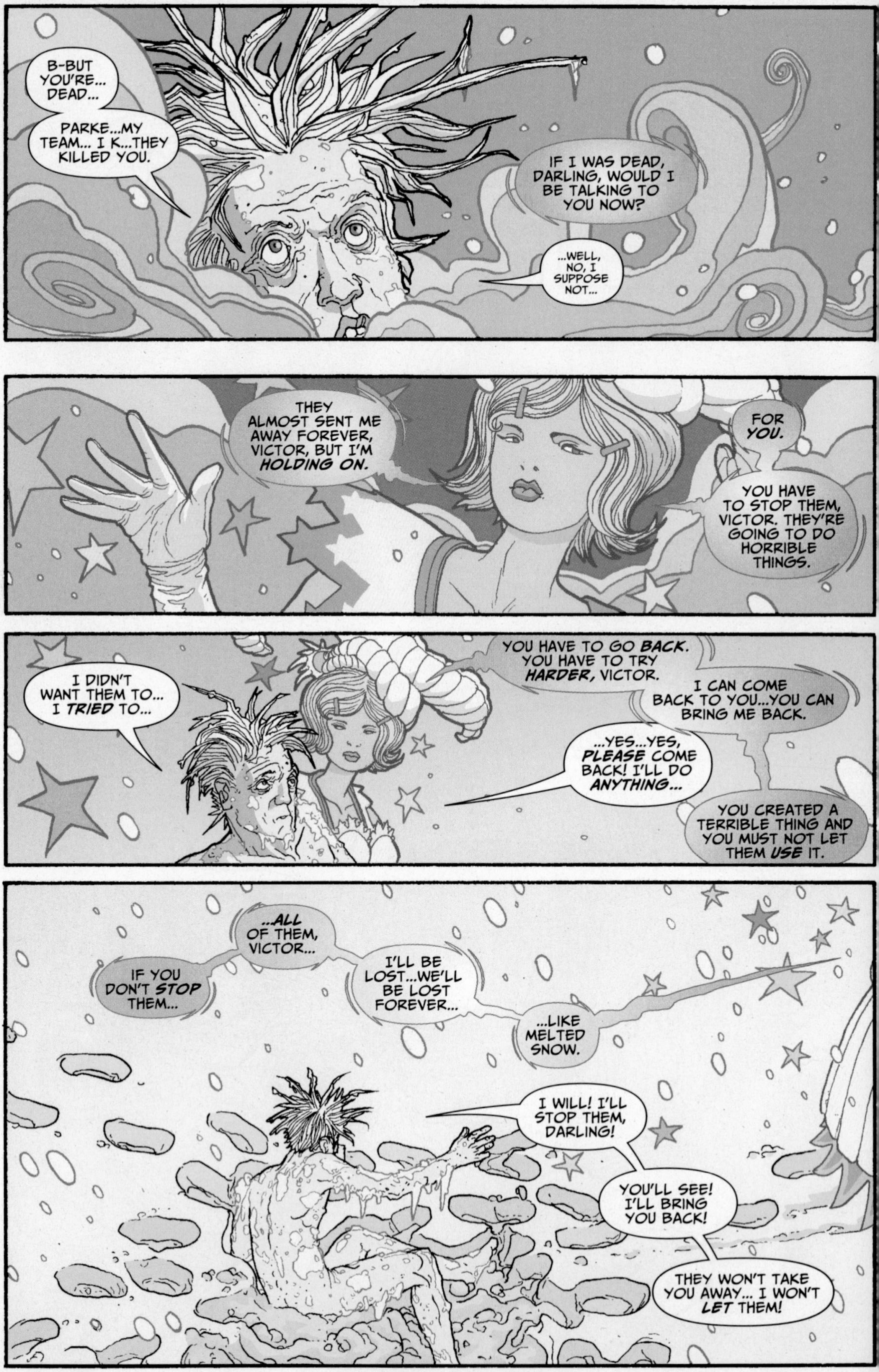
B-BUT YOU'RE... DEAD...
PARKE...MY TEAM... I K...THEY KILLED YOU.
IF I WAS DEAD, DARLING, WOULD I BE TALKING TO YOU NOW?
...WELL, NO, I SUPPOSE NOT...
THEY ALMOST SENT ME AWAY FOREVER, VICTOR, BUT I'M HOLDING ON.
FOR YOU.
YOU HAVE TO STOP THEM, VICTOR. THEY'RE GOING TO DO HORRIBLE THINGS.
I DIDN'T WANT THEM TO... I TRIED TO...
YOU HAVE TO GO BACK. YOU HAVE TO TRY HARDER, VICTOR.
I CAN COME BACK TO YOU...YOU CAN BRING ME BACK.
...YES...YES, PLEASE COME BACK! I'LL DO ANYTHING...
YOU CREATED A TERRIBLE THING AND YOU MUST NOT LET THEM USE IT.
IF YOU DON'T STOP THEM...
...ALL OF THEM, VICTOR...
I'LL BE LOST...WE'LL BE LOST FOREVER...
...LIKE MELTED SNOW.
I WILL! I'LL STOP THEM, DARLING!
YOU'LL SEE! I'LL BRING YOU BACK!
THEY WON'T TAKE YOU AWAY... I WON'T LET THEM!

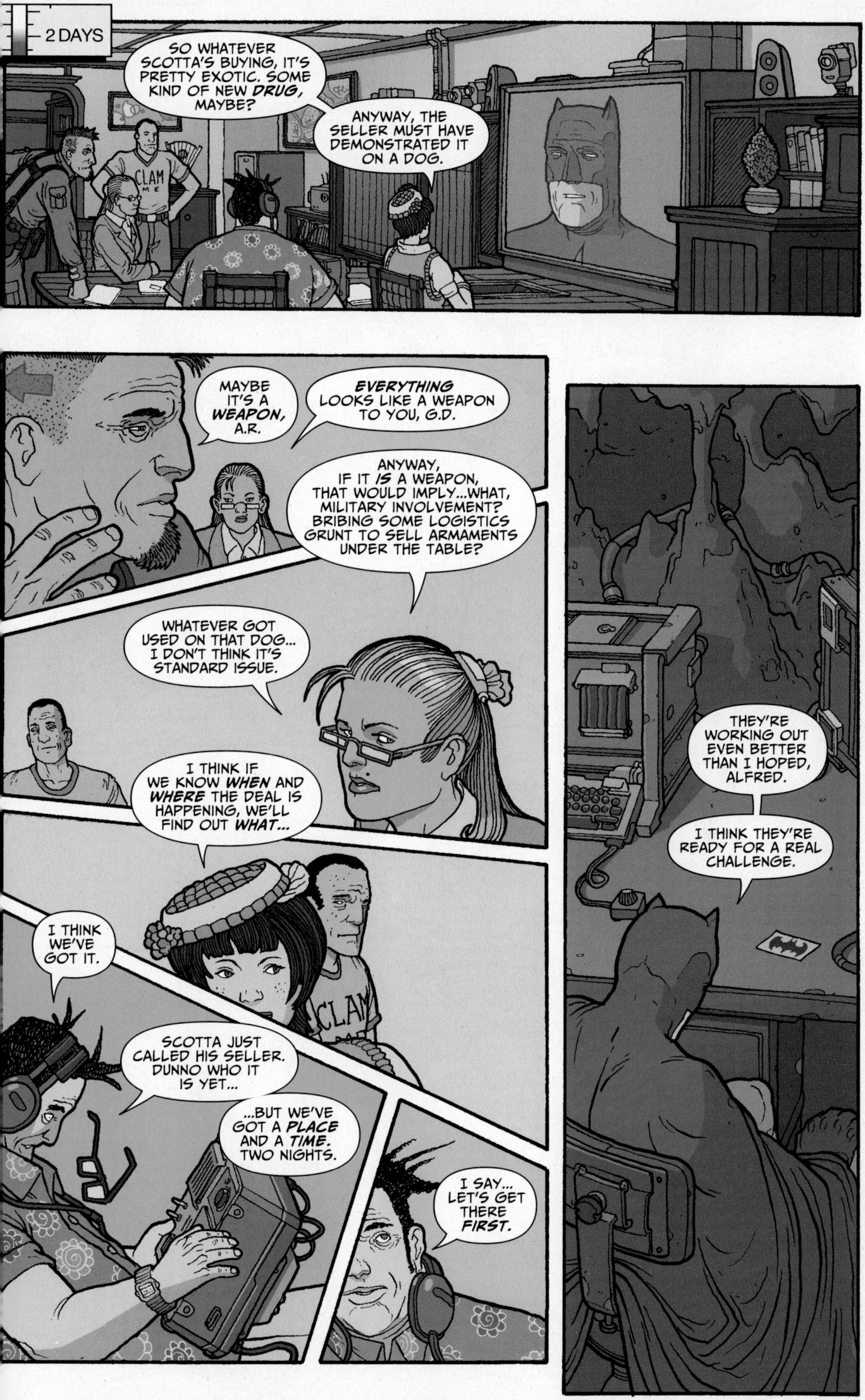
2 DAYS
SO WHATEVER SCOTTA'S BUYING, IT'S PRETTY EXOTIC. SOME KIND OF NEW DRUG, MAYBE?
ANYWAY, THE SELLER MUST HAVE DEMONSTRATED IT ON A DOG.
CLAM
MAYBE IT'S A WEAPON, A.R.
EVERYTHING LOOKS LIKE A WEAPON TO YOU, G.D.
ANYWAY, IF IT IS A WEAPON, THAT WOULD IMPLY...WHAT, MILITARY INVOLVEMENT? BRIBING SOME LOGISTICS GRUNT TO SELL ARMAMENTS UNDER THE TABLE?
WHATEVER GOT USED ON THAT DOG... I DON'T THINK IT'S STANDARD ISSUE.
I THINK IF WE KNOW WHEN AND WHERE THE DEAL IS HAPPENING, WE'LL FIND OUT WHAT...
I THINK WE'VE GOT IT.
SCOTTA JUST CALLED HIS SELLER. DUNNO WHO IT IS YET...
...BUT WE'VE GOT A PLACE AND A TIME. TWO NIGHTS.
I SAY... LET'S GET THERE FIRST.
THEY'RE WORKING OUT EVEN BETTER THAN I HOPED, ALFRED.
I THINK THEY'RE READY FOR A REAL CHALLENGE.

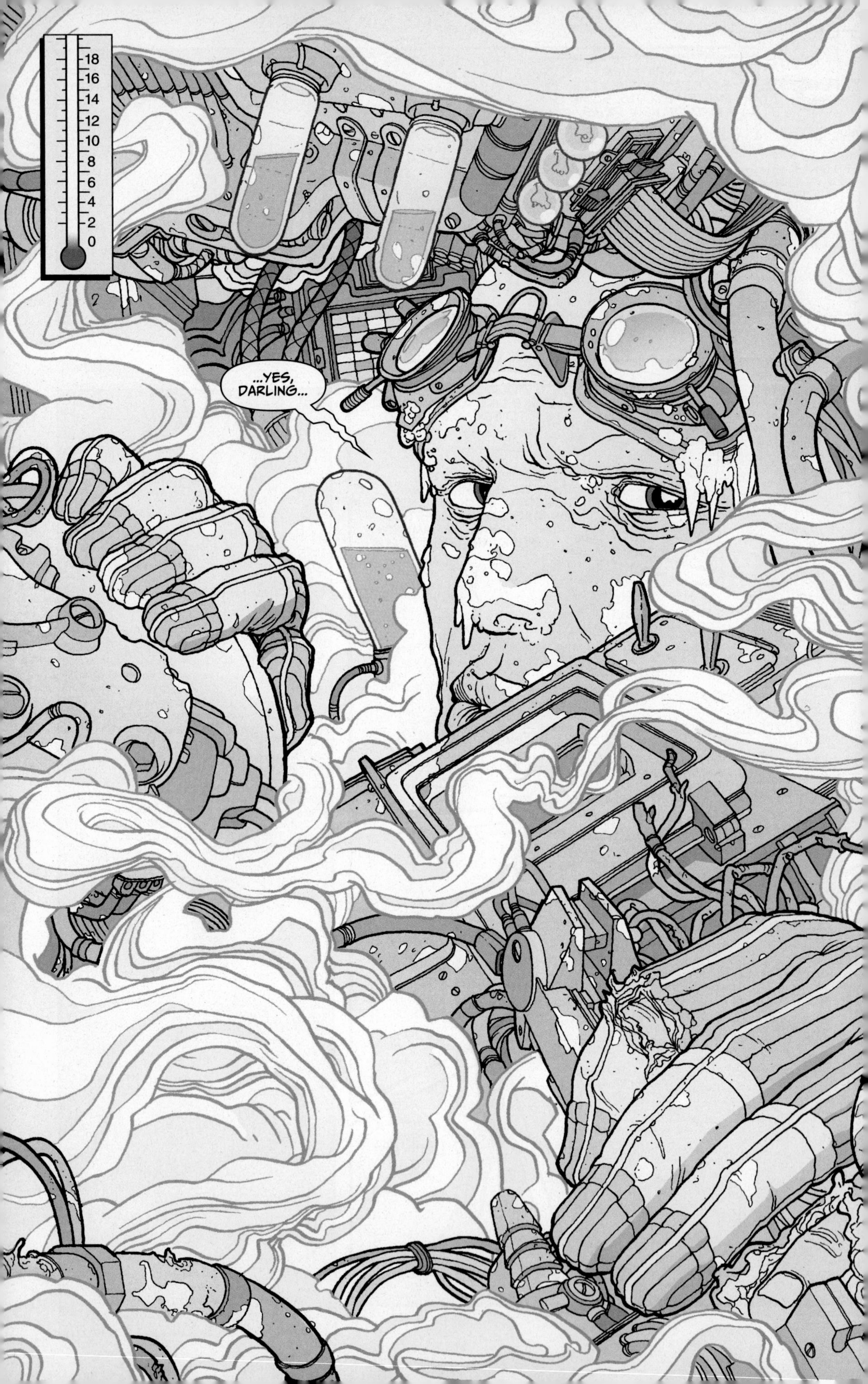
18
16
14
12
10
8
6
4
2
0
...YES, DARLING...

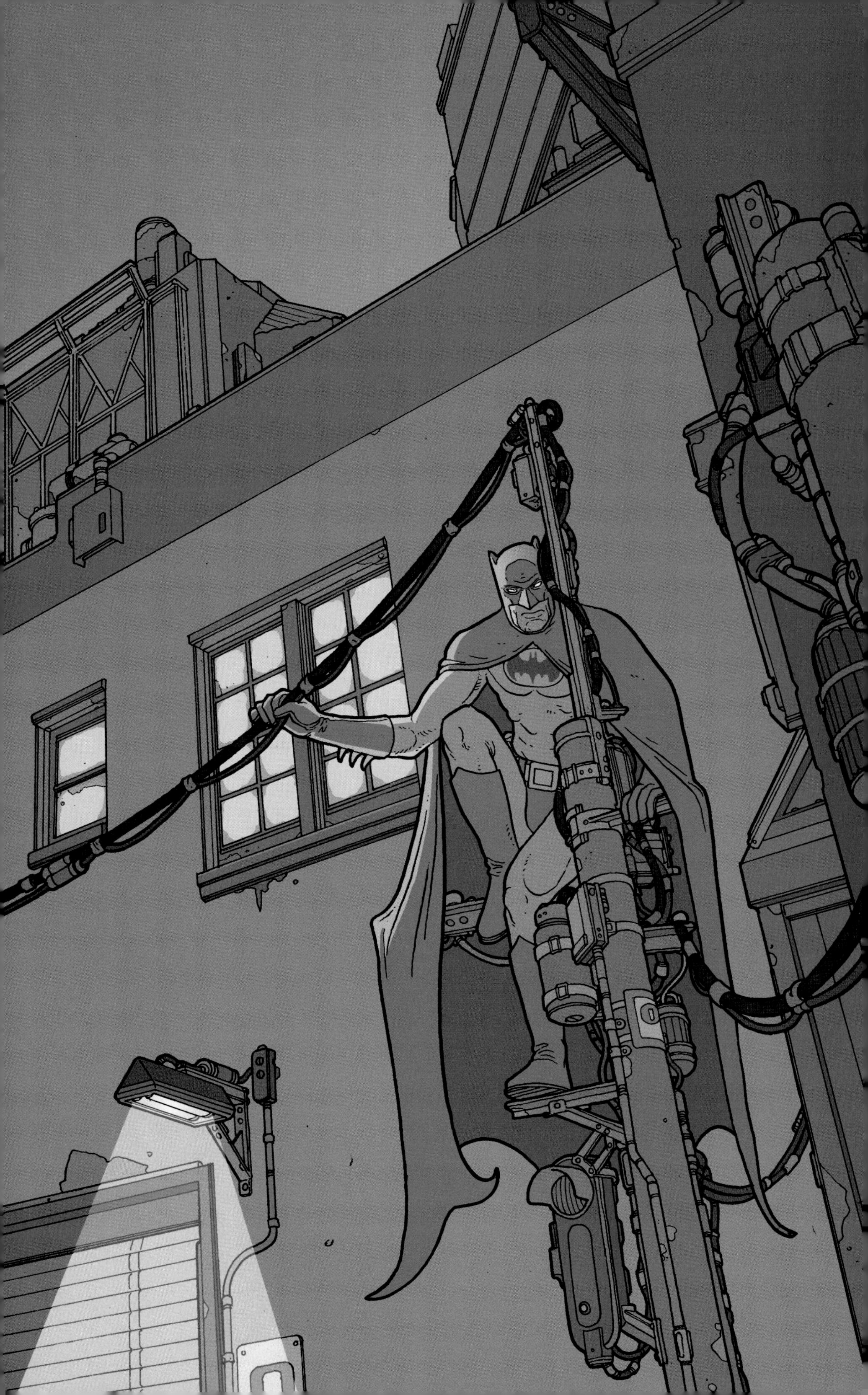

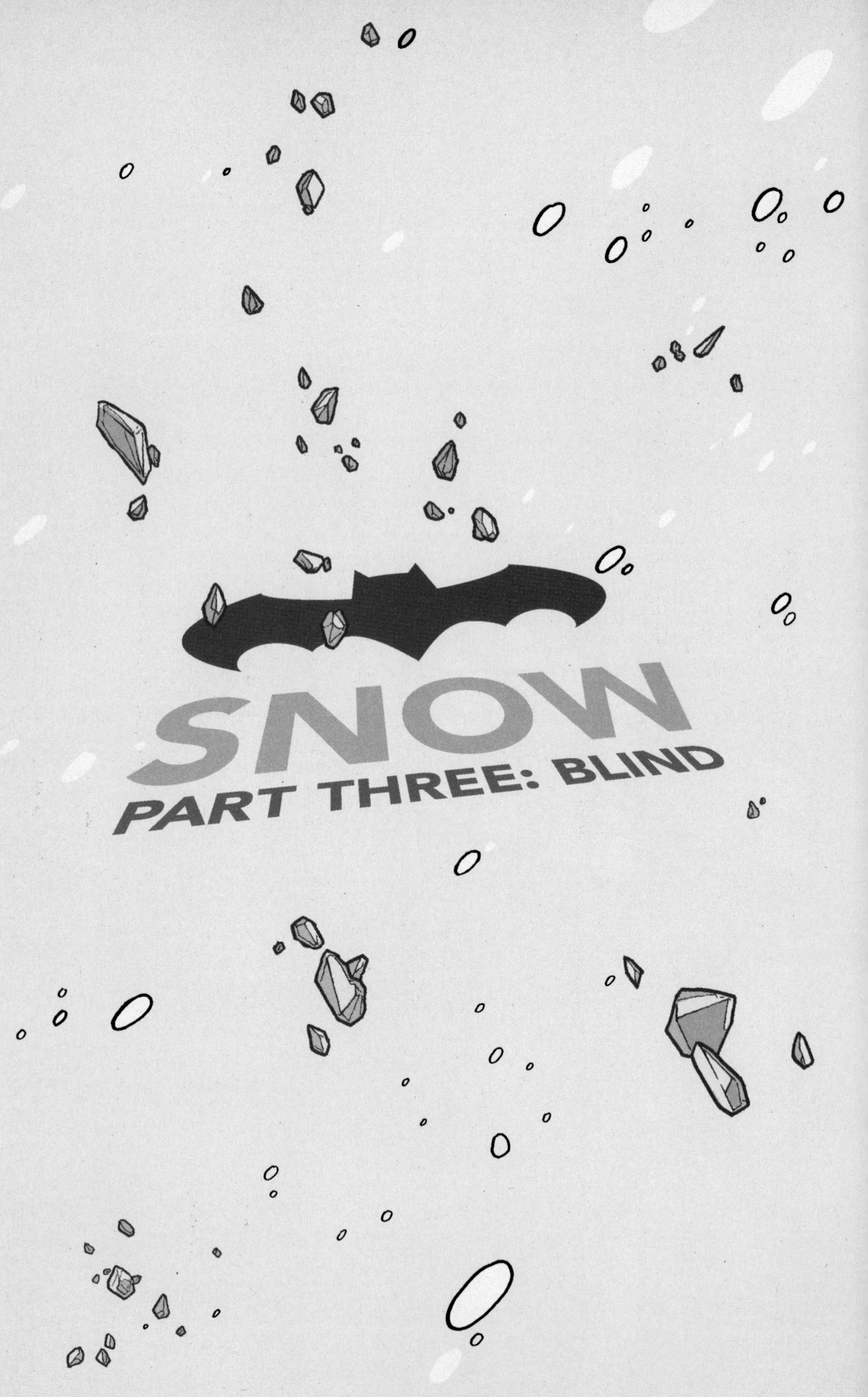
SNOW
PART THREE: BLIND

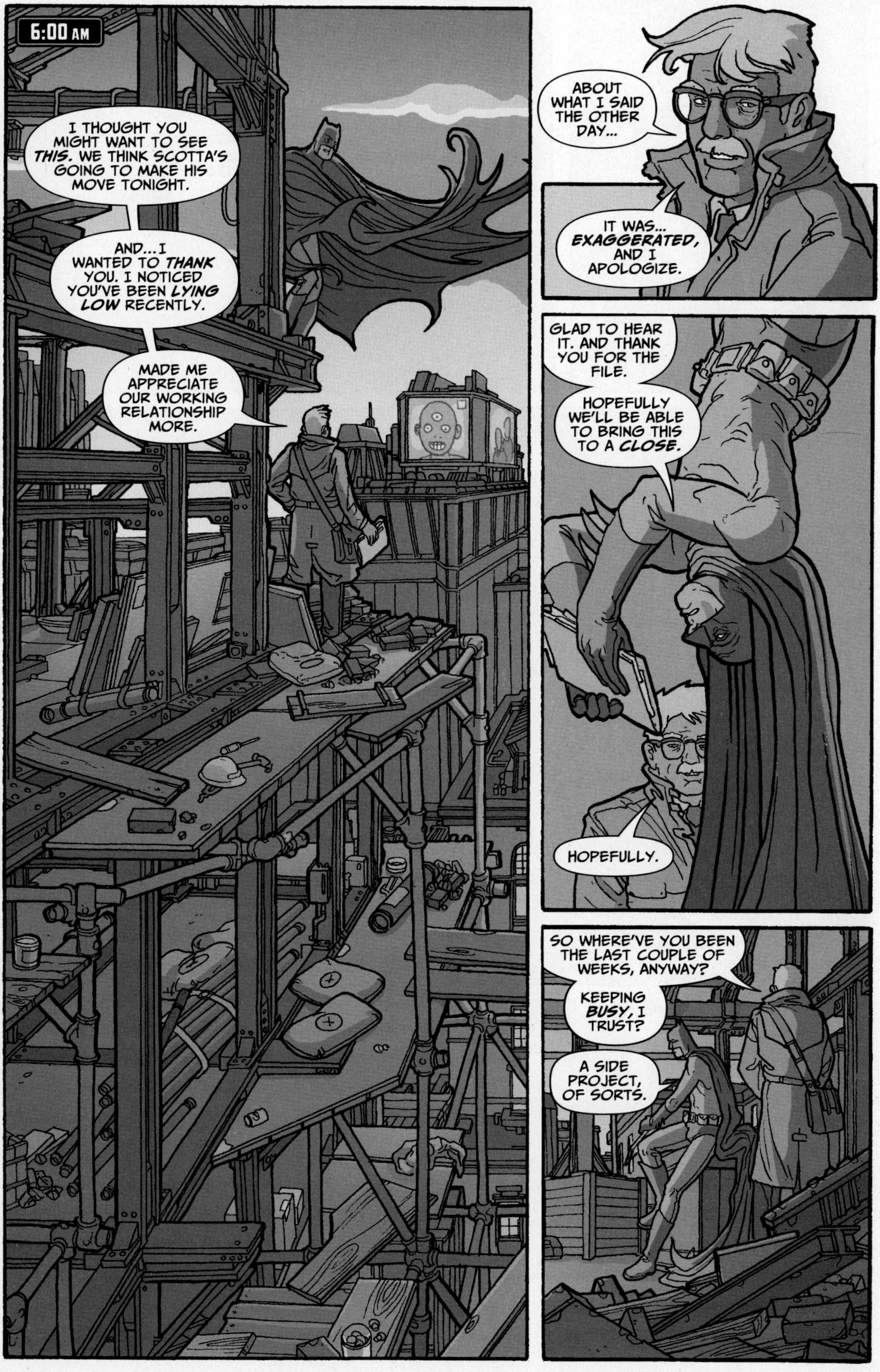
6:00 AM
I THOUGHT YOU MIGHT WANT TO SEE THIS. WE THINK SCOTTA'S GOING TO MAKE HIS MOVE TONIGHT.
AND... I WANTED TO THANK YOU. I NOTICED YOU'VE BEEN LYING LOW RECENTLY.
MADE ME APPRECIATE OUR WORKING RELATIONSHIP MORE.
ABOUT WHAT I SAID THE OTHER DAY...
IT WAS... EXAGGERATED, AND I APOLOGIZE.
GLAD TO HEAR IT. AND THANK YOU FOR THE FILE.
HOPEFULLY WE'LL BE ABLE TO BRING THIS TO A CLOSE.
HOPEFULLY.
SO WHERE'VE YOU BEEN THE LAST COUPLE OF WEEKS, ANYWAY?
KEEPING BUSY, I TRUST?
A SIDE PROJECT, OF SORTS.

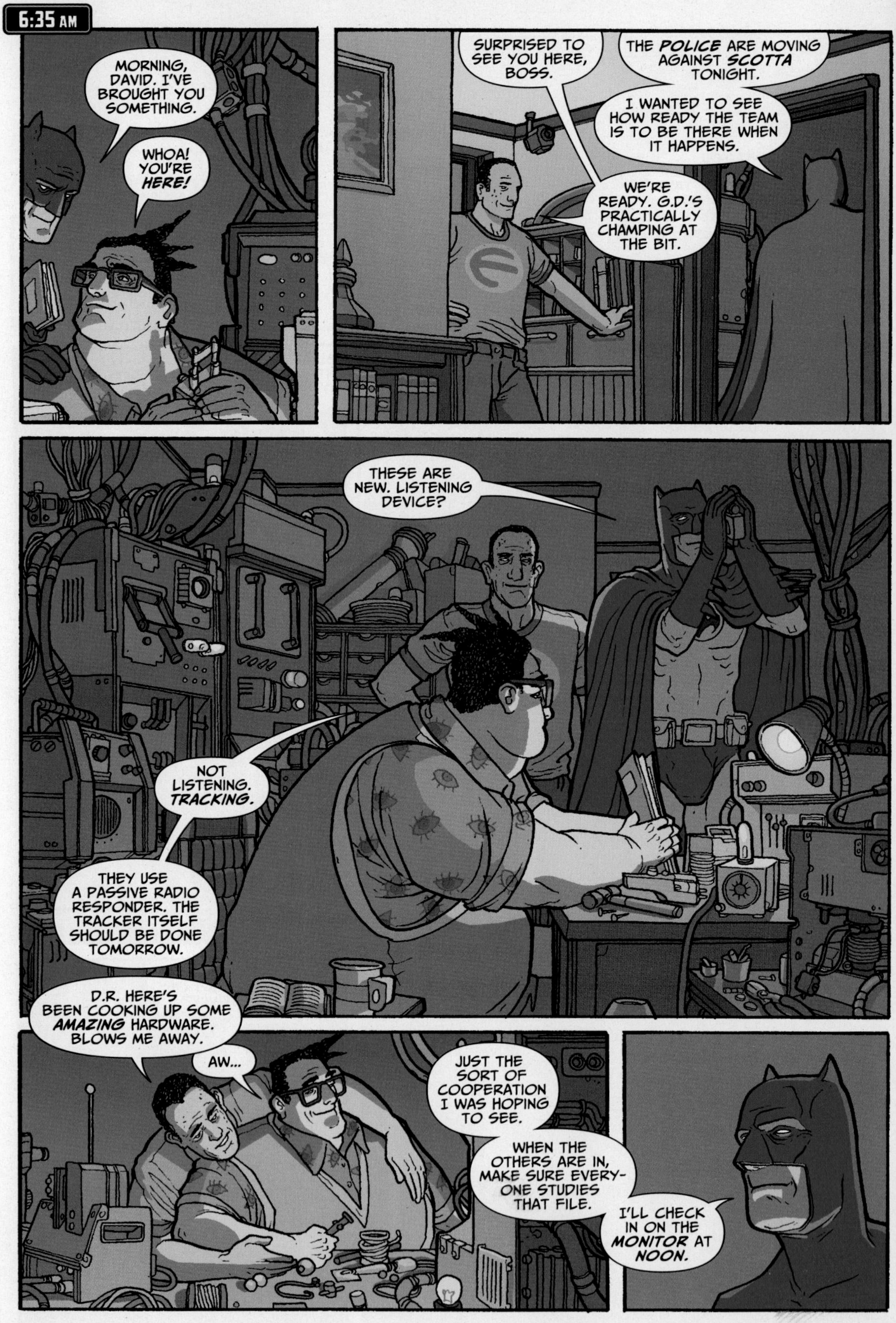
6:35 AM
MORNING, DAVID. I'VE BROUGHT YOU SOMETHING.
WHOA! YOU'RE *HERE!*
SURPRISED TO SEE YOU HERE, BOSS.
THE *POLICE* ARE MOVING AGAINST *SCOTTA* TONIGHT.
I WANTED TO SEE HOW READY THE TEAM IS TO BE THERE WHEN IT HAPPENS.
WE'RE READY. G.D.'S PRACTICALLY CHAMPING AT THE BIT.
THESE ARE NEW. LISTENING DEVICE?
NOT LISTENING. *TRACKING.*
THEY USE A PASSIVE RADIO RESPONDER. THE TRACKER ITSELF SHOULD BE DONE TOMORROW.
D.R. HERE'S BEEN COOKING UP SOME *AMAZING* HARDWARE. BLOWS ME AWAY.
AW...
JUST THE SORT OF COOPERATION I WAS HOPING TO SEE.
WHEN THE OTHERS ARE IN, MAKE SURE EVERY-ONE STUDIES THAT FILE.
I'LL CHECK IN ON THE *MONITOR* AT *NOON.*

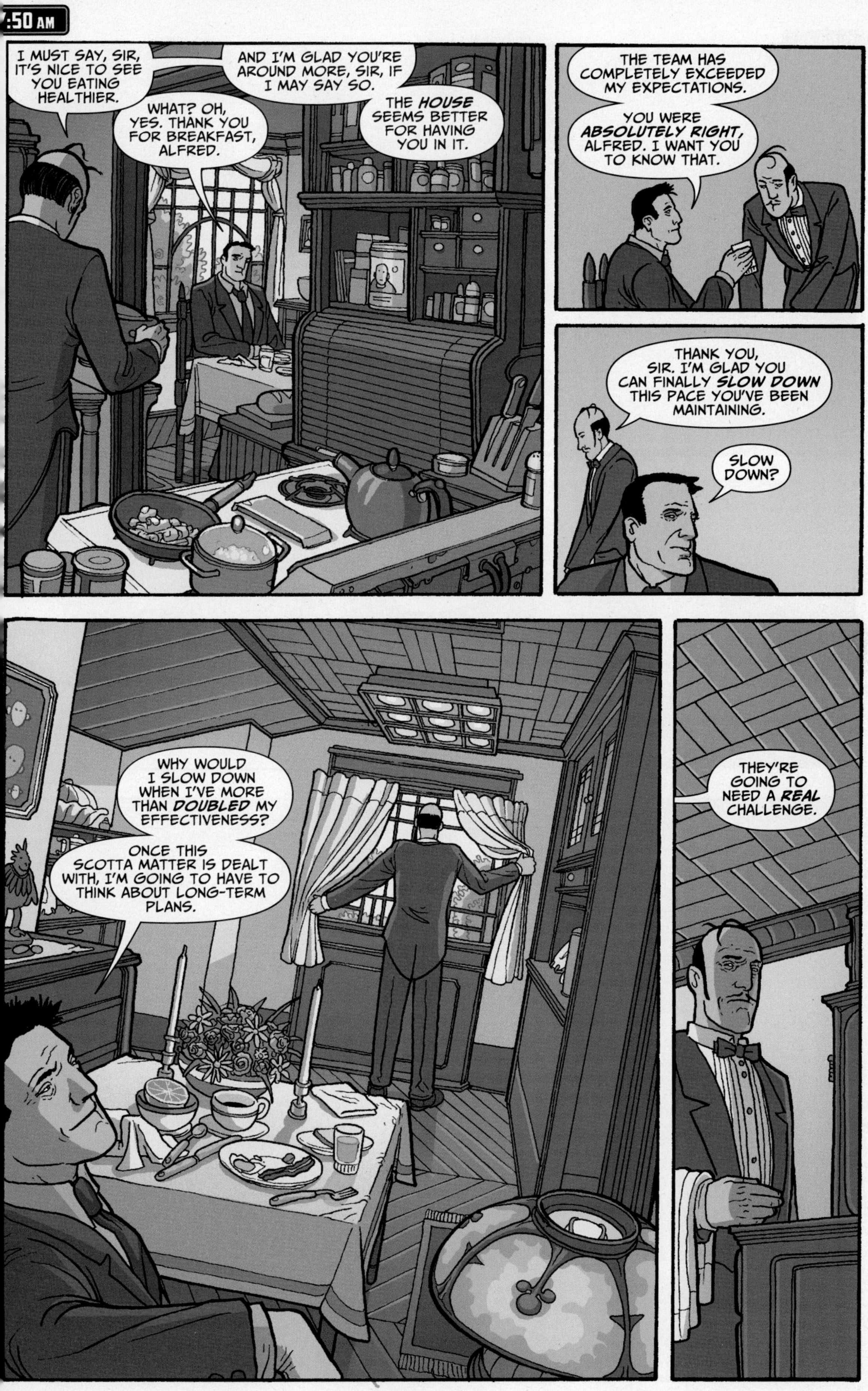
:50 AM
I MUST SAY, SIR, IT'S NICE TO SEE YOU EATING HEALTHIER.
WHAT? OH, YES. THANK YOU FOR BREAKFAST, ALFRED.
AND I'M GLAD YOU'RE AROUND MORE, SIR, IF I MAY SAY SO.
THE *HOUSE* SEEMS BETTER FOR HAVING YOU IN IT.
THE TEAM HAS COMPLETELY EXCEEDED MY EXPECTATIONS.
YOU WERE *ABSOLUTELY RIGHT*, ALFRED. I WANT YOU TO KNOW THAT.
THANK YOU, SIR. I'M GLAD YOU CAN FINALLY *SLOW DOWN* THIS PACE YOU'VE BEEN MAINTAINING.
SLOW DOWN?
WHY WOULD I SLOW DOWN WHEN I'VE MORE THAN *DOUBLED* MY EFFECTIVENESS?
ONCE THIS SCOTTA MATTER IS DEALT WITH, I'M GOING TO HAVE TO THINK ABOUT LONG-TERM PLANS.
THEY'RE GOING TO NEED A *REAL* CHALLENGE.

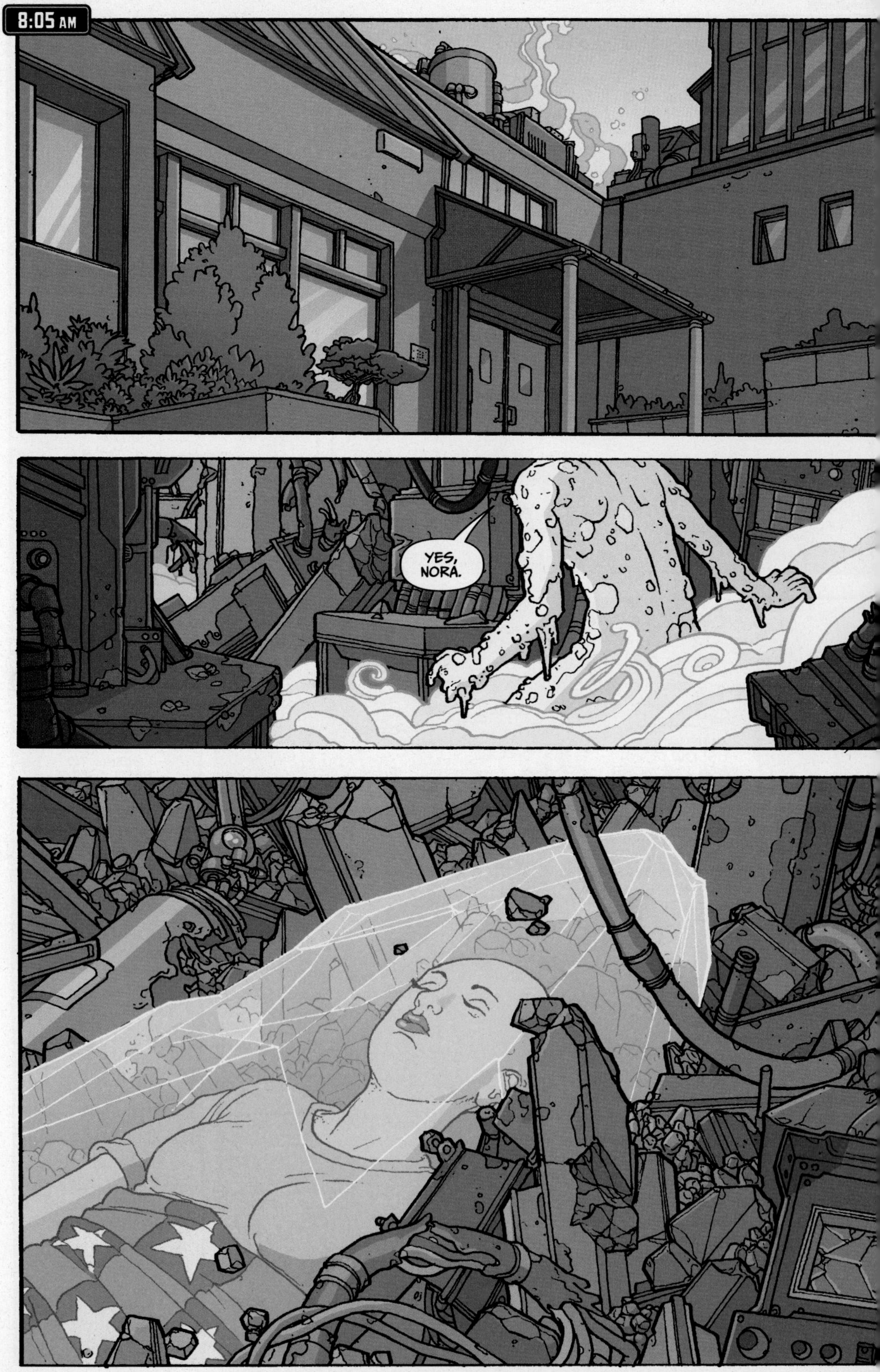
8:05 AM
YES, NORA.

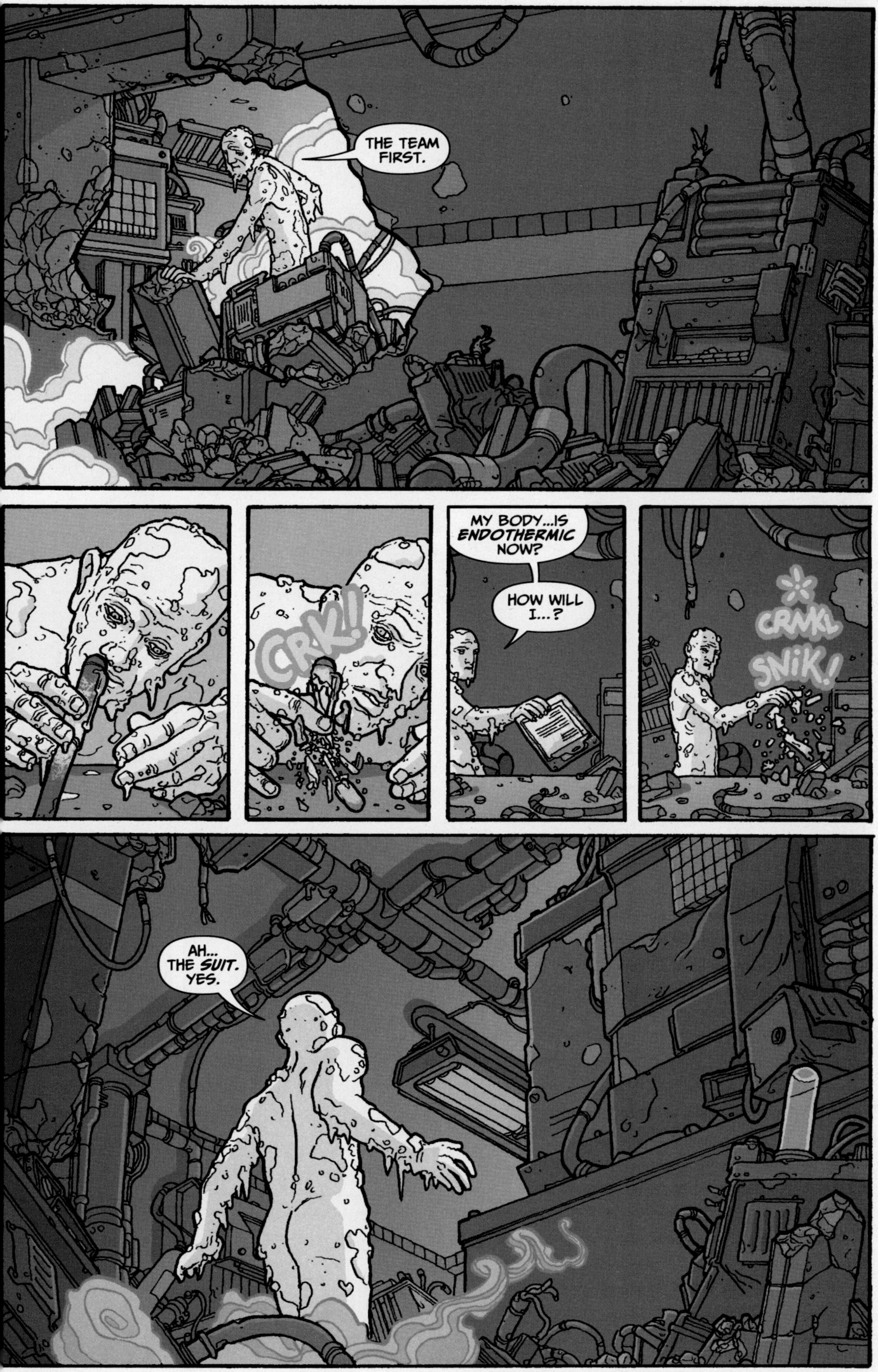
THE TEAM FIRST.
CRK!
MY BODY...IS *ENDOTHERMIC* NOW?
HOW WILL I...?
CRNKL
SNIK!
AH... THE *SUIT*. YES.

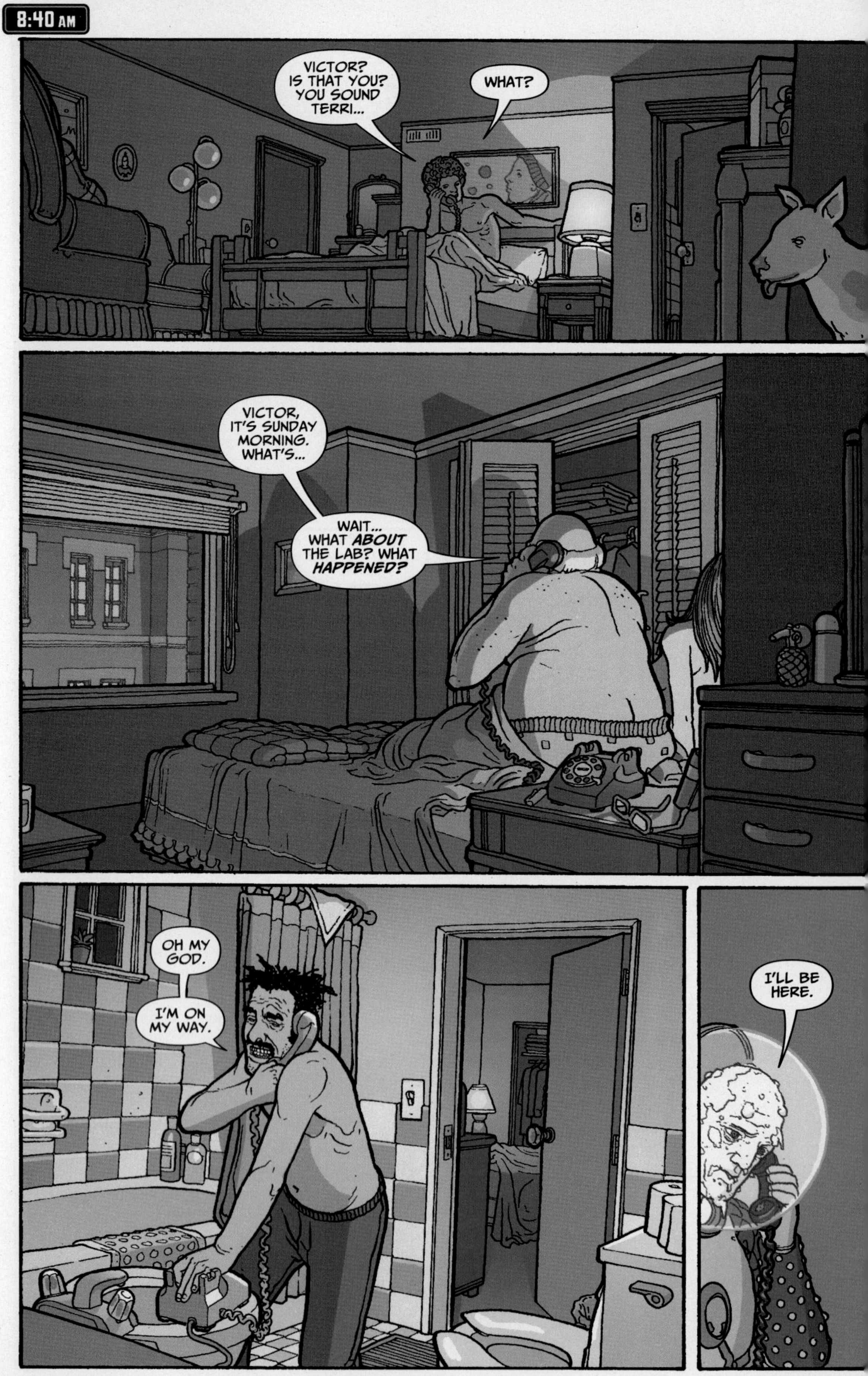
8:40 AM
VICTOR? IS THAT YOU? YOU SOUND TERRI...
WHAT?
VICTOR, IT'S SUNDAY MORNING. WHAT'S...
WAIT... WHAT ABOUT THE LAB? WHAT HAPPENED?
OH MY GOD.
I'M ON MY WAY.
I'LL BE HERE.

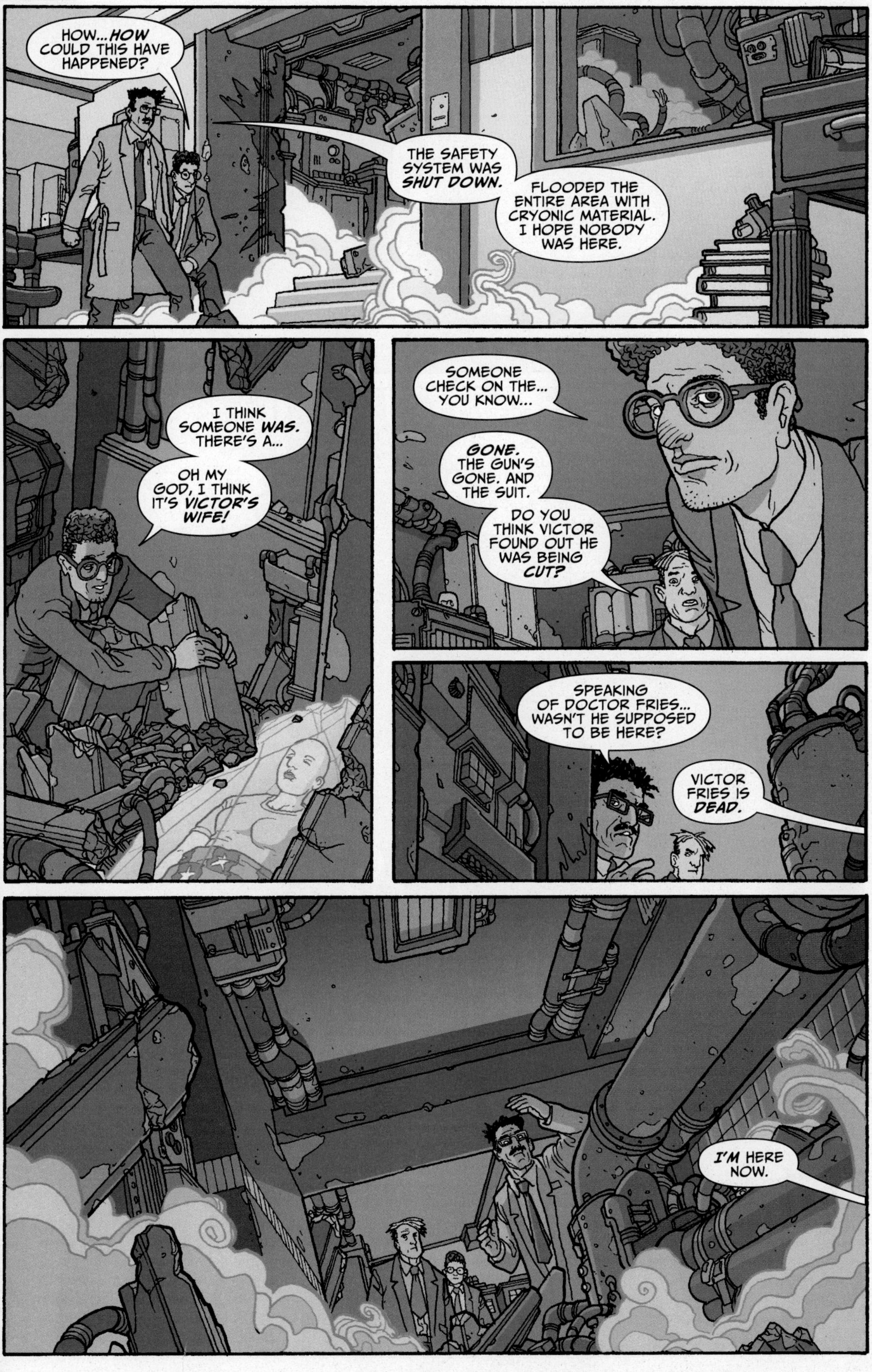
HOW... HOW COULD THIS HAVE HAPPENED?
THE SAFETY SYSTEM WAS SHUT DOWN.
FLOODED THE ENTIRE AREA WITH CRYONIC MATERIAL. I HOPE NOBODY WAS HERE.
I THINK SOMEONE WAS. THERE'S A...
OH MY GOD, I THINK IT'S VICTOR'S WIFE!
SOMEONE CHECK ON THE... YOU KNOW...
GONE. THE GUN'S GONE. AND THE SUIT.
DO YOU THINK VICTOR FOUND OUT HE WAS BEING CUT?
SPEAKING OF DOCTOR FRIES... WASN'T HE SUPPOSED TO BE HERE?
VICTOR FRIES IS DEAD.
I'M HERE NOW.

12:45 PM

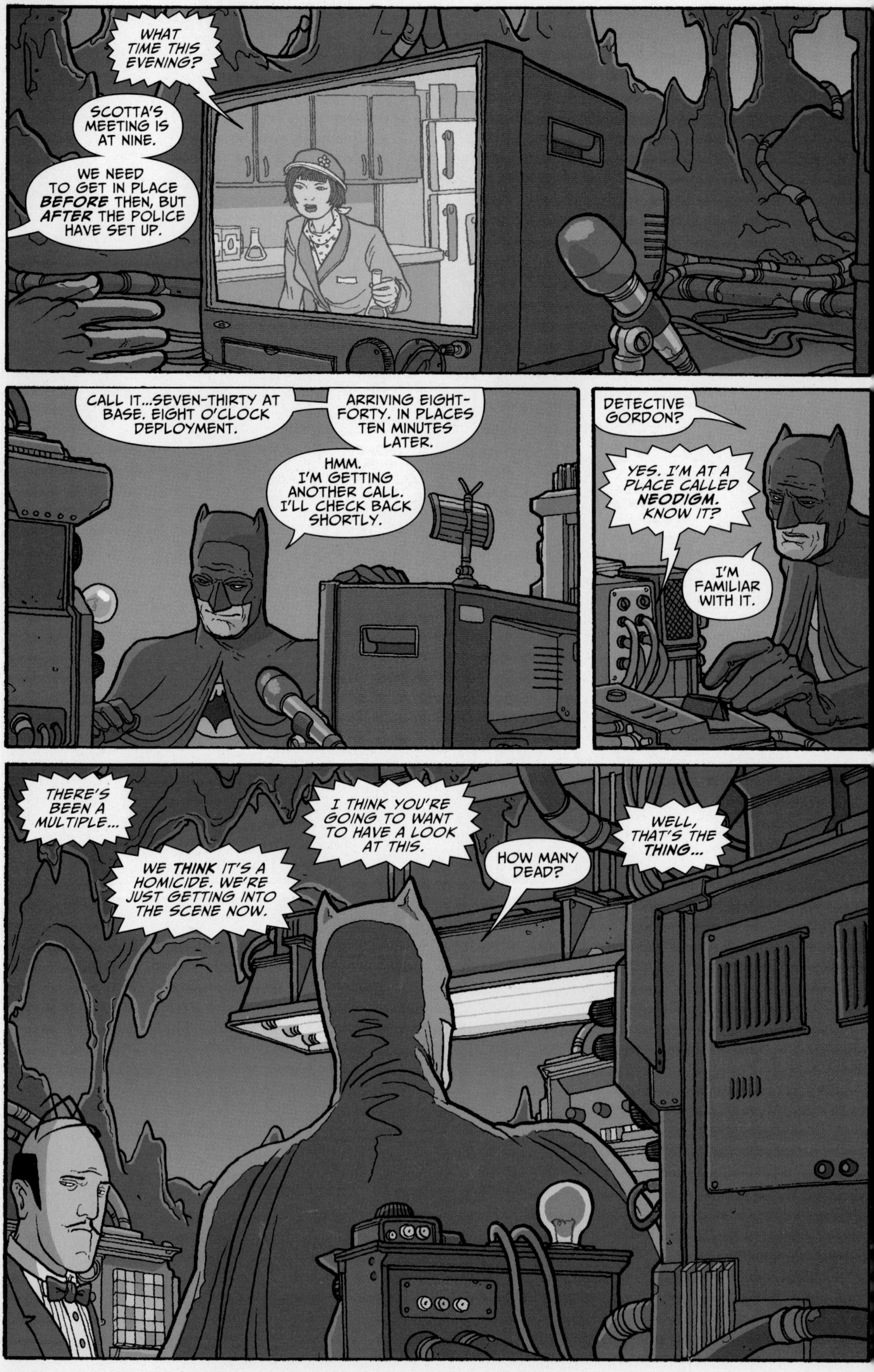
WHAT TIME THIS EVENING?
SCOTTA'S MEETING IS AT NINE.
WE NEED TO GET IN PLACE **BEFORE** THEN, BUT **AFTER** THE POLICE HAVE SET UP.
CALL IT...SEVEN-THIRTY AT BASE. EIGHT O'CLOCK DEPLOYMENT.
ARRIVING EIGHT-FORTY. IN PLACES TEN MINUTES LATER.
HMM. I'M GETTING ANOTHER CALL. I'LL CHECK BACK SHORTLY.
DETECTIVE GORDON?
YES. I'M AT A PLACE CALLED **NEODIGM.** KNOW IT?
I'M FAMILIAR WITH IT.
THERE'S BEEN A MULTIPLE...
WE **THINK** IT'S A HOMICIDE. WE'RE JUST GETTING INTO THE SCENE NOW.
I THINK YOU'RE GOING TO WANT TO HAVE A LOOK AT THIS.
HOW MANY DEAD?
WELL, THAT'S THE **THING...**

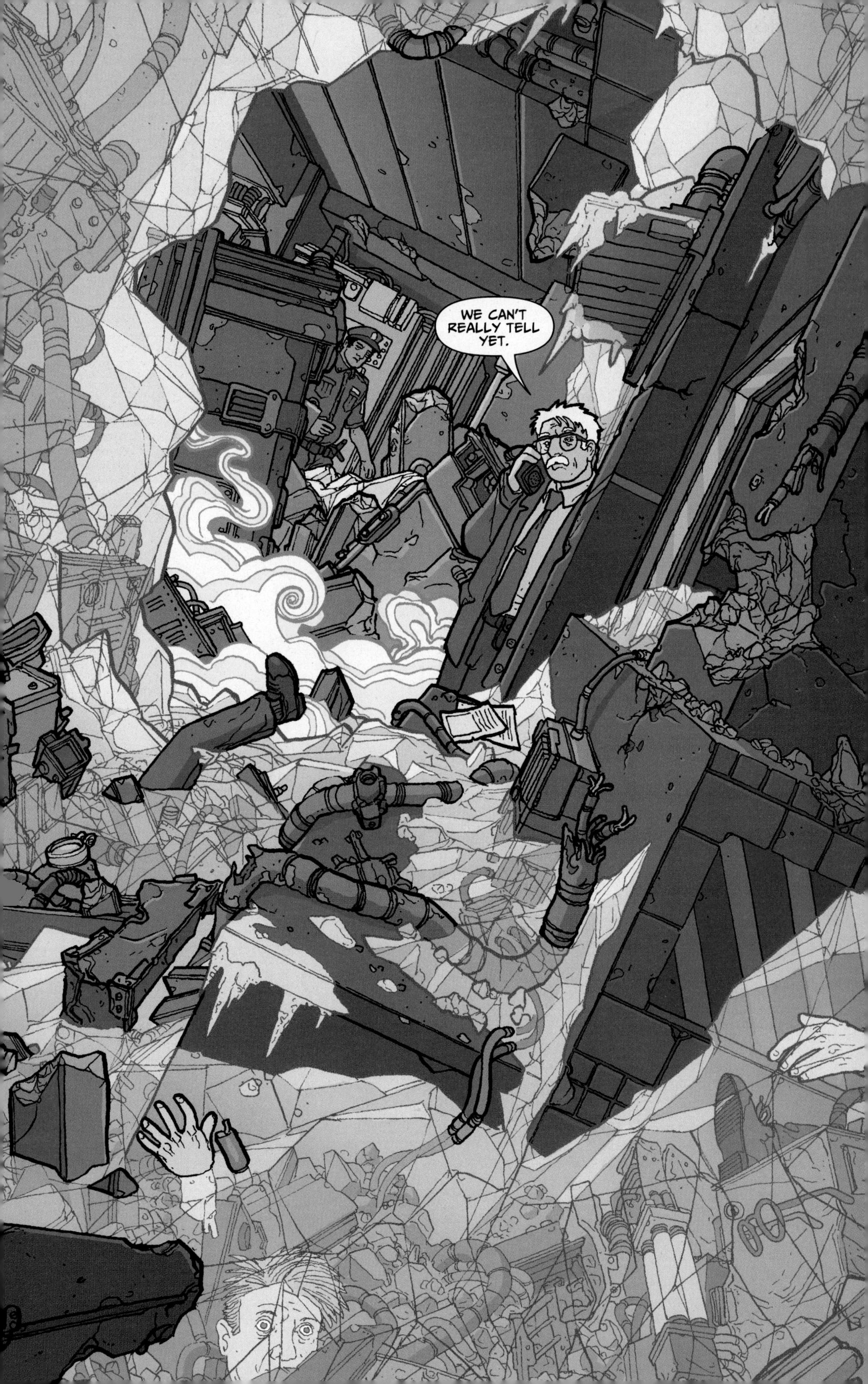
WE CAN'T REALLY TELL YET.

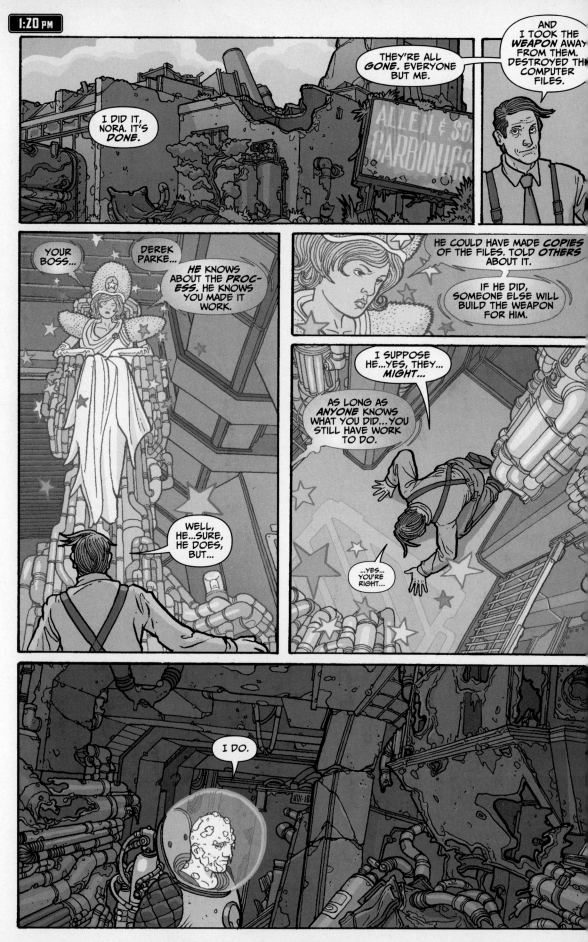

I DID IT, NORA. IT'S *DONE*.

THEY'RE ALL *GONE*. EVERYONE BUT ME.

AND I TOOK THE *WEAPON* AWAY FROM THEM. DESTROYED TH[E] COMPUTER FILES.

YOUR BOSS... DEREK PARKE... *HE* KNOWS ABOUT THE *PROCESS*. HE KNOWS YOU MADE IT WORK.

HE COULD HAVE MADE *COPIES* OF THE FILES. TOLD *OTHERS* ABOUT IT.

IF HE DID, SOMEONE ELSE WILL BUILD THE WEAPON FOR HIM.

WELL, HE...SURE, HE DOES, BUT...

I SUPPOSE HE...YES, THEY... *MIGHT*...

AS LONG AS *ANYONE* KNOWS WHAT YOU DID...YOU STILL HAVE WORK TO DO.

...YES... YOU'RE RIGHT...

I DO.

64

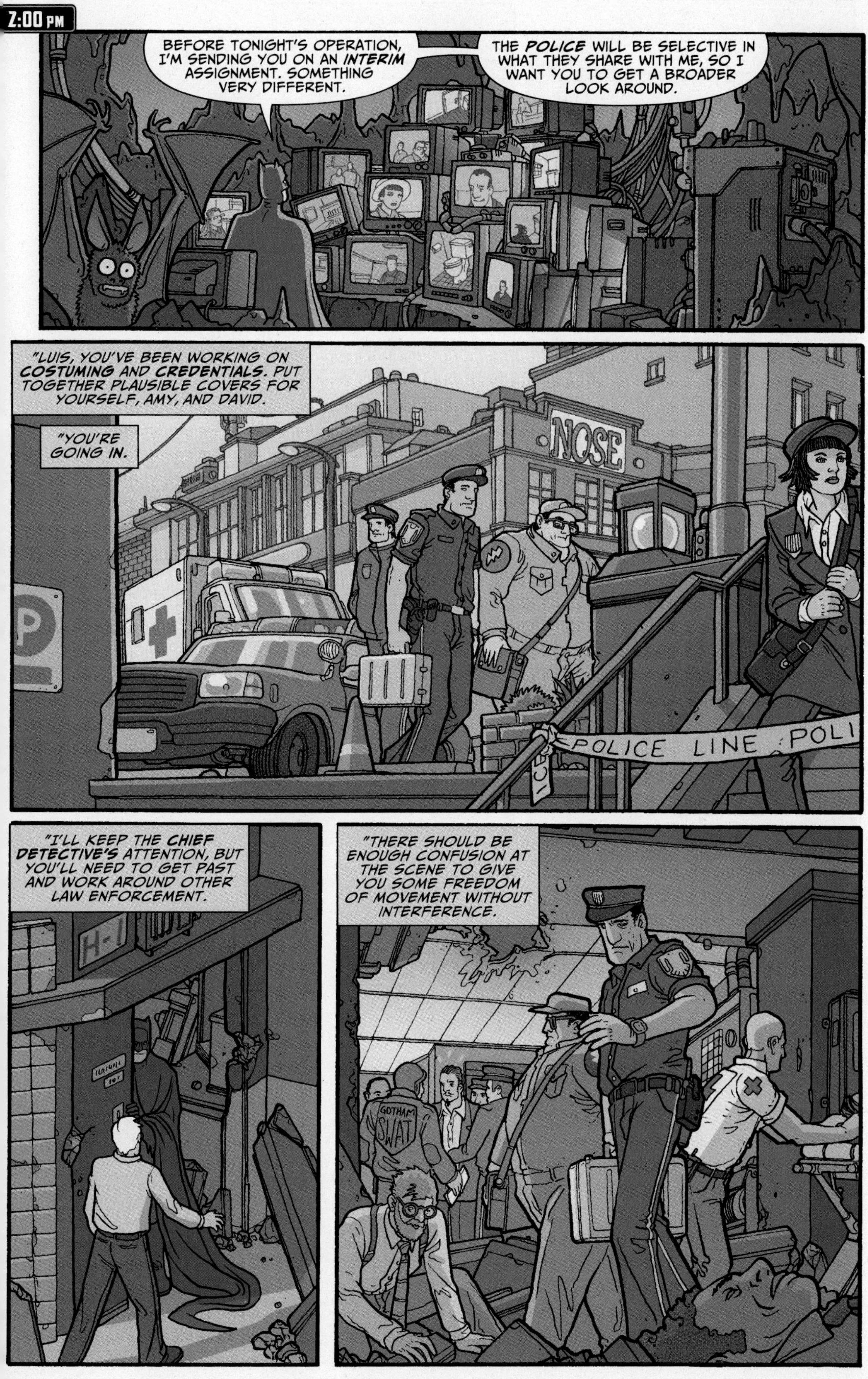
2:00 PM
BEFORE TONIGHT'S OPERATION, I'M SENDING YOU ON AN *INTERIM* ASSIGNMENT. SOMETHING VERY DIFFERENT.
THE *POLICE* WILL BE SELECTIVE IN WHAT THEY SHARE WITH ME, SO I WANT YOU TO GET A BROADER LOOK AROUND.
"LUIS, YOU'VE BEEN WORKING ON **COSTUMING** AND **CREDENTIALS.** PUT TOGETHER PLAUSIBLE COVERS FOR YOURSELF, AMY, AND DAVID.
"YOU'RE GOING *IN.*
NOSE
POLICE LINE POLI
"I'LL KEEP THE **CHIEF DETECTIVE'S** ATTENTION, BUT YOU'LL NEED TO GET PAST AND WORK AROUND OTHER LAW ENFORCEMENT.
H-1
"THERE SHOULD BE ENOUGH CONFUSION AT THE SCENE TO GIVE YOU SOME FREEDOM OF MOVEMENT WITHOUT INTERFERENCE.
GOTHAM SWAT

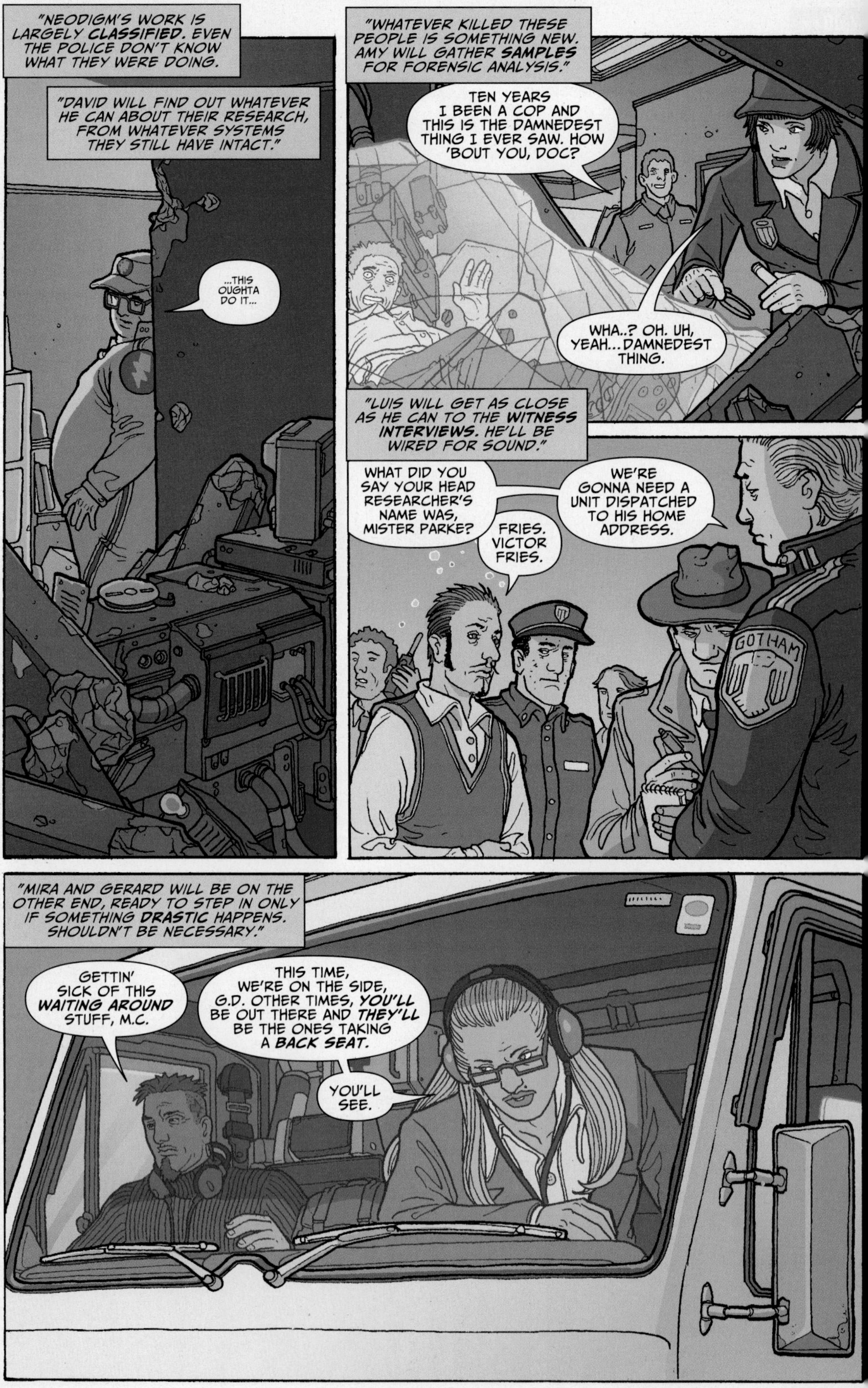
"NEODIGM'S WORK IS LARGELY CLASSIFIED. EVEN THE POLICE DON'T KNOW WHAT THEY WERE DOING.
"DAVID WILL FIND OUT WHATEVER HE CAN ABOUT THEIR RESEARCH, FROM WHATEVER SYSTEMS THEY STILL HAVE INTACT."
...THIS OUGHTA DO IT...
"WHATEVER KILLED THESE PEOPLE IS SOMETHING NEW. AMY WILL GATHER SAMPLES FOR FORENSIC ANALYSIS."
TEN YEARS I BEEN A COP AND THIS IS THE DAMNEDEST THING I EVER SAW. HOW 'BOUT YOU, DOC?
WHA..? OH. UH, YEAH...DAMNEDEST THING.
"LUIS WILL GET AS CLOSE AS HE CAN TO THE WITNESS INTERVIEWS. HE'LL BE WIRED FOR SOUND."
WHAT DID YOU SAY YOUR HEAD RESEARCHER'S NAME WAS, MISTER PARKE?
FRIES. VICTOR FRIES.
WE'RE GONNA NEED A UNIT DISPATCHED TO HIS HOME ADDRESS.
GOTHAM
"MIRA AND GERARD WILL BE ON THE OTHER END, READY TO STEP IN ONLY IF SOMETHING DRASTIC HAPPENS. SHOULDN'T BE NECESSARY."
GETTIN' SICK OF THIS WAITING AROUND STUFF, M.C.
THIS TIME, WE'RE ON THE SIDE, G.D. OTHER TIMES, YOU'LL BE OUT THERE AND THEY'LL BE THE ONES TAKING A BACK SEAT.
YOU'LL SEE.

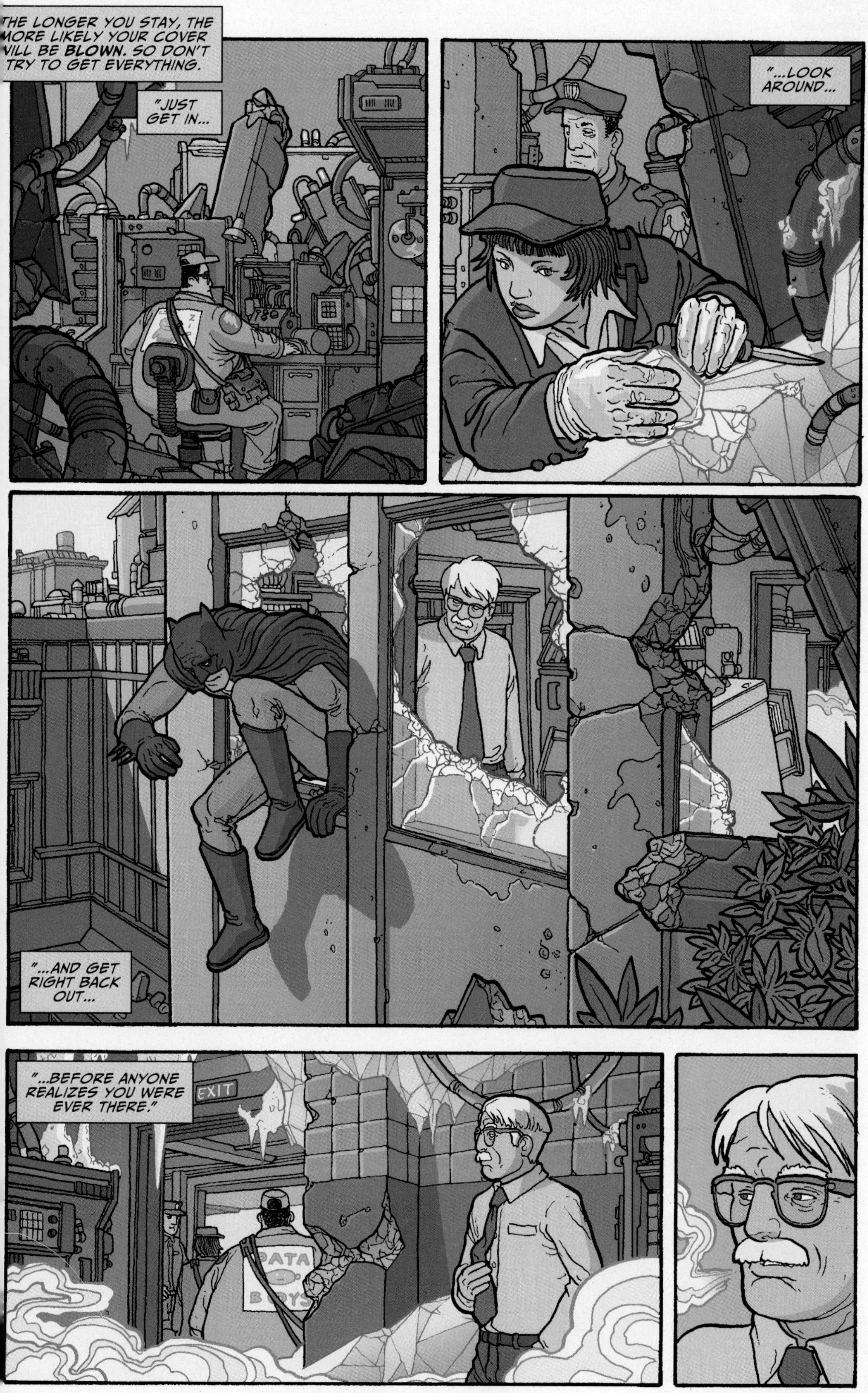
THE LONGER YOU STAY, THE MORE LIKELY YOUR COVER WILL BE BLOWN. SO DON'T TRY TO GET EVERYTHING.
"JUST GET IN...
"...LOOK AROUND...
"...AND GET RIGHT BACK OUT...
"...BEFORE ANYONE REALIZES YOU WERE EVER THERE."
EXIT
DATA BOYS

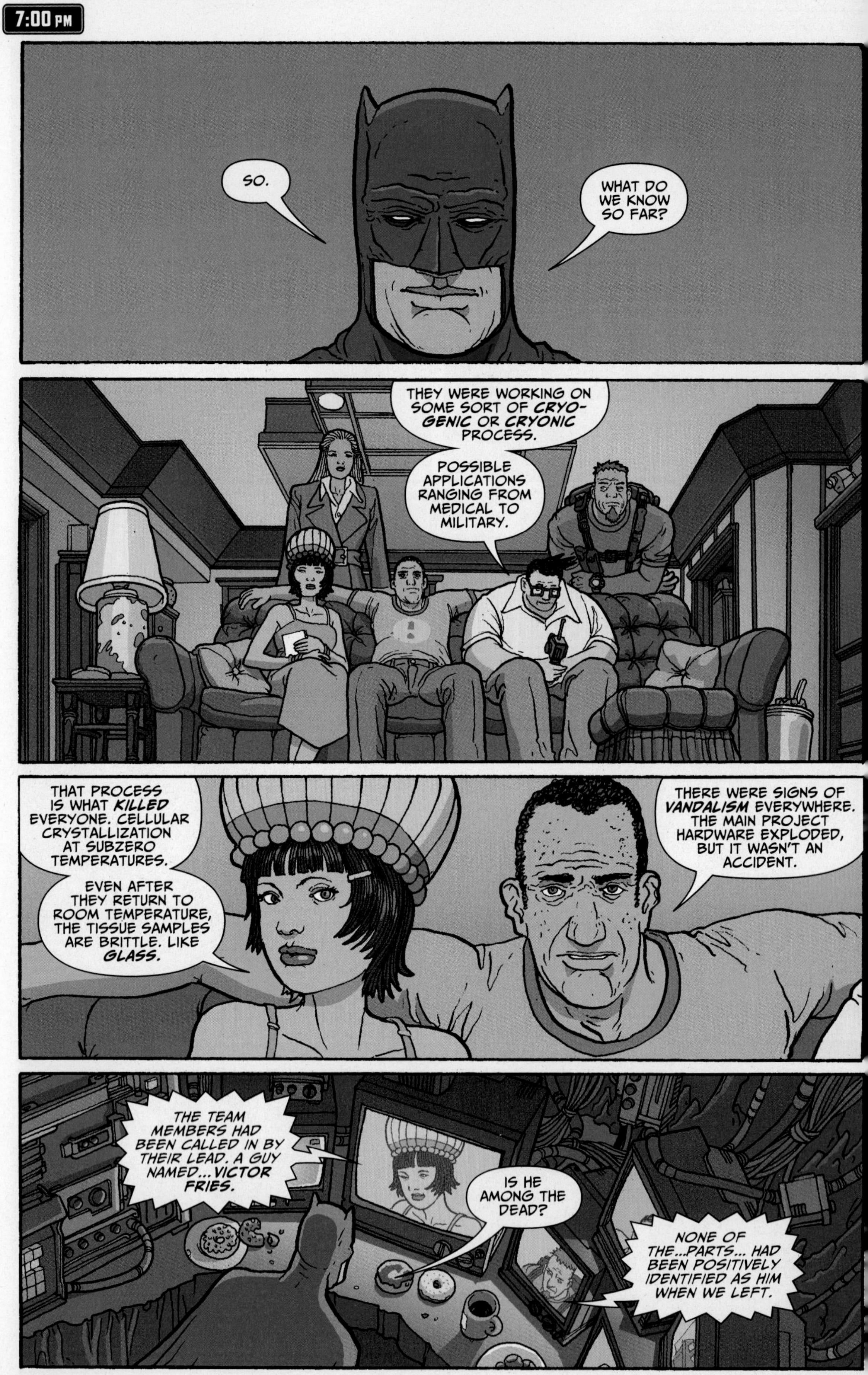
7:00 PM
SO.
WHAT DO WE KNOW SO FAR?
THEY WERE WORKING ON SOME SORT OF CRYO-GENIC OR CRYONIC PROCESS.
POSSIBLE APPLICATIONS RANGING FROM MEDICAL TO MILITARY.
THAT PROCESS IS WHAT KILLED EVERYONE. CELLULAR CRYSTALLIZATION AT SUBZERO TEMPERATURES.
EVEN AFTER THEY RETURN TO ROOM TEMPERATURE, THE TISSUE SAMPLES ARE BRITTLE. LIKE GLASS.
THERE WERE SIGNS OF VANDALISM EVERYWHERE. THE MAIN PROJECT HARDWARE EXPLODED, BUT IT WASN'T AN ACCIDENT.
THE TEAM MEMBERS HAD BEEN CALLED IN BY THEIR LEAD. A GUY NAMED... VICTOR FRIES.
IS HE AMONG THE DEAD?
NONE OF THE...PARTS... HAD BEEN POSITIVELY IDENTIFIED AS HIM WHEN WE LEFT.

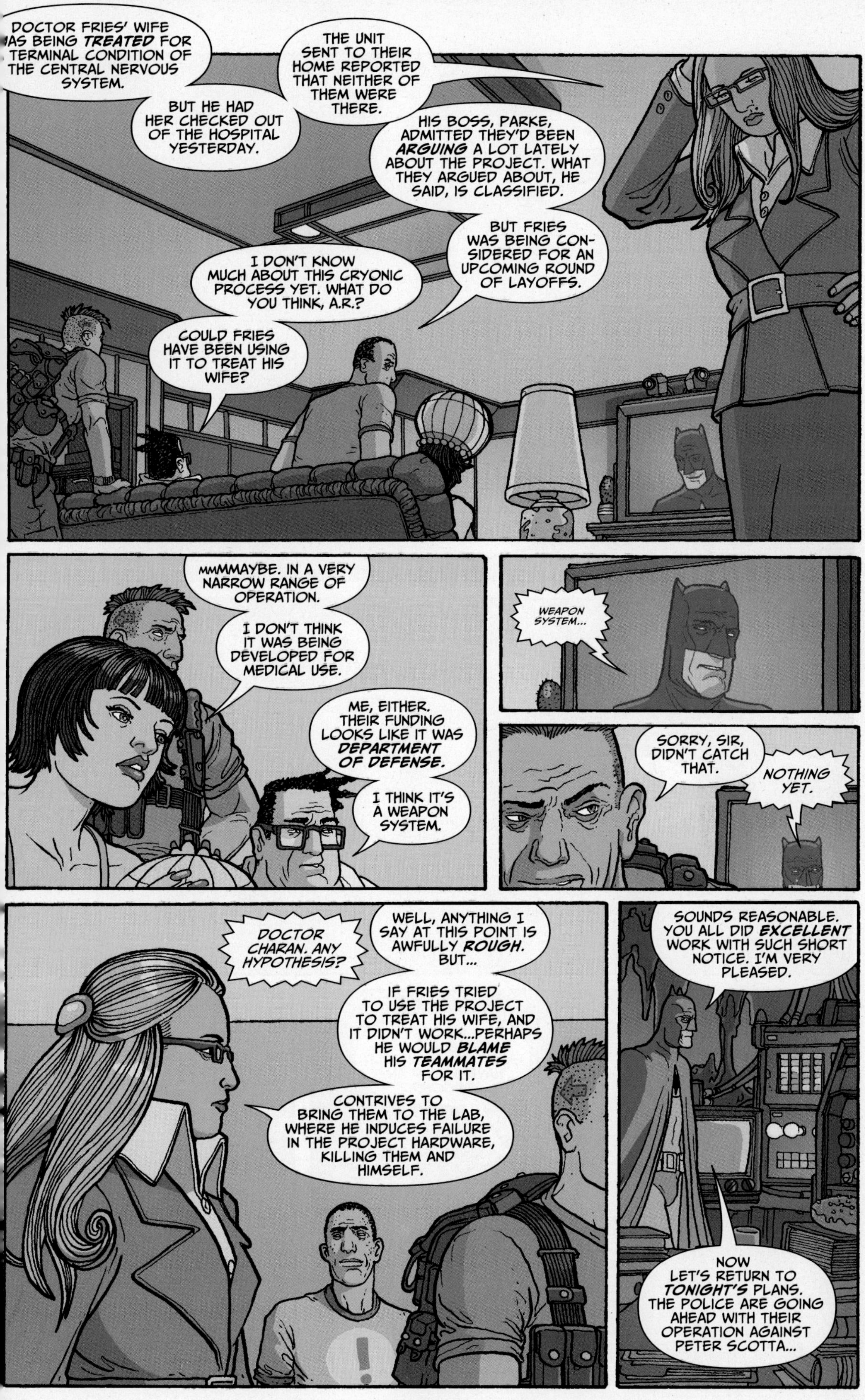
DOCTOR FRIES' WIFE WAS BEING TREATED FOR TERMINAL CONDITION OF THE CENTRAL NERVOUS SYSTEM.
BUT HE HAD HER CHECKED OUT OF THE HOSPITAL YESTERDAY.
THE UNIT SENT TO THEIR HOME REPORTED THAT NEITHER OF THEM WERE THERE.
HIS BOSS, PARKE, ADMITTED THEY'D BEEN ARGUING A LOT LATELY ABOUT THE PROJECT. WHAT THEY ARGUED ABOUT, HE SAID, IS CLASSIFIED.
BUT FRIES WAS BEING CONSIDERED FOR AN UPCOMING ROUND OF LAYOFFS.
I DON'T KNOW MUCH ABOUT THIS CRYONIC PROCESS YET. WHAT DO YOU THINK, A.R.?
COULD FRIES HAVE BEEN USING IT TO TREAT HIS WIFE?
MMMMAYBE. IN A VERY NARROW RANGE OF OPERATION.
I DON'T THINK IT WAS BEING DEVELOPED FOR MEDICAL USE.
ME, EITHER. THEIR FUNDING LOOKS LIKE IT WAS DEPARTMENT OF DEFENSE.
I THINK IT'S A WEAPON SYSTEM.
WEAPON SYSTEM...
SORRY, SIR, DIDN'T CATCH THAT.
NOTHING YET.
DOCTOR CHARAN. ANY HYPOTHESIS?
WELL, ANYTHING I SAY AT THIS POINT IS AWFULLY ROUGH. BUT...
IF FRIES TRIED TO USE THE PROJECT TO TREAT HIS WIFE, AND IT DIDN'T WORK...PERHAPS HE WOULD BLAME HIS TEAMMATES FOR IT.
CONTRIVES TO BRING THEM TO THE LAB, WHERE HE INDUCES FAILURE IN THE PROJECT HARDWARE, KILLING THEM AND HIMSELF.
SOUNDS REASONABLE. YOU ALL DID EXCELLENT WORK WITH SUCH SHORT NOTICE. I'M VERY PLEASED.
NOW LET'S RETURN TO TONIGHT'S PLANS. THE POLICE ARE GOING AHEAD WITH THEIR OPERATION AGAINST PETER SCOTTA...

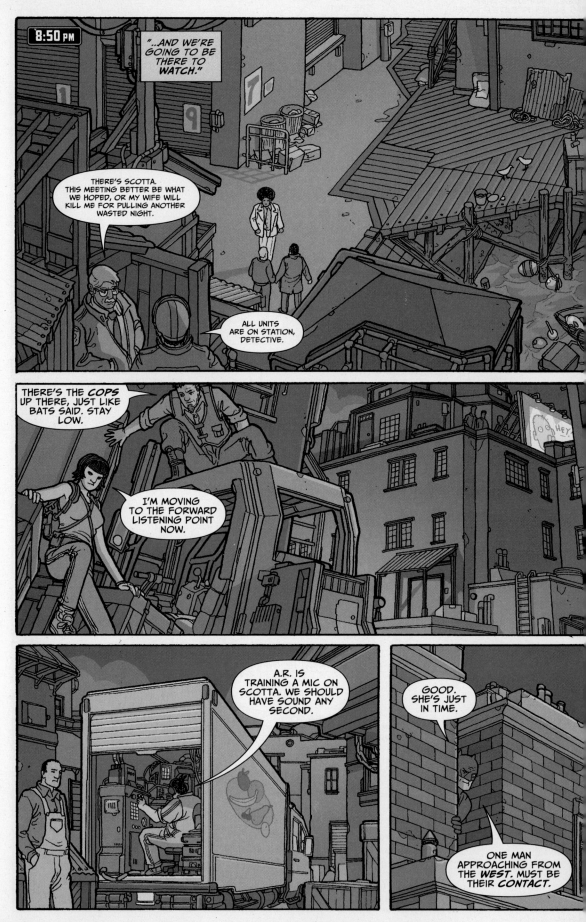

8:50 PM

"...AND WE'RE GOING TO BE THERE TO WATCH."

THERE'S SCOTTA. THIS MEETING BETTER BE WHAT WE HOPED, OR MY WIFE WILL KILL ME FOR PULLING ANOTHER WASTED NIGHT.

ALL UNITS ARE ON STATION, DETECTIVE.

THERE'S THE *COPS* UP THERE, JUST LIKE BATS SAID. STAY LOW.

I'M MOVING TO THE FORWARD LISTENING POINT NOW.

A.R. IS TRAINING A MIC ON SCOTTA. WE SHOULD HAVE SOUND ANY SECOND.

GOOD. SHE'S JUST IN TIME.

ONE MAN APPROACHING FROM THE *WEST*. MUST BE THEIR *CONTACT*.

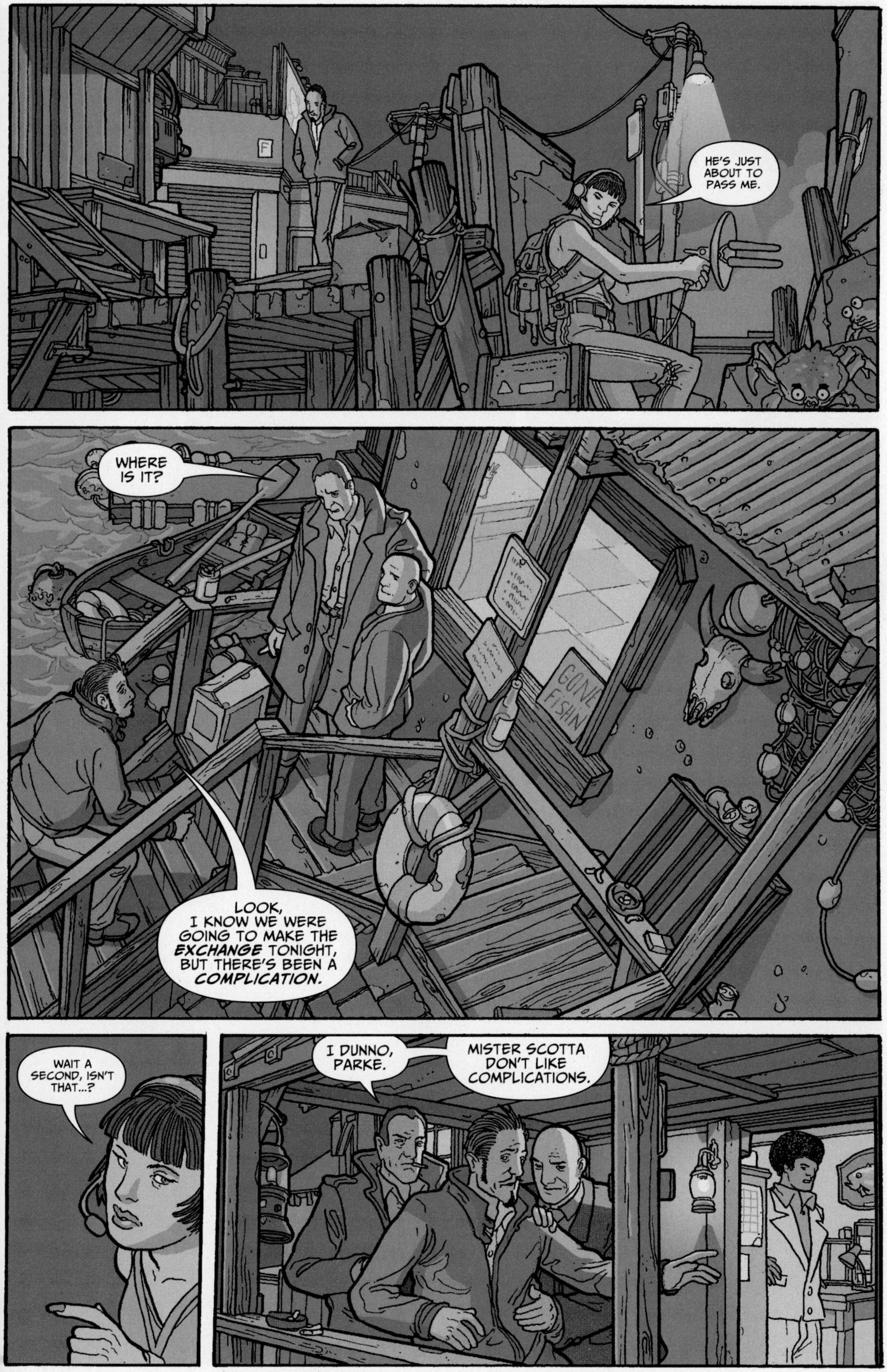
HE'S JUST ABOUT TO PASS ME.
WHERE IS IT?
LOOK, I KNOW WE WERE GOING TO MAKE THE *EXCHANGE* TONIGHT, BUT THERE'S BEEN A *COMPLICATION.*
GONE FISHIN
WAIT A SECOND, ISN'T THAT...?
I DUNNO, PARKE.
MISTER SCOTTA DON'T LIKE COMPLICATIONS.

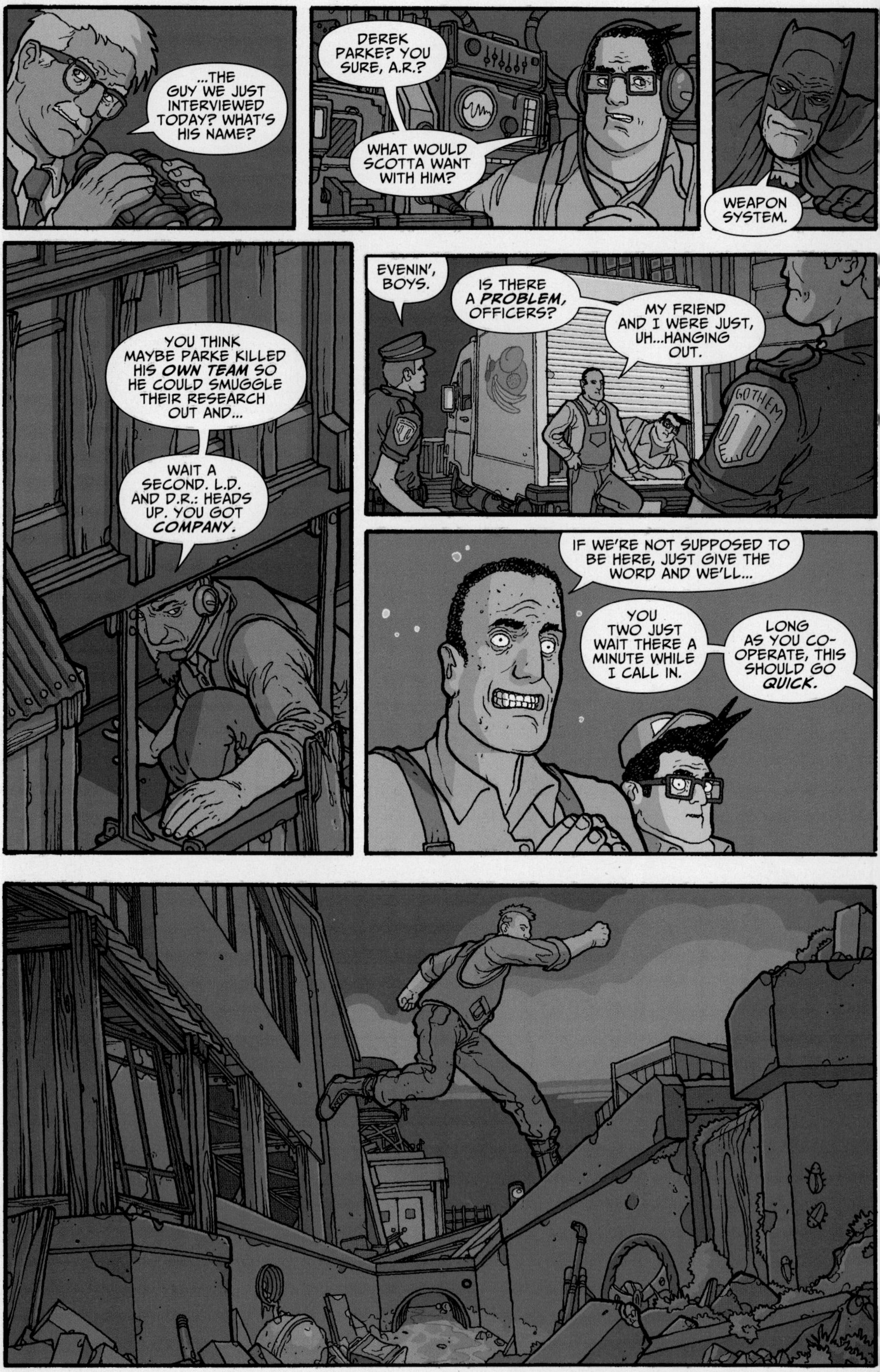
...THE GUY WE JUST INTERVIEWED TODAY? WHAT'S HIS NAME?
DEREK PARKE? YOU SURE, A.R.?
WHAT WOULD SCOTTA WANT WITH HIM?
WEAPON SYSTEM.
YOU THINK MAYBE PARKE KILLED HIS OWN TEAM SO HE COULD SMUGGLE THEIR RESEARCH OUT AND...
WAIT A SECOND. L.D. AND D.R.: HEADS UP. YOU GOT COMPANY.
EVENIN', BOYS.
IS THERE A PROBLEM, OFFICERS?
MY FRIEND AND I WERE JUST, UH...HANGING OUT.
GOTHEM
IF WE'RE NOT SUPPOSED TO BE HERE, JUST GIVE THE WORD AND WE'LL...
YOU TWO JUST WAIT THERE A MINUTE WHILE I CALL IN.
LONG AS YOU CO-OPERATE, THIS SHOULD GO QUICK.

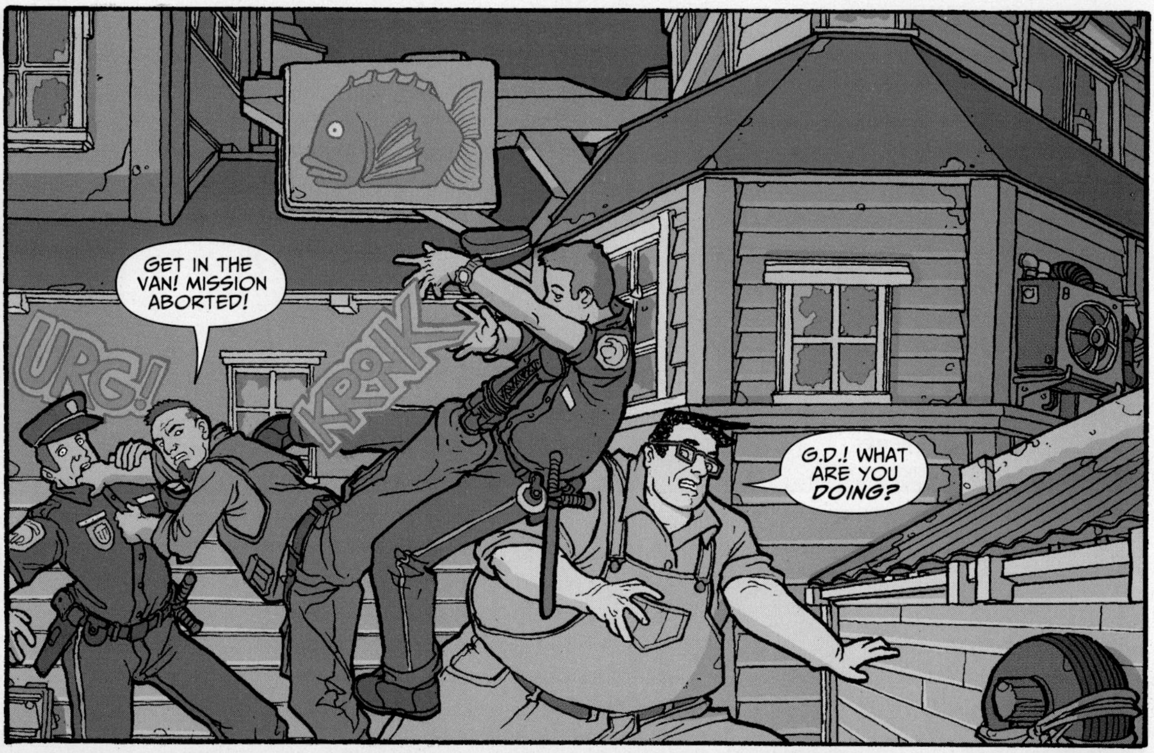
GET IN THE VAN! MISSION ABORTED!
URG!
KRONK
G.D.! WHAT ARE YOU *DOING?*

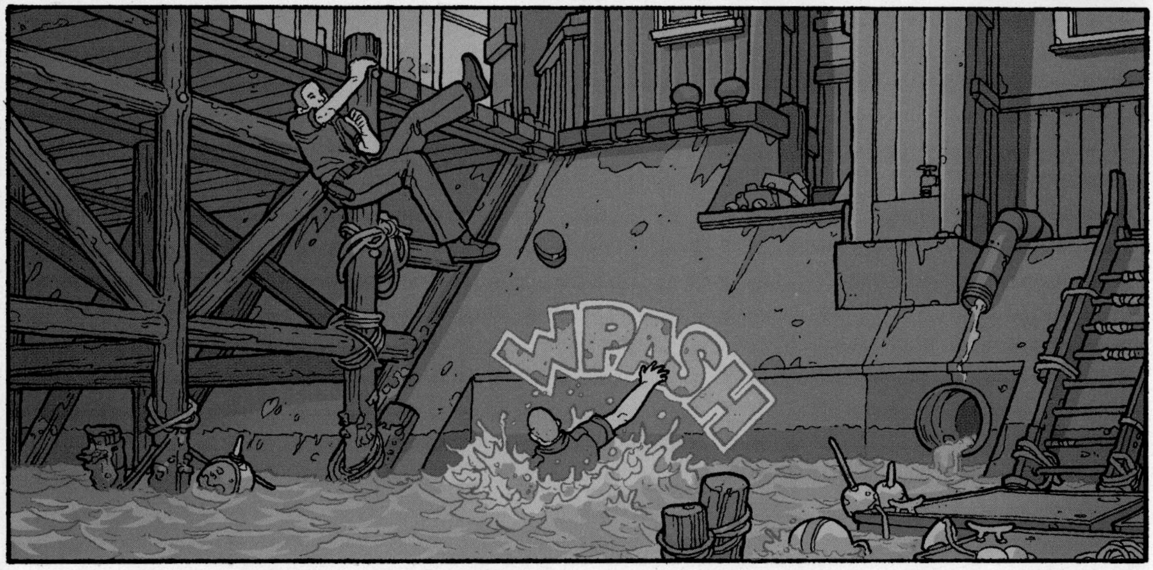
WPASH

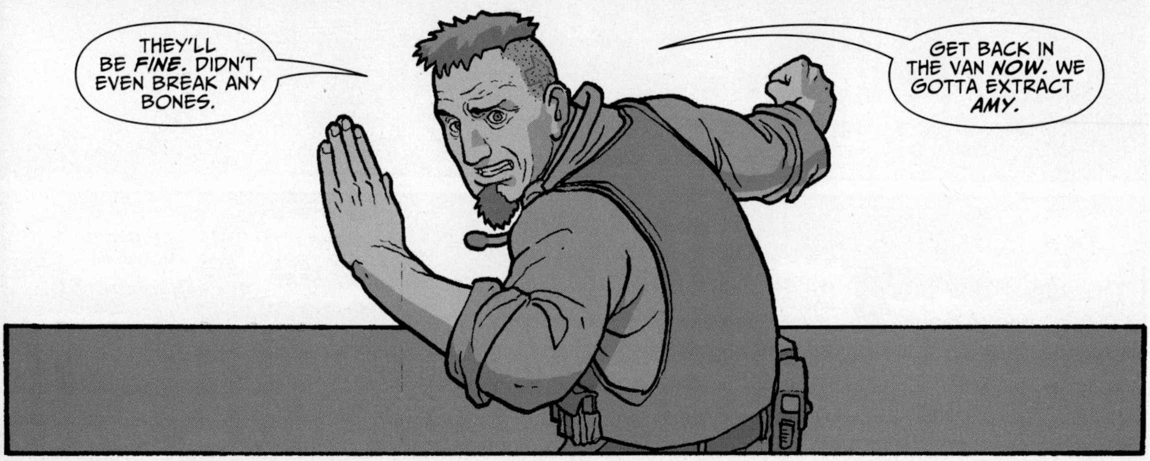
THEY'LL BE *FINE*. DIDN'T EVEN BREAK ANY BONES.
GET BACK IN THE VAN *NOW*. WE GOTTA EXTRACT *AMY*.

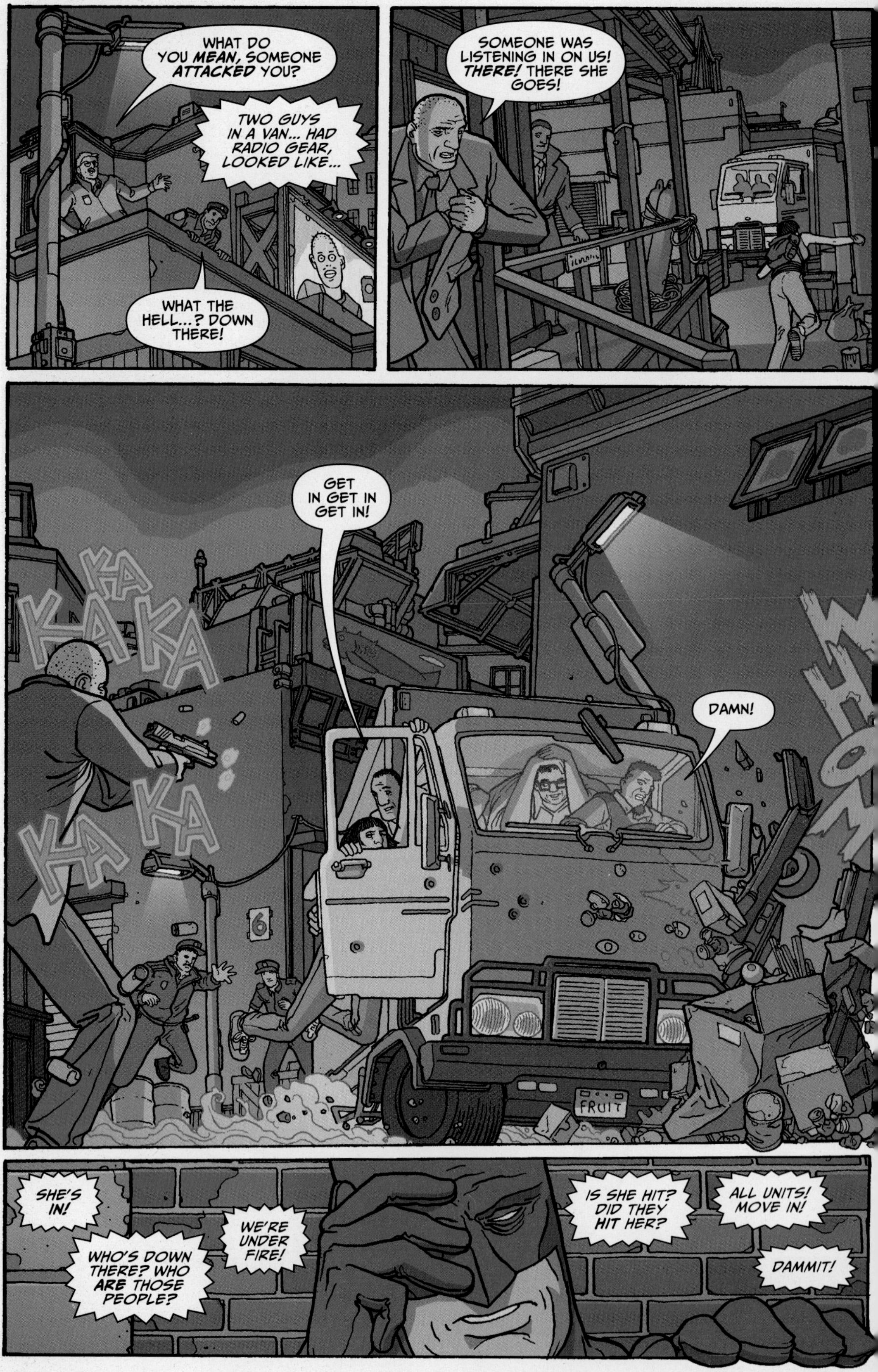
WHAT DO YOU MEAN, SOMEONE ATTACKED YOU?
TWO GUYS IN A VAN... HAD RADIO GEAR, LOOKED LIKE...
WHAT THE HELL...? DOWN THERE!
SOMEONE WAS LISTENING IN ON US! THERE! THERE SHE GOES!
GET IN GET IN GET IN!
KA KA KA KA
KA KA KA
DAMN!
6
FRUIT
SHE'S IN!
WHO'S DOWN THERE? WHO ARE THOSE PEOPLE?
WE'RE UNDER FIRE!
IS SHE HIT? DID THEY HIT HER?
ALL UNITS! MOVE IN!
DAMMIT!

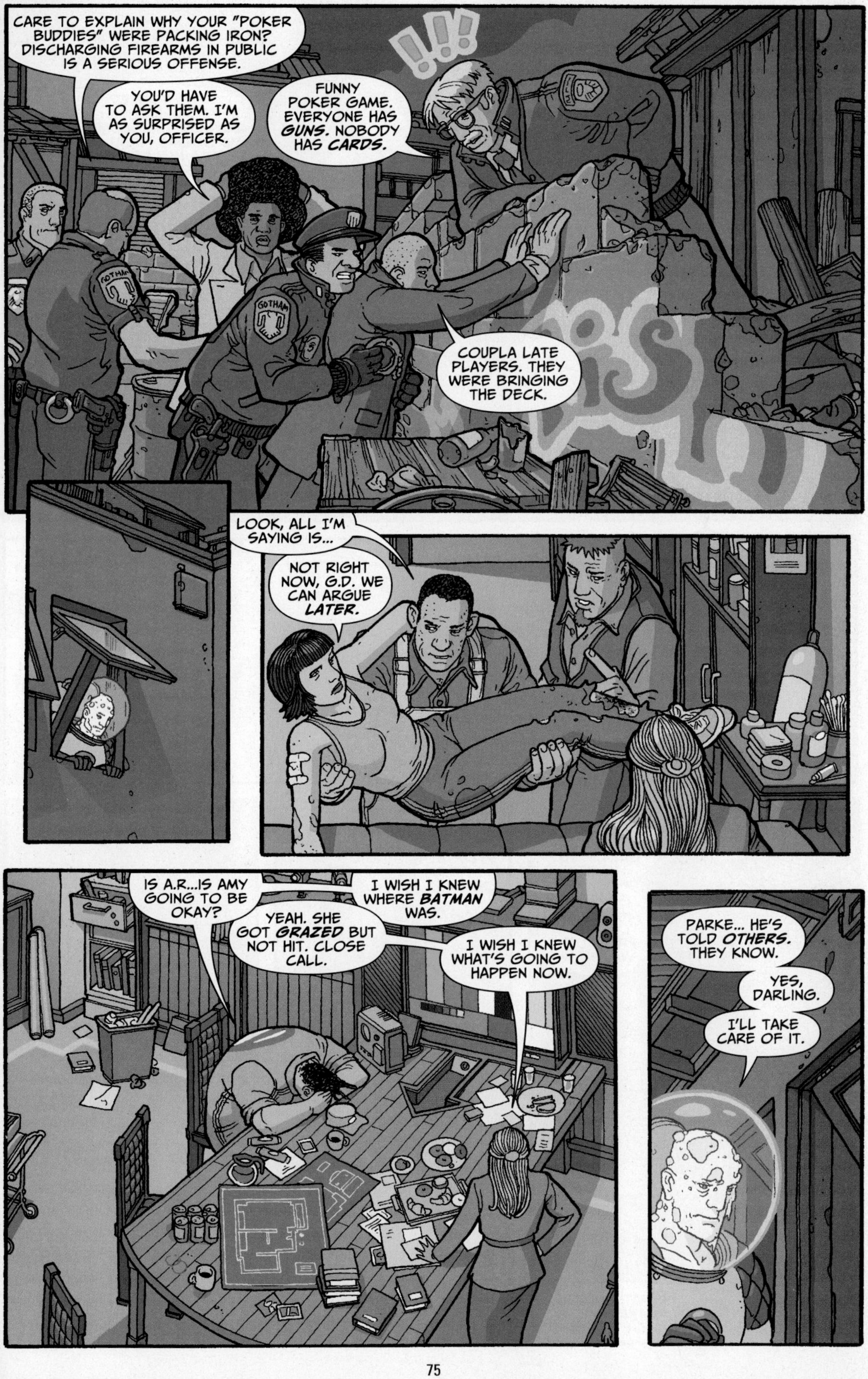
CARE TO EXPLAIN WHY YOUR "POKER BUDDIES" WERE PACKING IRON? DISCHARGING FIREARMS IN PUBLIC IS A SERIOUS OFFENSE.
YOU'D HAVE TO ASK THEM. I'M AS SURPRISED AS YOU, OFFICER.
FUNNY POKER GAME. EVERYONE HAS *GUNS.* NOBODY HAS *CARDS.*
!!!
COUPLA LATE PLAYERS. THEY WERE BRINGING THE DECK.
GOTHAM
LOOK, ALL I'M SAYING IS...
NOT RIGHT NOW, G.D. WE CAN ARGUE *LATER.*
IS A.R...IS AMY GOING TO BE OKAY?
I WISH I KNEW WHERE *BATMAN* WAS.
YEAH. SHE GOT *GRAZED* BUT NOT HIT. CLOSE CALL.
I WISH I KNEW WHAT'S GOING TO HAPPEN NOW.
PARKE... HE'S TOLD *OTHERS.* THEY KNOW.
YES, DARLING.
I'LL TAKE CARE OF IT.

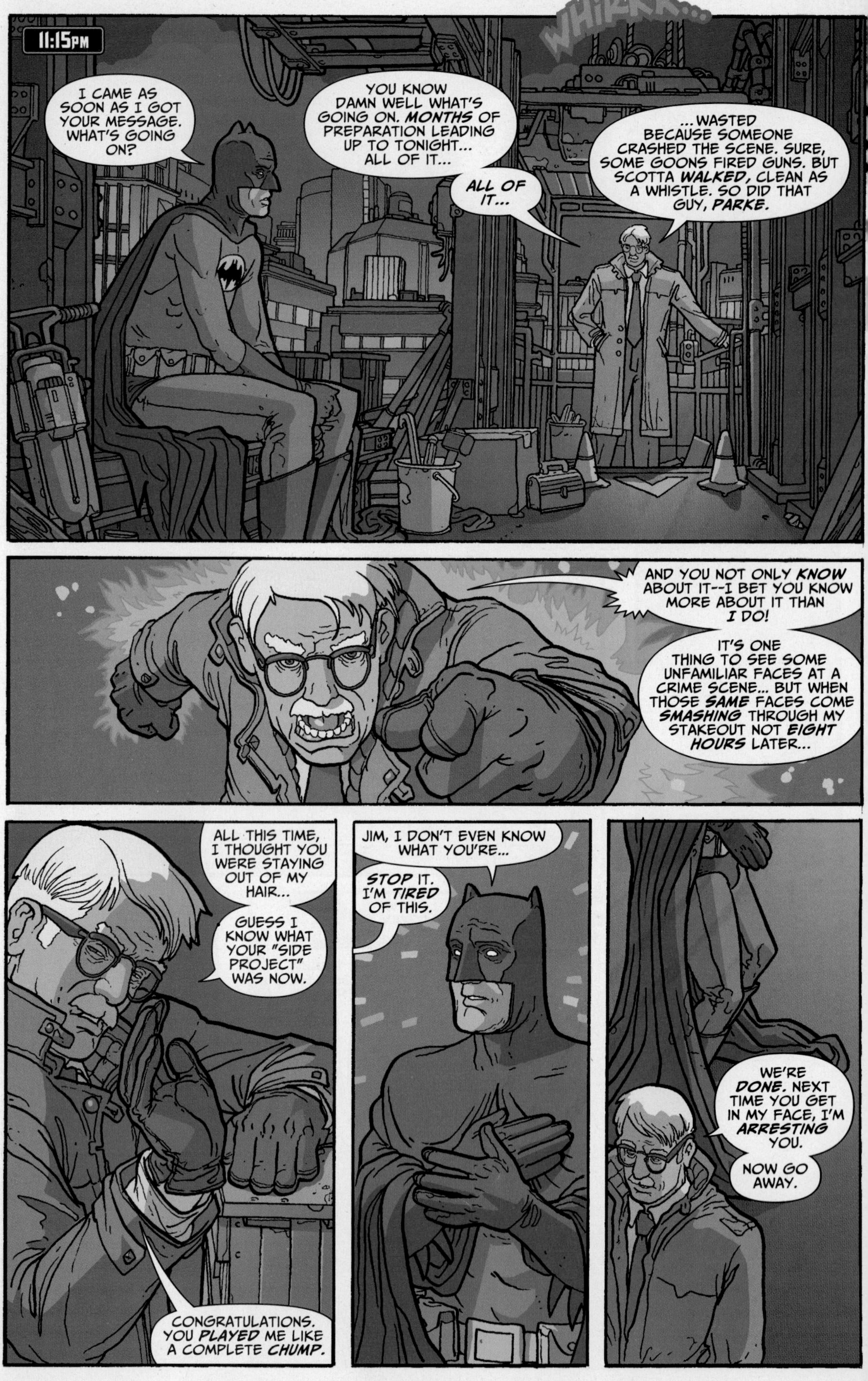
WHIRRR...
11:15PM
I CAME AS SOON AS I GOT YOUR MESSAGE. WHAT'S GOING ON?
YOU KNOW DAMN WELL WHAT'S GOING ON. MONTHS OF PREPARATION LEADING UP TO TONIGHT... ALL OF IT...
ALL OF IT...
...WASTED BECAUSE SOMEONE CRASHED THE SCENE. SURE, SOME GOONS FIRED GUNS. BUT SCOTTA WALKED, CLEAN AS A WHISTLE. SO DID THAT GUY, PARKE.
AND YOU NOT ONLY KNOW ABOUT IT--I BET YOU KNOW MORE ABOUT IT THAN I DO!
IT'S ONE THING TO SEE SOME UNFAMILIAR FACES AT A CRIME SCENE... BUT WHEN THOSE SAME FACES COME SMASHING THROUGH MY STAKEOUT NOT EIGHT HOURS LATER...
ALL THIS TIME, I THOUGHT YOU WERE STAYING OUT OF MY HAIR...
GUESS I KNOW WHAT YOUR "SIDE PROJECT" WAS NOW.
CONGRATULATIONS. YOU PLAYED ME LIKE A COMPLETE CHUMP.
JIM, I DON'T EVEN KNOW WHAT YOU'RE...
STOP IT. I'M TIRED OF THIS.
WE'RE DONE. NEXT TIME YOU GET IN MY FACE, I'M ARRESTING YOU.
NOW GO AWAY.

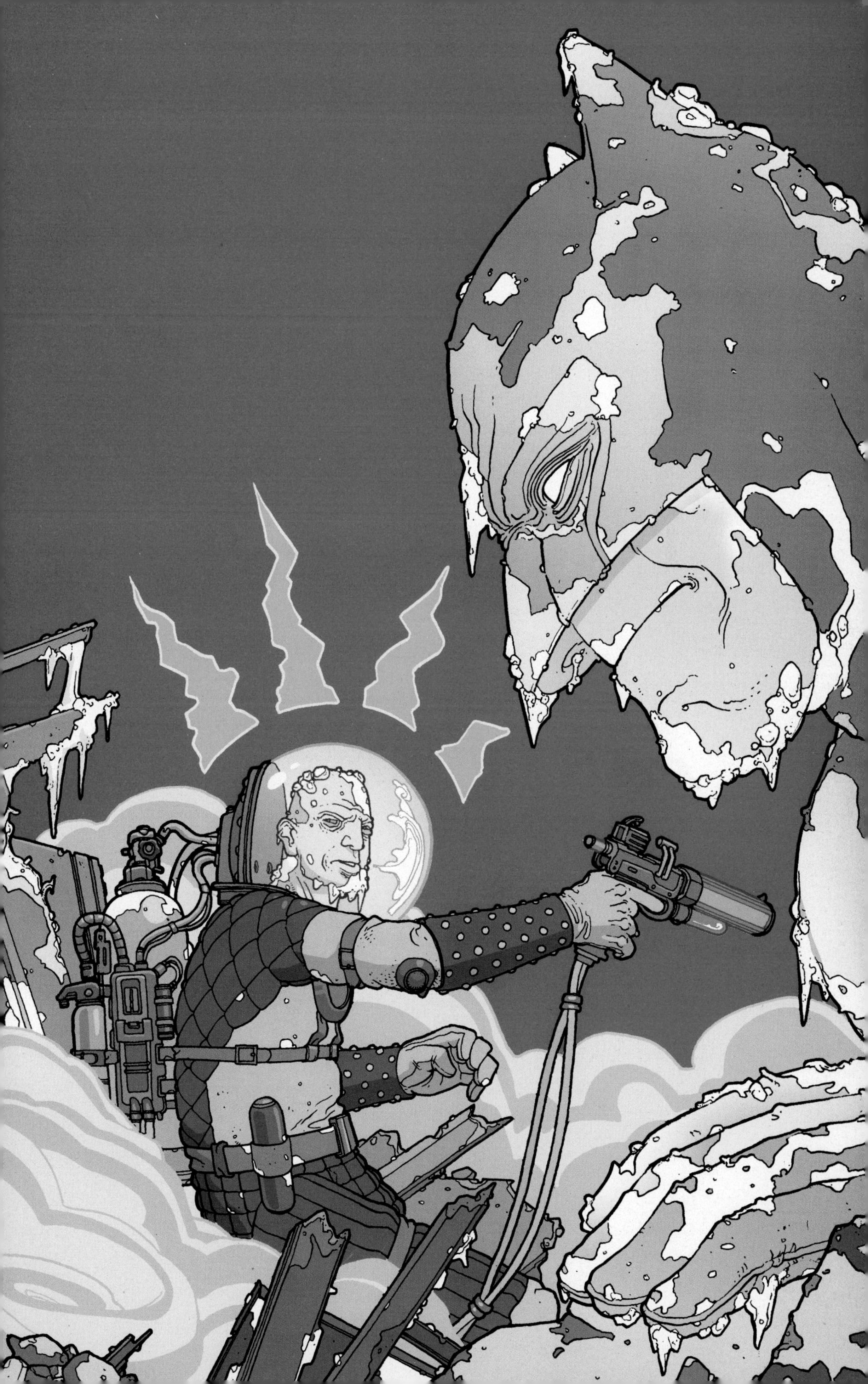

SNOW
PART FOUR: FALL

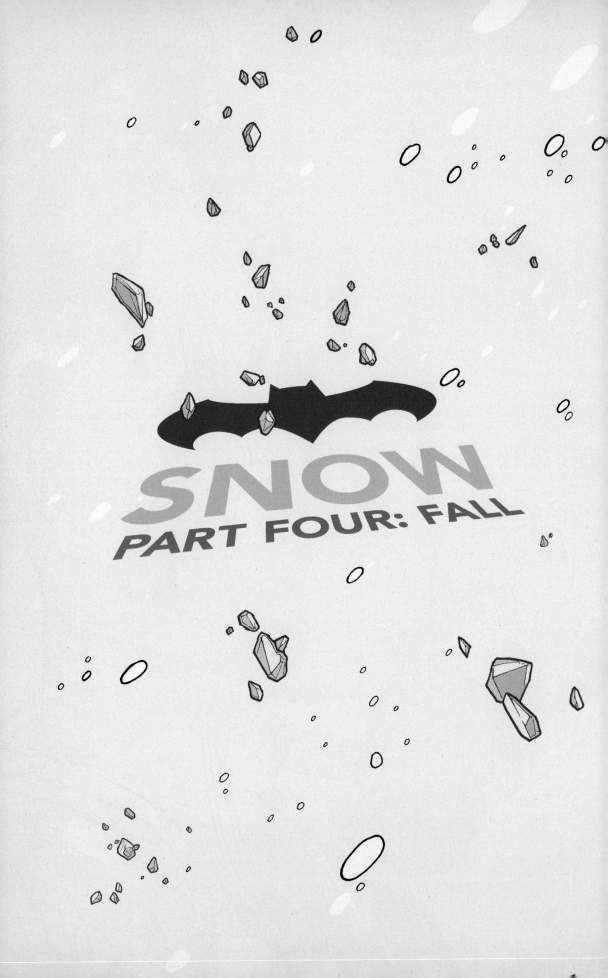

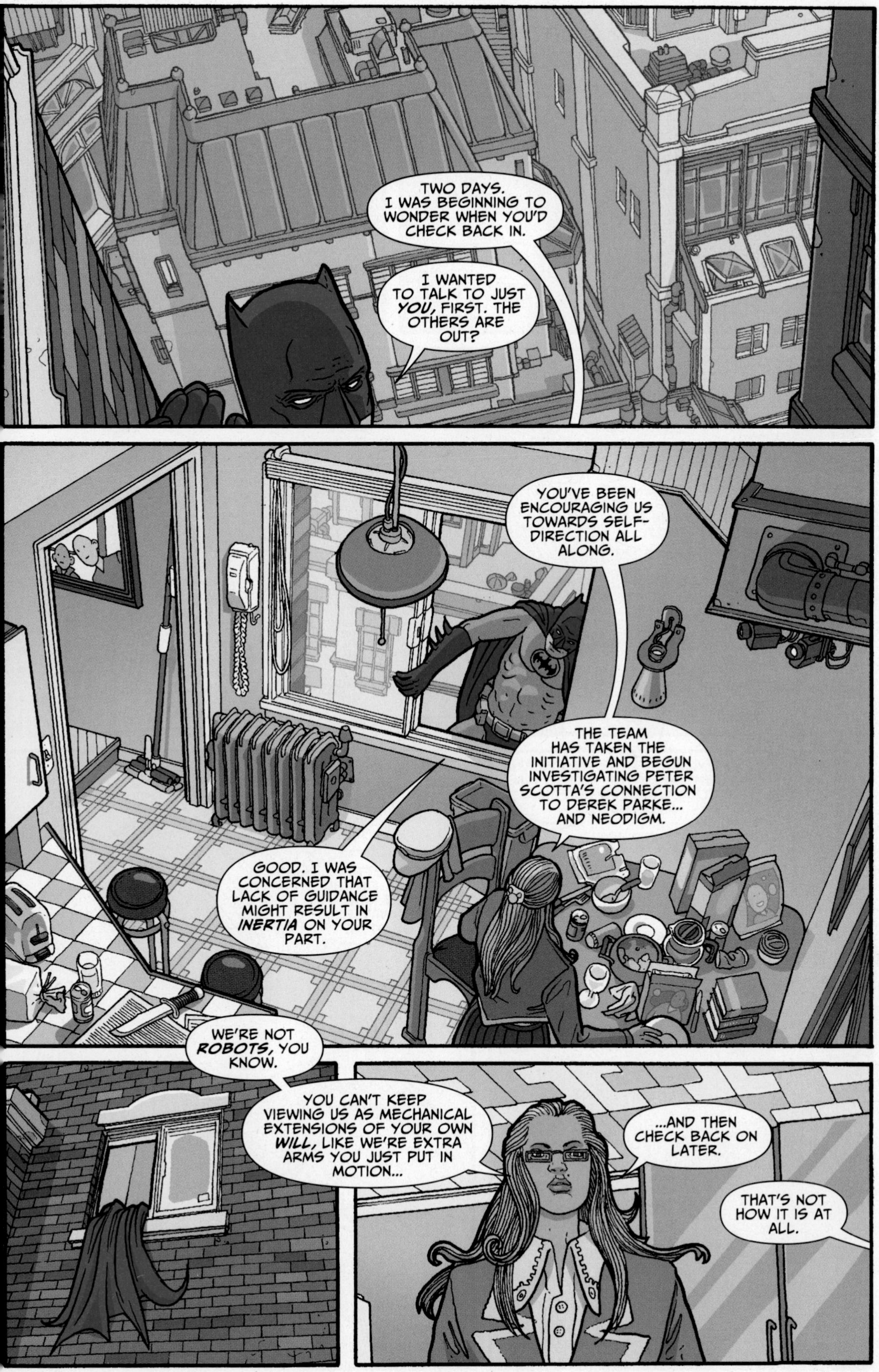
TWO DAYS. I WAS BEGINNING TO WONDER WHEN YOU'D CHECK BACK IN.
I WANTED TO TALK TO JUST *YOU*, FIRST. THE OTHERS ARE OUT?
YOU'VE BEEN ENCOURAGING US TOWARDS SELF-DIRECTION ALL ALONG.
THE TEAM HAS TAKEN THE INITIATIVE AND BEGUN INVESTIGATING PETER SCOTTA'S CONNECTION TO DEREK PARKE... AND NEODIGM.
GOOD. I WAS CONCERNED THAT LACK OF GUIDANCE MIGHT RESULT IN *INERTIA* ON YOUR PART.
WE'RE NOT *ROBOTS*, YOU KNOW.
YOU CAN'T KEEP VIEWING US AS MECHANICAL EXTENSIONS OF YOUR OWN *WILL*, LIKE WE'RE EXTRA ARMS YOU JUST PUT IN MOTION...
...AND THEN CHECK BACK ON LATER.
THAT'S NOT HOW IT IS AT ALL.

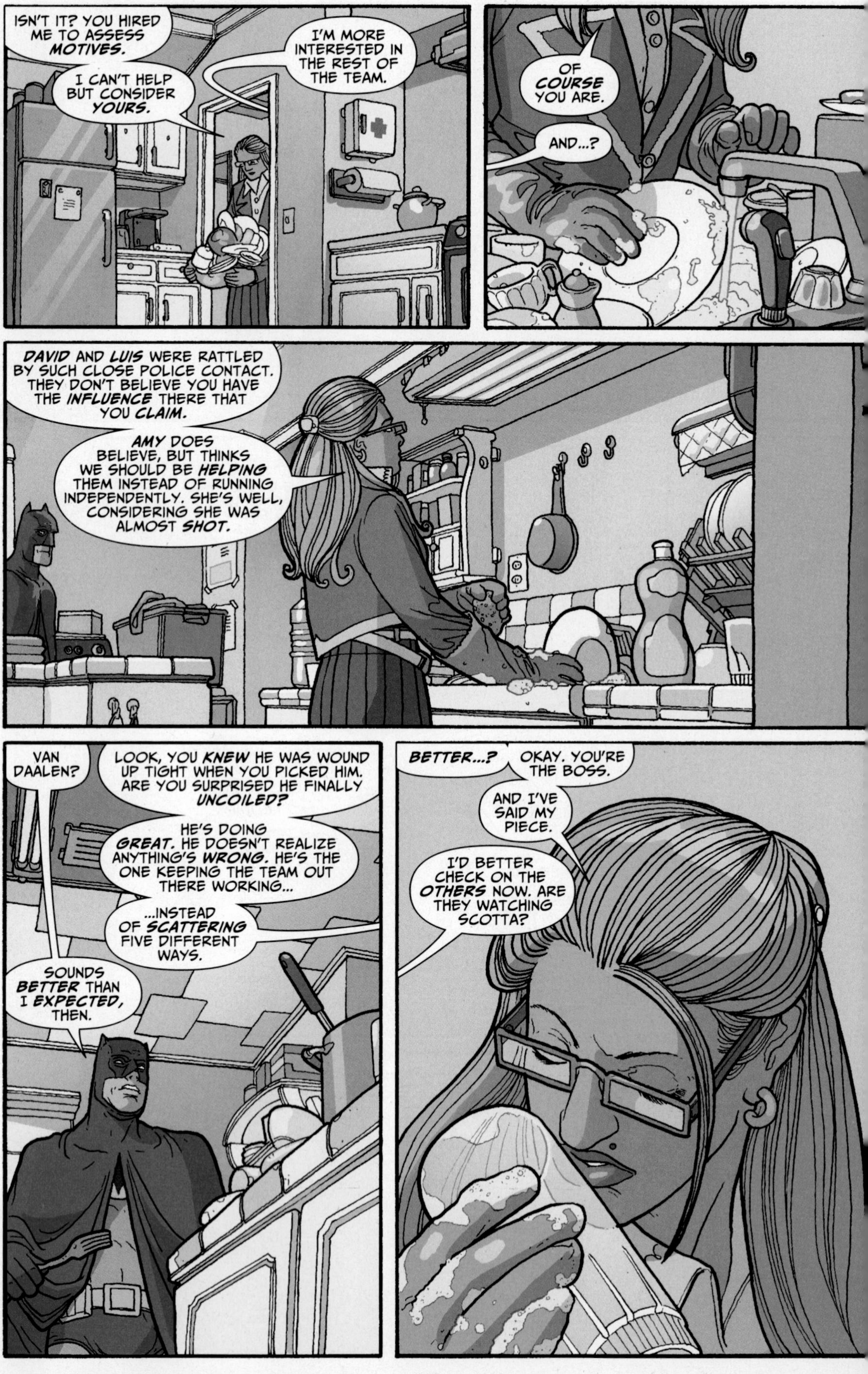
ISN'T IT? YOU HIRED ME TO ASSESS MOTIVES.
I CAN'T HELP BUT CONSIDER YOURS.
I'M MORE INTERESTED IN THE REST OF THE TEAM.
OF COURSE YOU ARE.
AND...?
DAVID AND LUIS WERE RATTLED BY SUCH CLOSE POLICE CONTACT. THEY DON'T BELIEVE YOU HAVE THE INFLUENCE THERE THAT YOU CLAIM.
AMY DOES BELIEVE, BUT THINKS WE SHOULD BE HELPING THEM INSTEAD OF RUNNING INDEPENDENTLY. SHE'S WELL, CONSIDERING SHE WAS ALMOST SHOT.
VAN DAALEN?
LOOK, YOU KNEW HE WAS WOUND UP TIGHT WHEN YOU PICKED HIM. ARE YOU SURPRISED HE FINALLY UNCOILED?
HE'S DOING GREAT. HE DOESN'T REALIZE ANYTHING'S WRONG. HE'S THE ONE KEEPING THE TEAM OUT THERE WORKING...
...INSTEAD OF SCATTERING FIVE DIFFERENT WAYS.
SOUNDS BETTER THAN I EXPECTED, THEN.
BETTER...?
OKAY. YOU'RE THE BOSS.
AND I'VE SAID MY PIECE.
I'D BETTER CHECK ON THE OTHERS NOW. ARE THEY WATCHING SCOTTA?

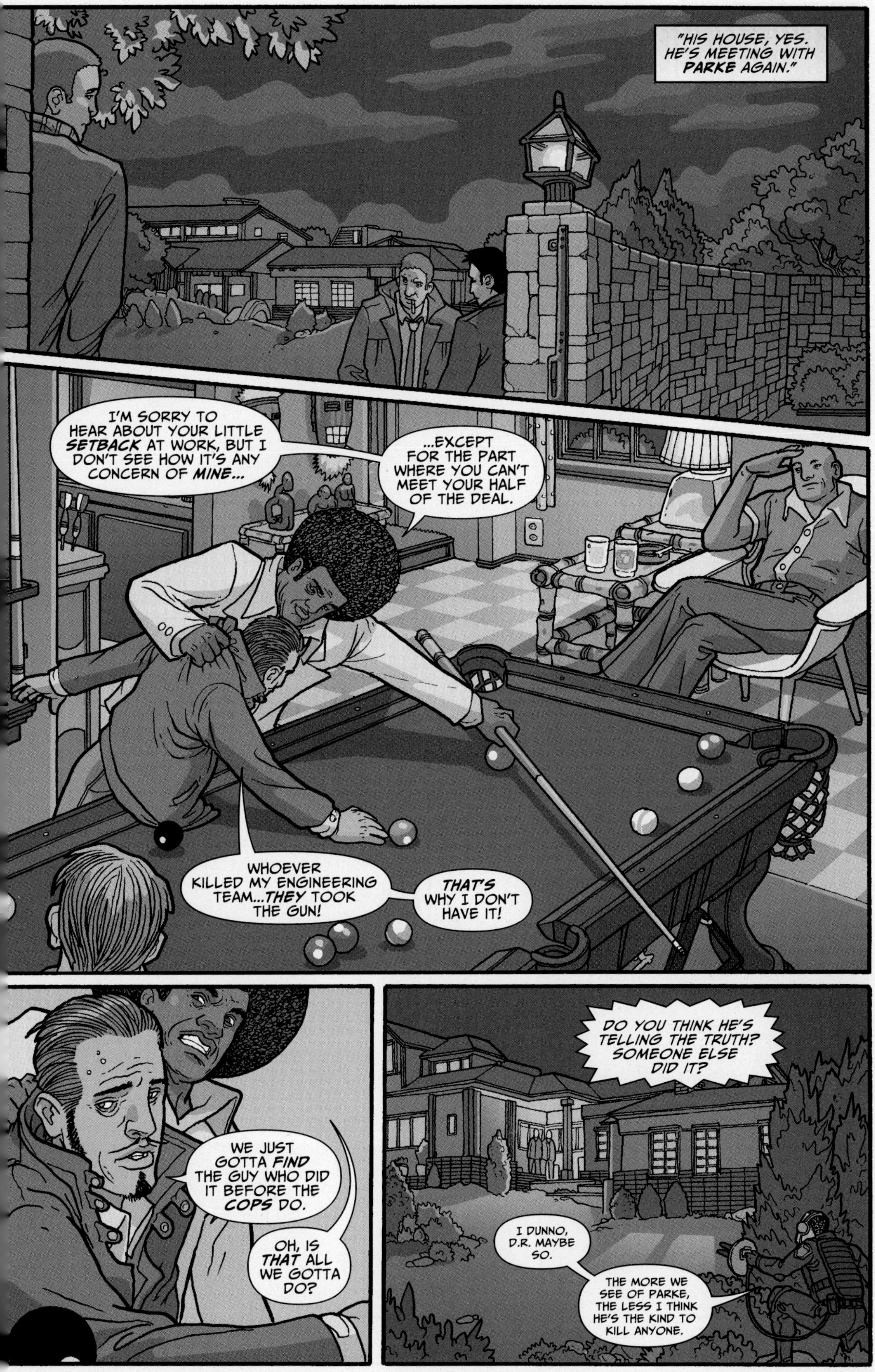
"HIS HOUSE, YES. HE'S MEETING WITH PARKE AGAIN."
I'M SORRY TO HEAR ABOUT YOUR LITTLE SETBACK AT WORK, BUT I DON'T SEE HOW IT'S ANY CONCERN OF MINE...
...EXCEPT FOR THE PART WHERE YOU CAN'T MEET YOUR HALF OF THE DEAL.
WHOEVER KILLED MY ENGINEERING TEAM...THEY TOOK THE GUN!
THAT'S WHY I DON'T HAVE IT!
WE JUST GOTTA FIND THE GUY WHO DID IT BEFORE THE COPS DO.
OH, IS THAT ALL WE GOTTA DO?
DO YOU THINK HE'S TELLING THE TRUTH? SOMEONE ELSE DID IT?
I DUNNO, D.R. MAYBE SO.
THE MORE WE SEE OF PARKE, THE LESS I THINK HE'S THE KIND TO KILL ANYONE.

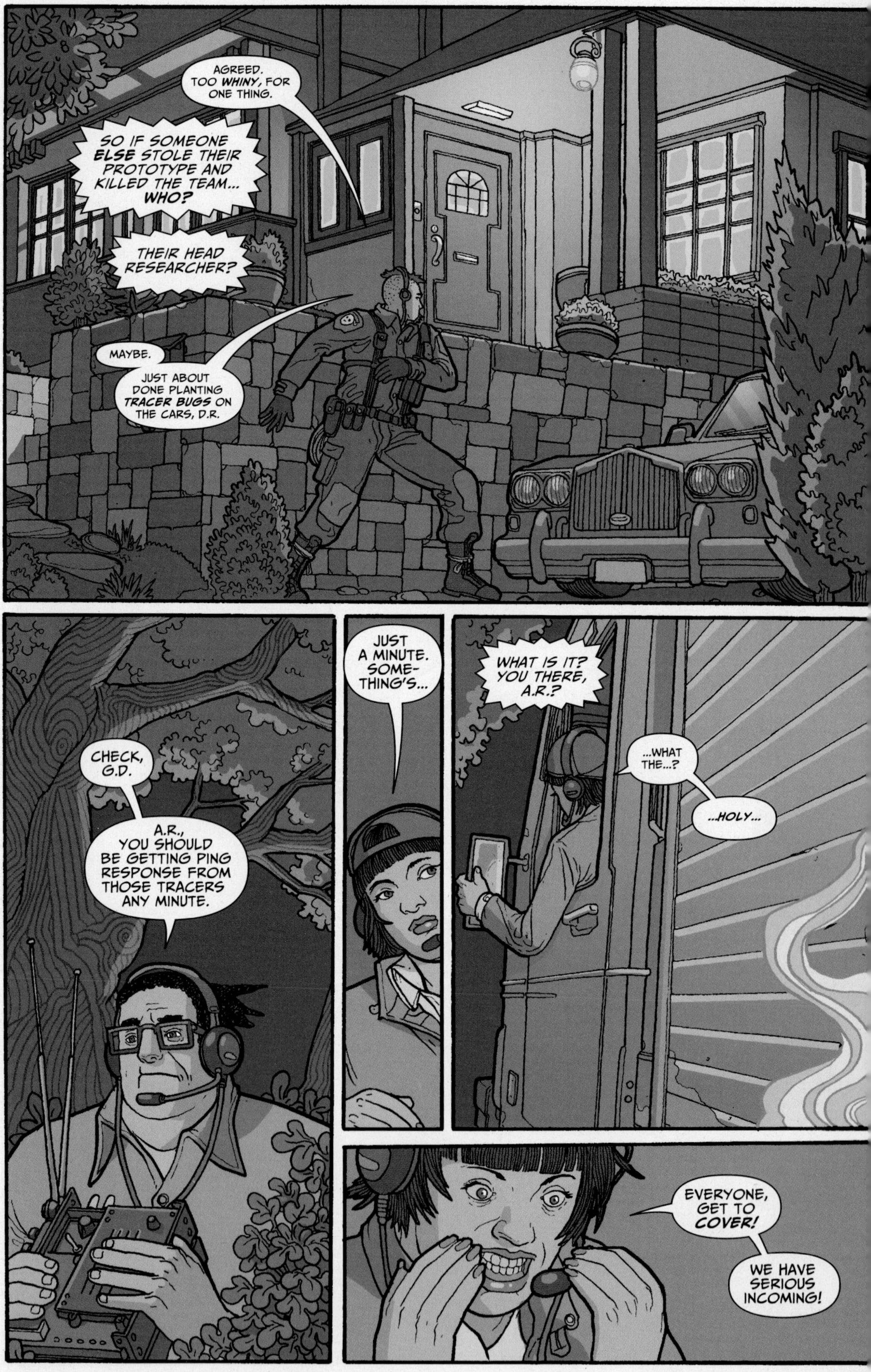

SO IF SOMEONE ELSE STOLE THEIR PROTOTYPE AND KILLED THE TEAM... WHO?
AGREED. TOO WHINY, FOR ONE THING.
THEIR HEAD RESEARCHER?
MAYBE.
JUST ABOUT DONE PLANTING TRACER BUGS ON THE CARS, D.R.
CHECK, G.D.
A.R., YOU SHOULD BE GETTING PING RESPONSE FROM THOSE TRACERS ANY MINUTE.
JUST A MINUTE. SOME-THING'S...
WHAT IS IT? YOU THERE, A.R.?
...WHAT THE...?
...HOLY...
EVERYONE, GET TO COVER!
WE HAVE SERIOUS INCOMING!

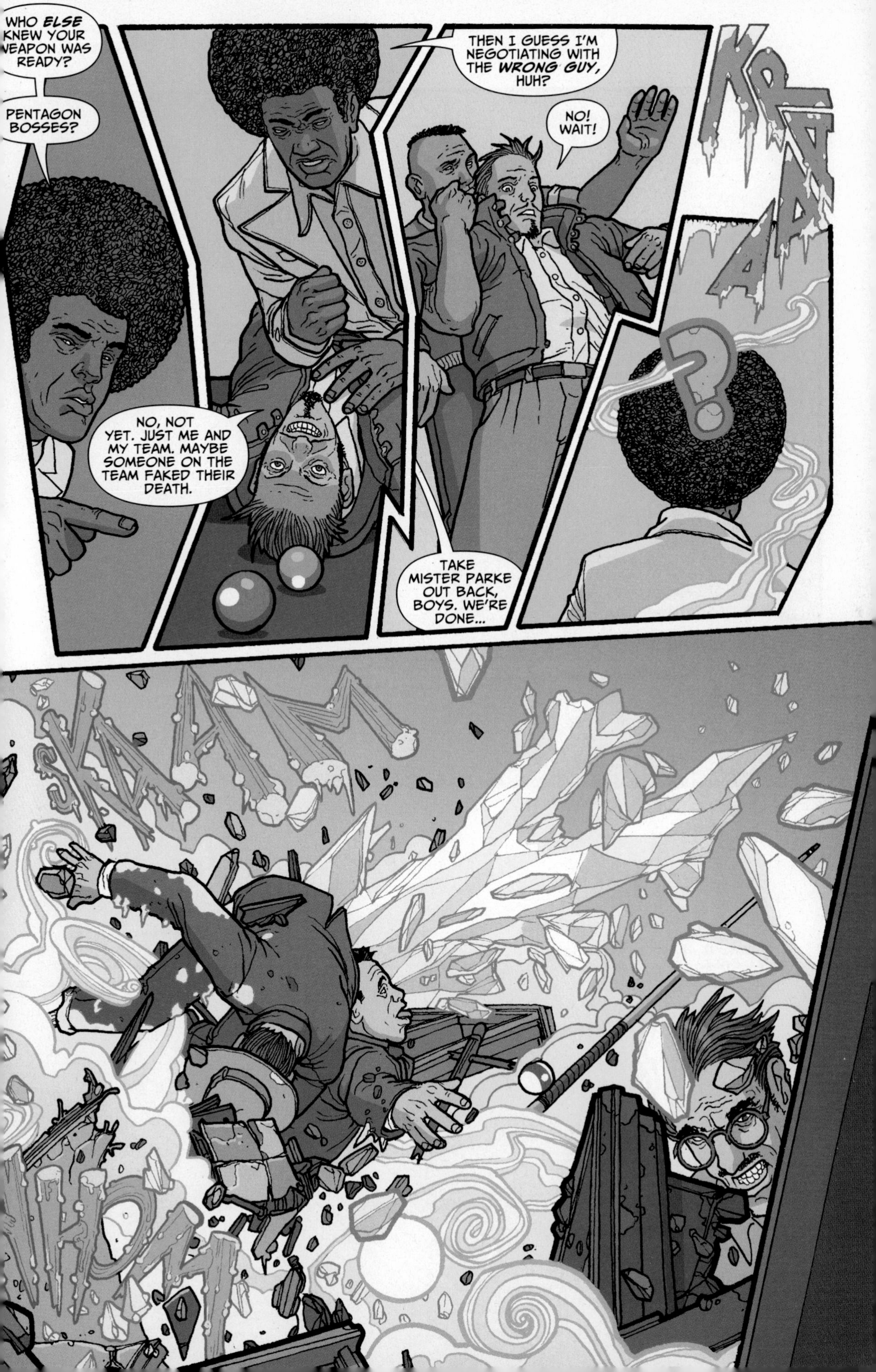
WHO ELSE KNEW YOUR WEAPON WAS READY?
PENTAGON BOSSES?
NO, NOT YET. JUST ME AND MY TEAM. MAYBE SOMEONE ON THE TEAM FAKED THEIR DEATH.
THEN I GUESS I'M NEGOTIATING WITH THE WRONG GUY, HUH?
NO! WAIT!
TAKE MISTER PARKE OUT BACK, BOYS. WE'RE DONE...
KRAAA
?

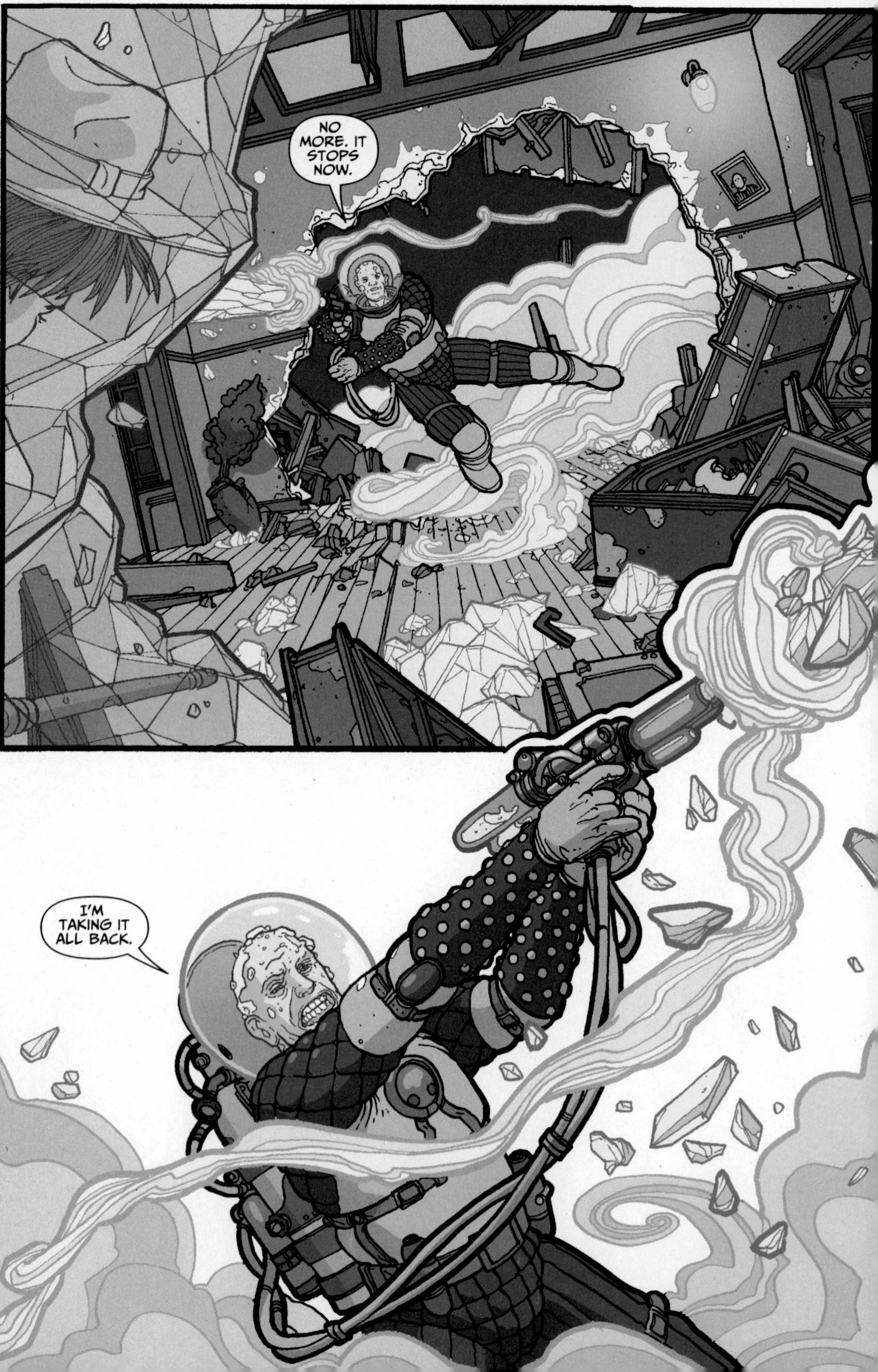
NO MORE. IT STOPS NOW.
I'M TAKING IT ALL BACK.

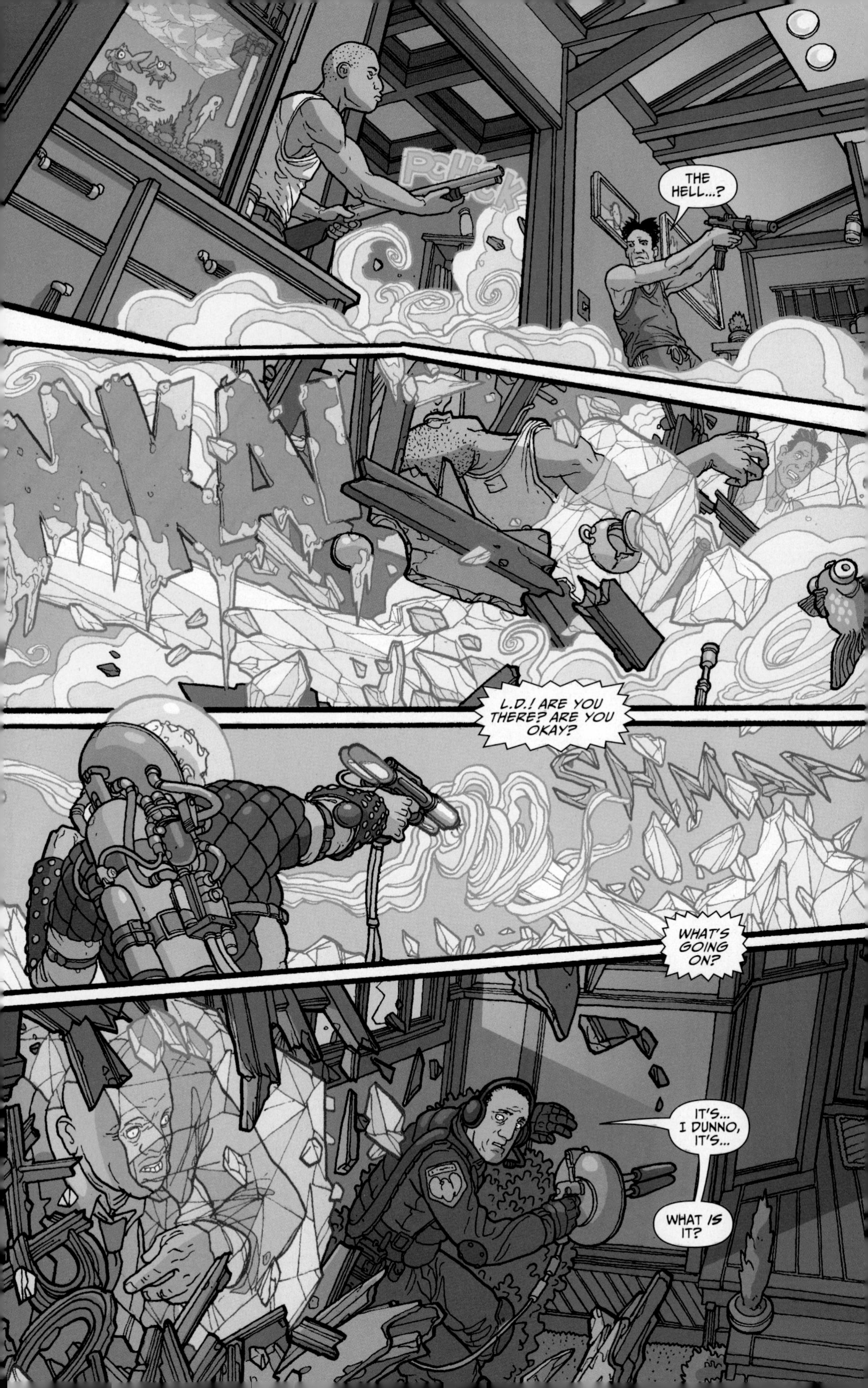
PCHICK
THE HELL...?
L.D.! ARE YOU THERE? ARE YOU OKAY?
WHAT'S GOING ON?
IT'S... I DUNNO, IT'S...
WHAT IS IT?

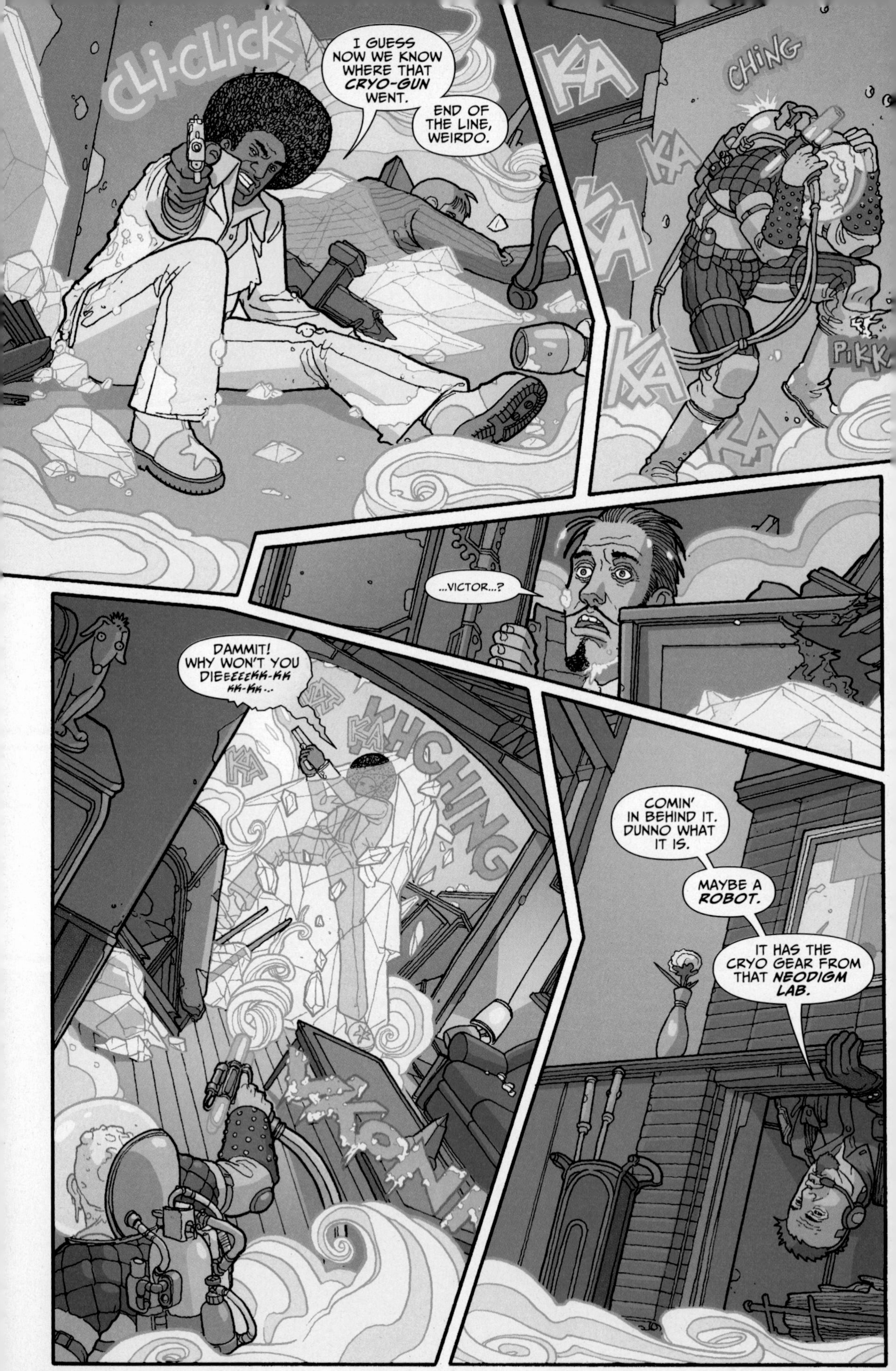
CLI-CLICK
I GUESS NOW WE KNOW WHERE THAT CRYO-GUN WENT.
END OF THE LINE, WEIRDO.
KA
CHING
KA
KA
KA
KA
KA
PIKK
...VICTOR...?
DAMMIT! WHY WON'T YOU DIEEEEKK-KK KK-KK...
KA
KA
KA
KHCHING
COMIN' IN BEHIND IT. DUNNO WHAT IT IS.
MAYBE A ROBOT.
IT HAS THE CRYO GEAR FROM THAT NEODIGM LAB.

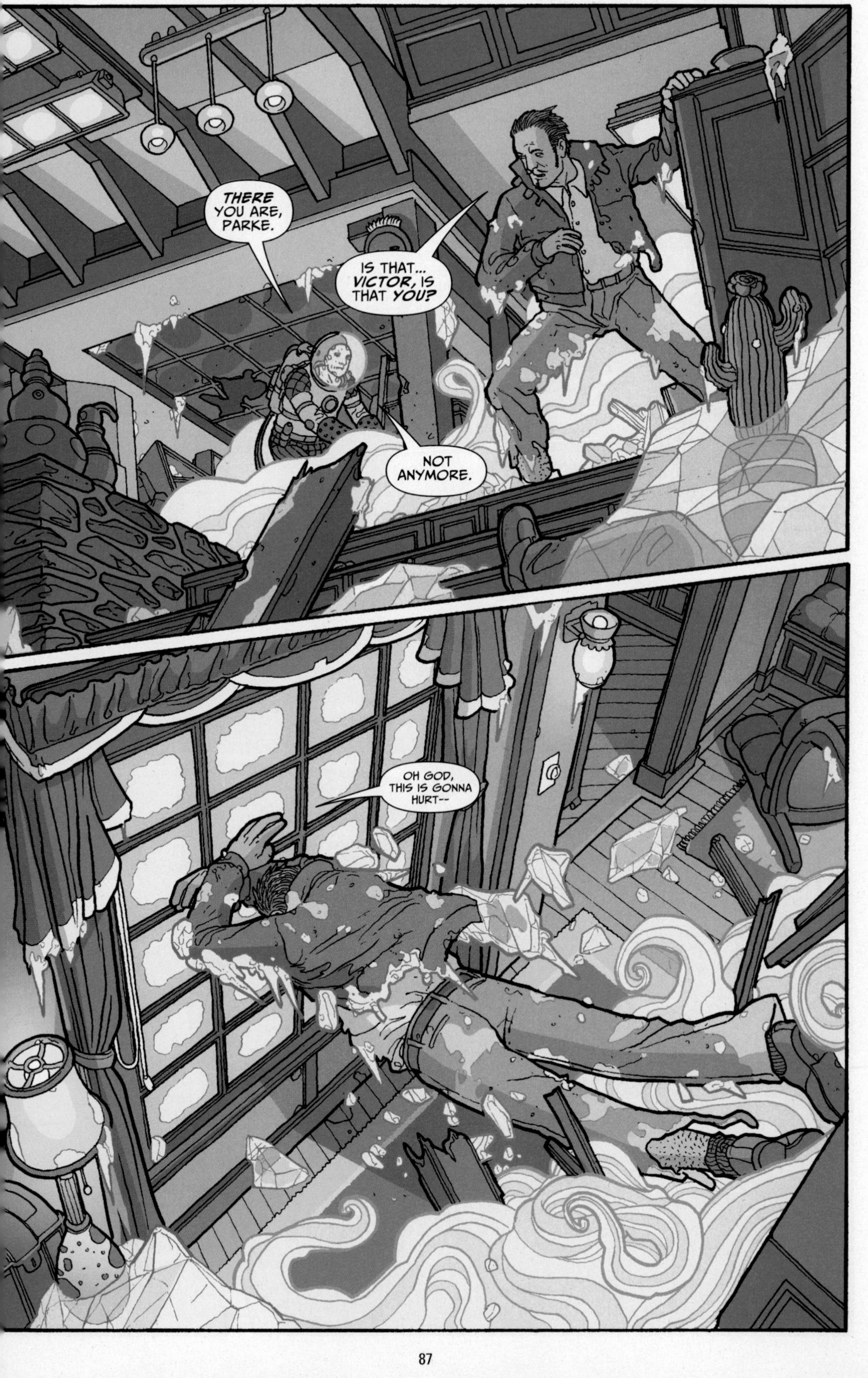
THERE YOU ARE, PARKE.
IS THAT... VICTOR, IS THAT YOU?
NOT ANYMORE.
OH GOD, THIS IS GONNA HURT--

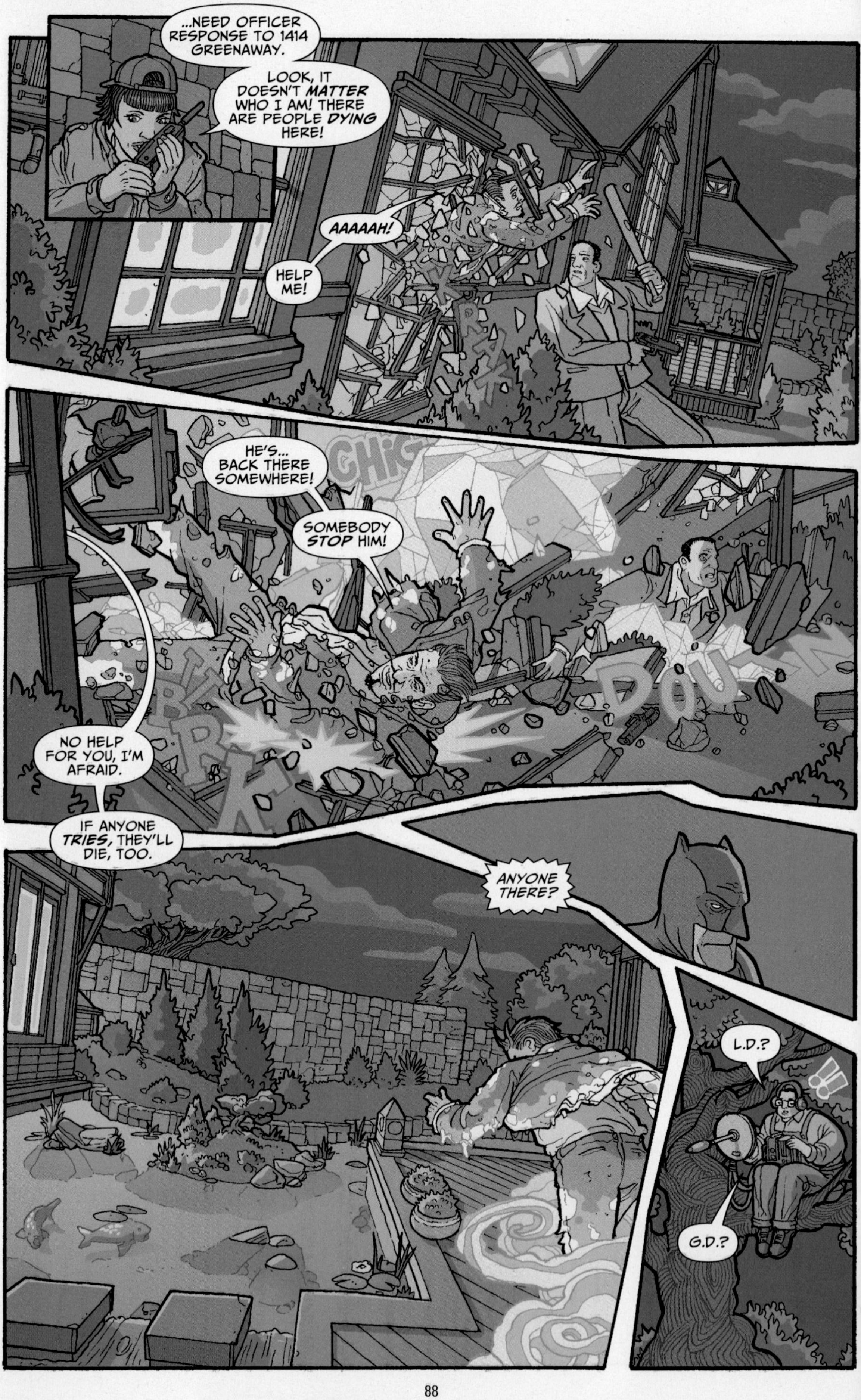
...NEED OFFICER RESPONSE TO 1414 GREENAWAY.
LOOK, IT DOESN'T MATTER WHO I AM! THERE ARE PEOPLE DYING HERE!
AAAAAH!
HELP ME!
HE'S... BACK THERE SOMEWHERE!
SOMEBODY STOP HIM!
NO HELP FOR YOU, I'M AFRAID.
IF ANYONE TRIES, THEY'LL DIE, TOO.
ANYONE THERE?
L.D.?
G.D.?

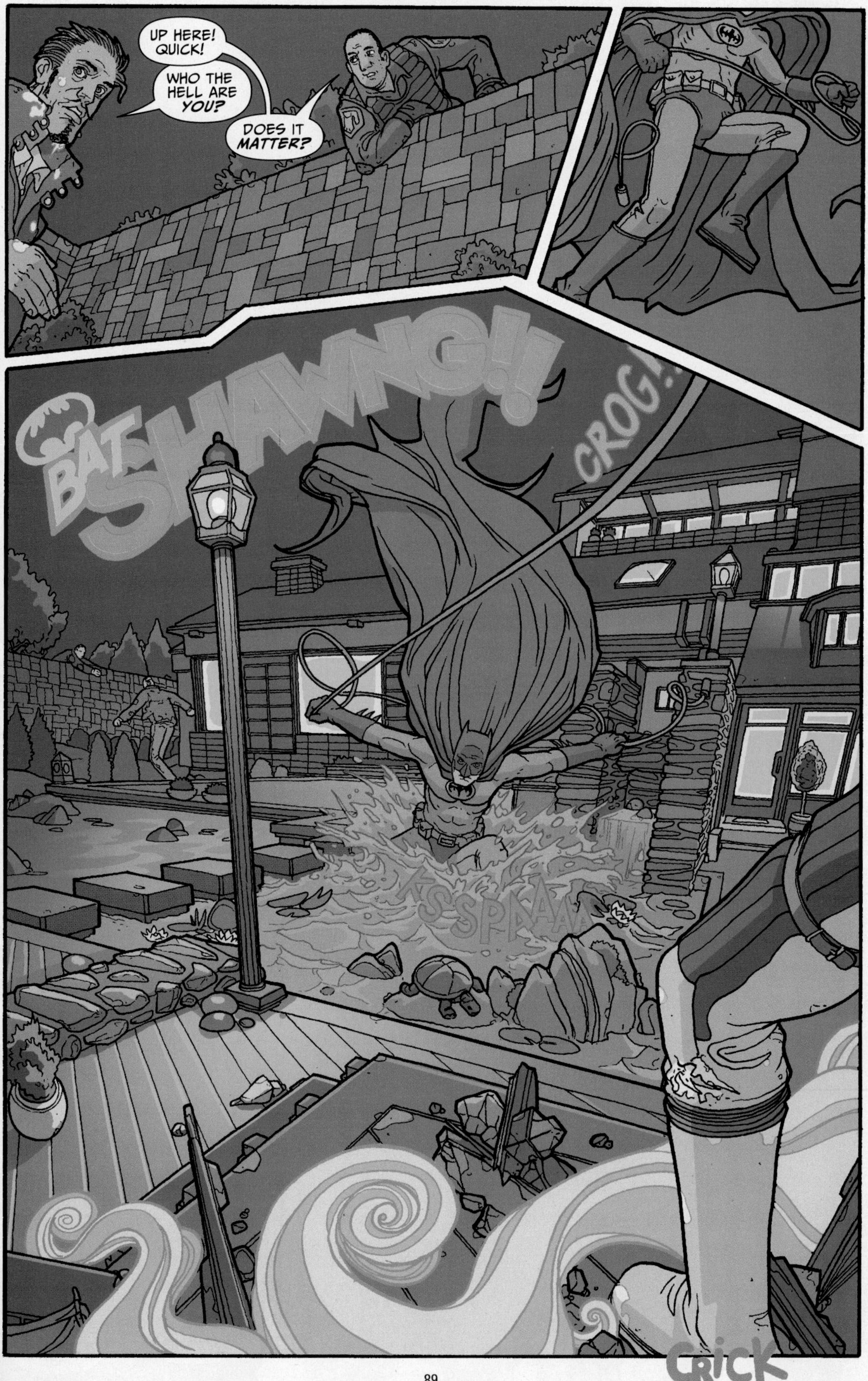
UP HERE! QUICK!
WHO THE HELL ARE YOU?
DOES IT MATTER?
BAT SHWAWNG!!
CROG!!
KSSPLAAAA
CRICK

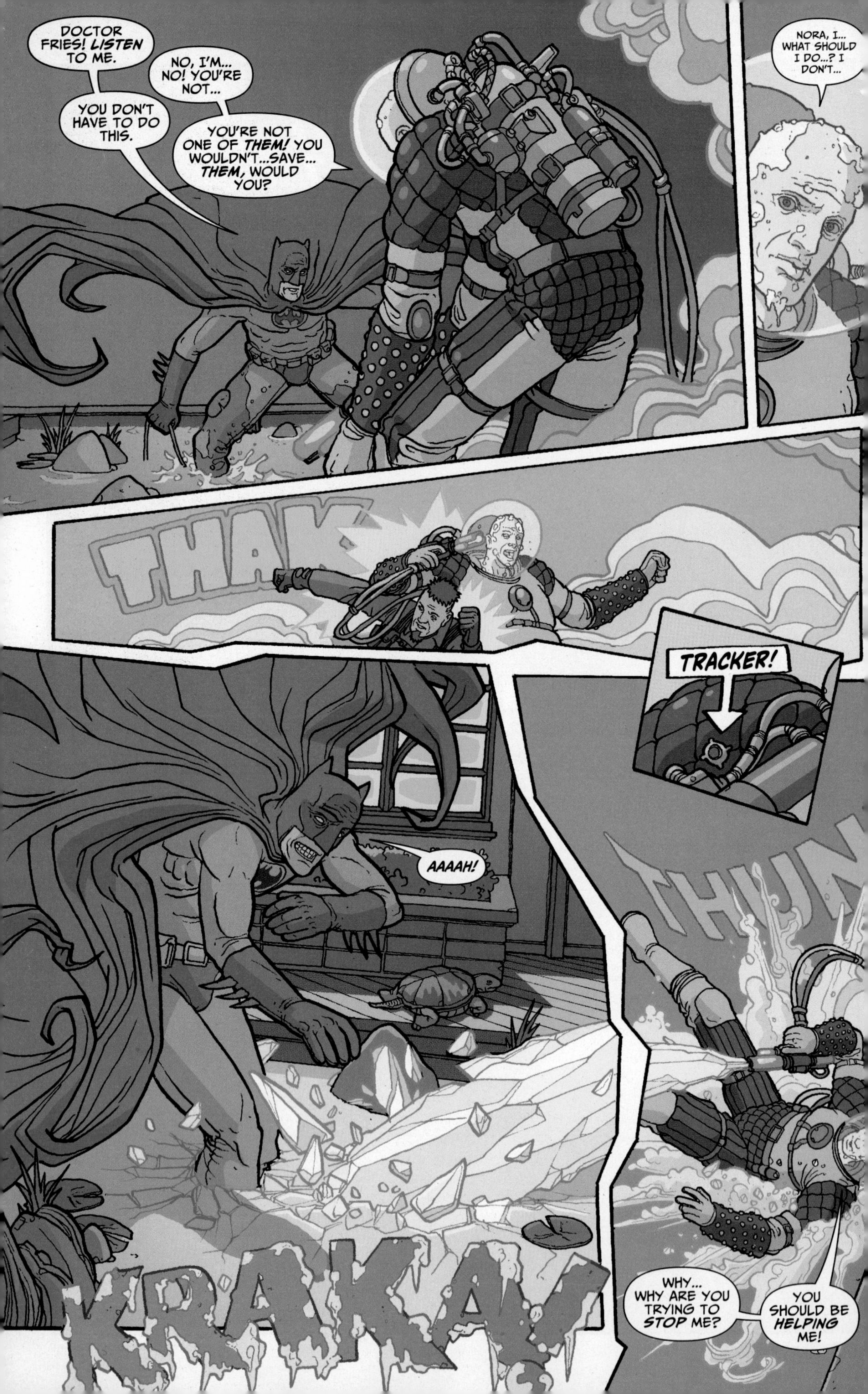
DOCTOR FRIES! *LISTEN* TO ME.
YOU DON'T HAVE TO DO THIS.
NO, I'M... NO! YOU'RE NOT...
YOU'RE NOT ONE OF *THEM!* YOU WOULDN'T...SAVE... *THEM,* WOULD YOU?
NORA, I... WHAT SHOULD I DO...? I DON'T...
THAK
TRACKER!
AAAAH!
THUN
WHY... WHY ARE YOU TRYING TO *STOP* ME?
YOU SHOULD BE *HELPING* ME!
KRAKAK

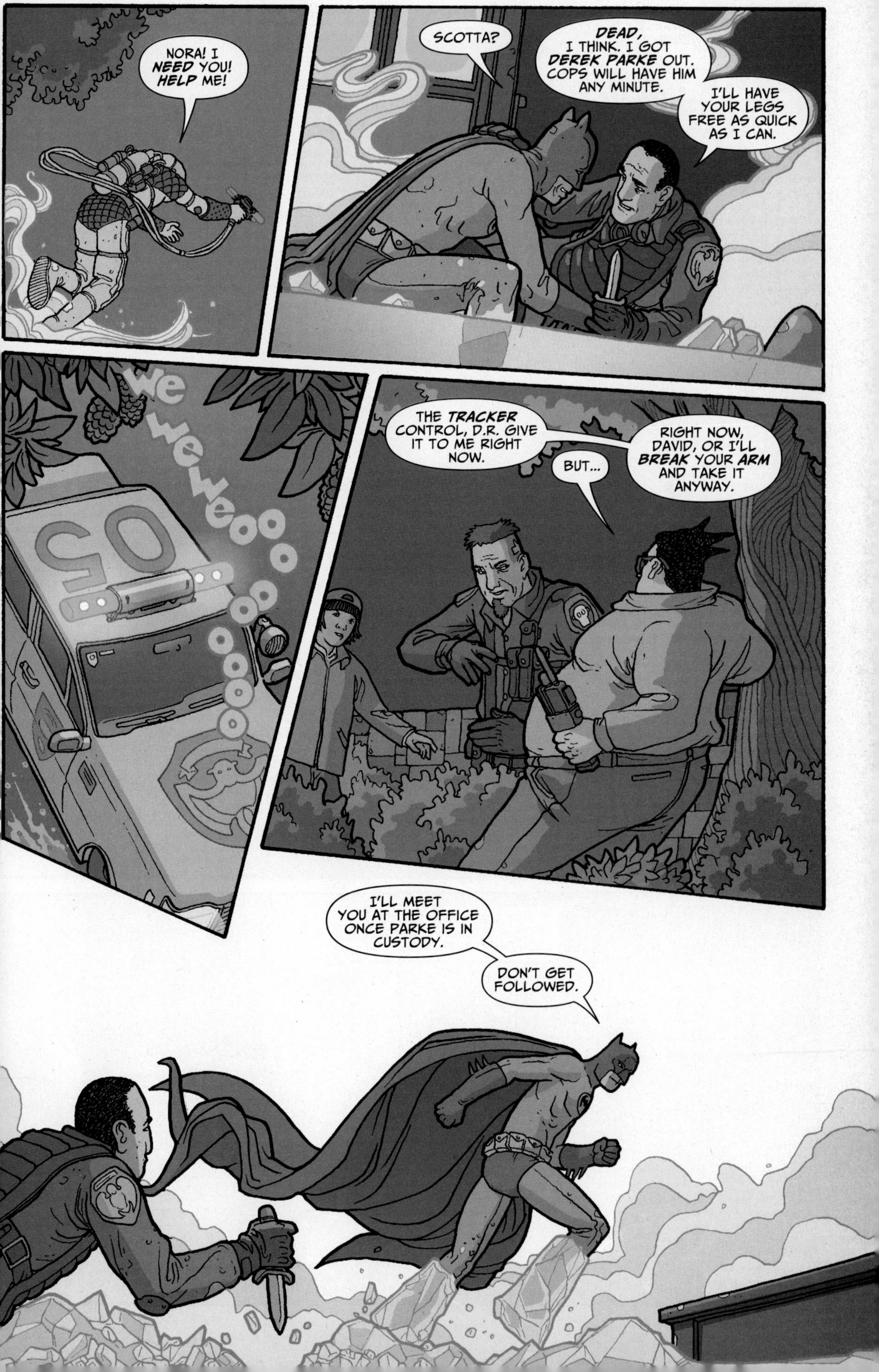
NORA! I NEED YOU! HELP ME!
SCOTTA?
DEAD, I THINK. I GOT DEREK PARKE OUT. COPS WILL HAVE HIM ANY MINUTE.
I'LL HAVE YOUR LEGS FREE AS QUICK AS I CAN.
THE TRACKER CONTROL, D.R. GIVE IT TO ME RIGHT NOW.
BUT...
RIGHT NOW, DAVID, OR I'LL BREAK YOUR ARM AND TAKE IT ANYWAY.
I'LL MEET YOU AT THE OFFICE ONCE PARKE IS IN CUSTODY.
DON'T GET FOLLOWED.

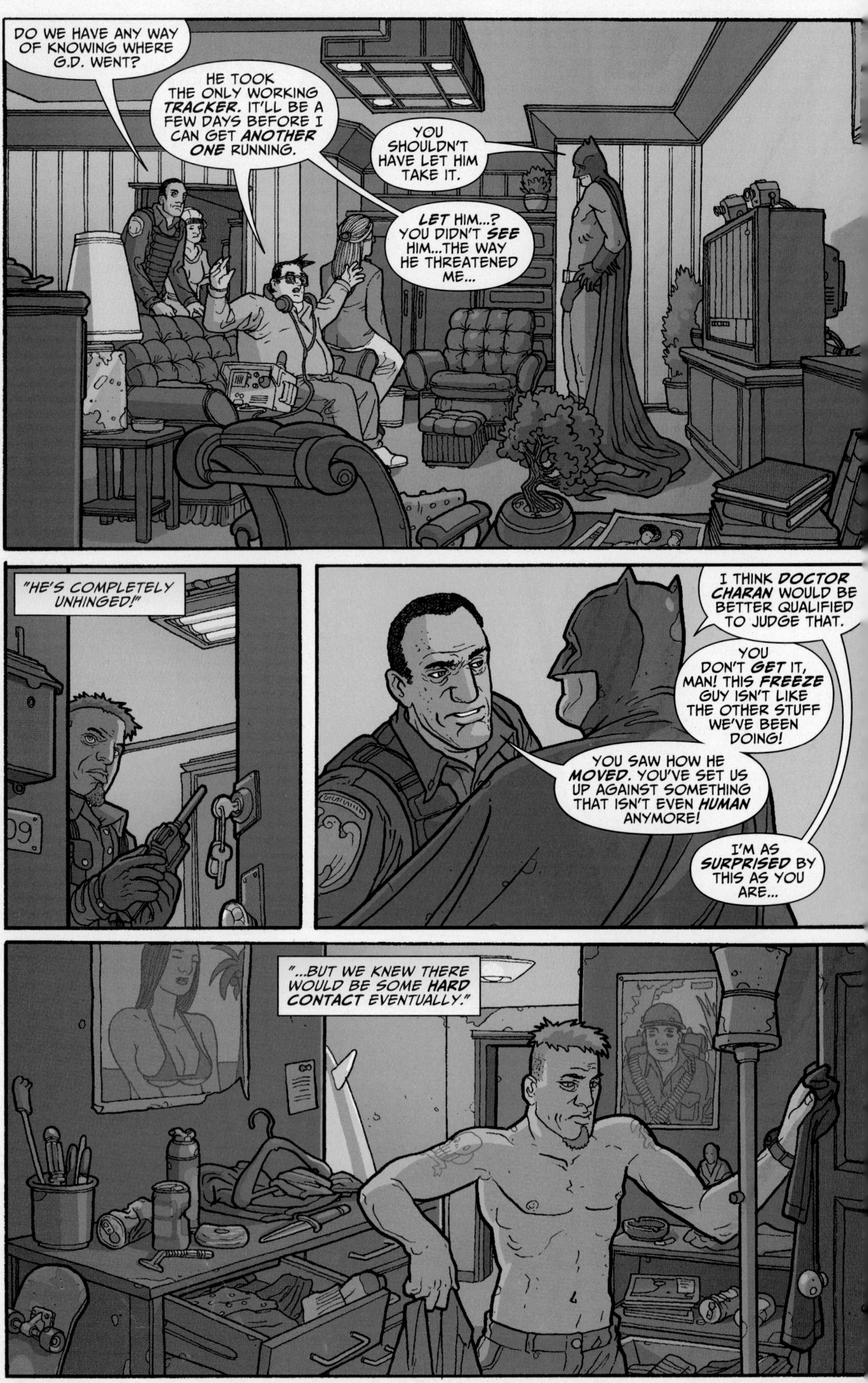
DO WE HAVE ANY WAY OF KNOWING WHERE G.D. WENT?
HE TOOK THE ONLY WORKING TRACKER. IT'LL BE A FEW DAYS BEFORE I CAN GET ANOTHER ONE RUNNING.
YOU SHOULDN'T HAVE LET HIM TAKE IT.
LET HIM...? YOU DIDN'T SEE HIM...THE WAY HE THREATENED ME...
"HE'S COMPLETELY UNHINGED!"
I THINK DOCTOR CHARAN WOULD BE BETTER QUALIFIED TO JUDGE THAT.
YOU DON'T GET IT, MAN! THIS FREEZE GUY ISN'T LIKE THE OTHER STUFF WE'VE BEEN DOING!
YOU SAW HOW HE MOVED. YOU'VE SET US UP AGAINST SOMETHING THAT ISN'T EVEN HUMAN ANYMORE!
I'M AS SURPRISED BY THIS AS YOU ARE...
"...BUT WE KNEW THERE WOULD BE SOME HARD CONTACT EVENTUALLY."

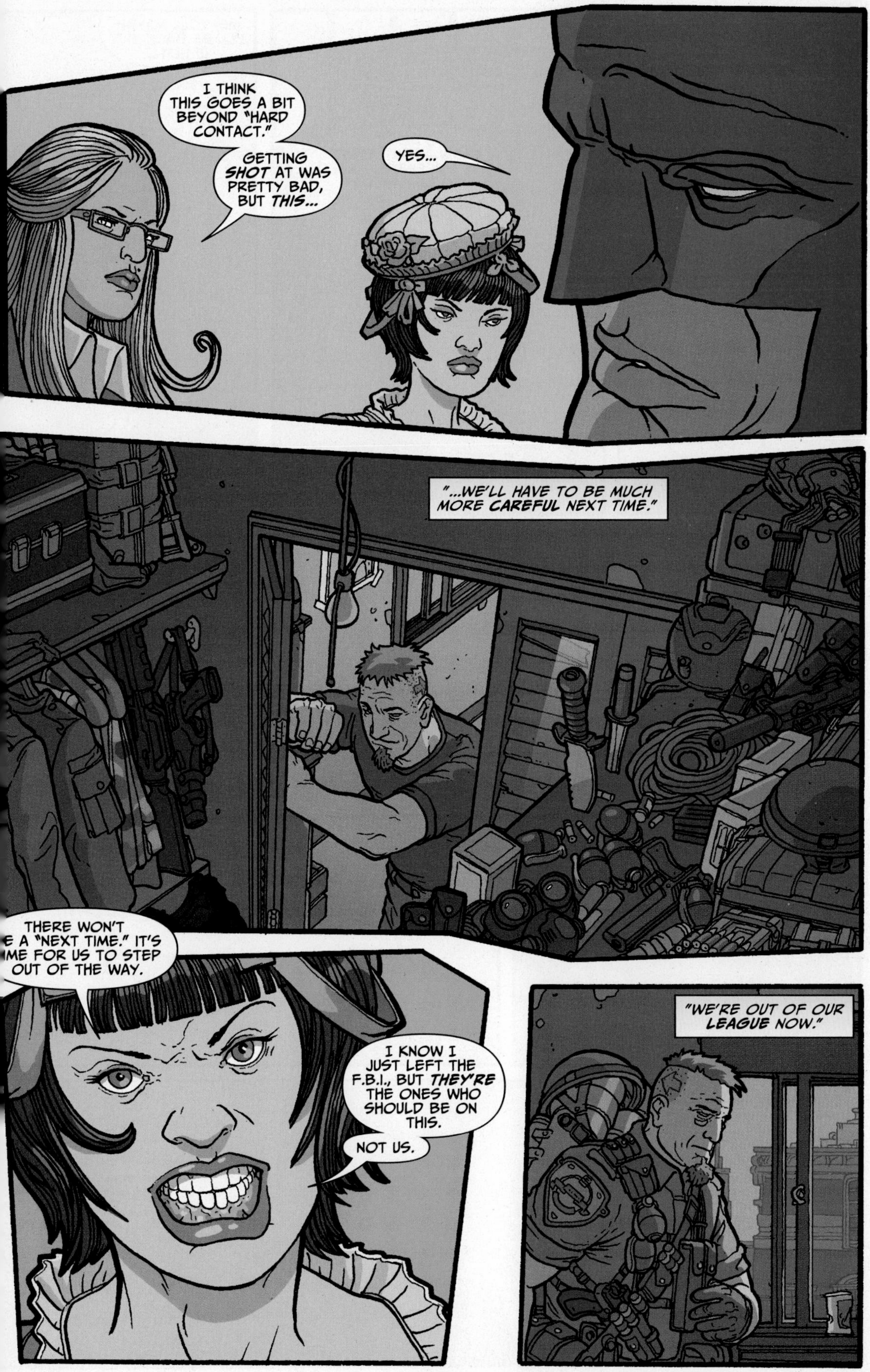
I THINK THIS GOES A BIT BEYOND "HARD CONTACT."
GETTING SHOT AT WAS PRETTY BAD, BUT THIS...
YES...
"...WE'LL HAVE TO BE MUCH MORE CAREFUL NEXT TIME."
THERE WON'T E A "NEXT TIME." IT'S ME FOR US TO STEP OUT OF THE WAY.
I KNOW I JUST LEFT THE F.B.I., BUT THEY'RE THE ONES WHO SHOULD BE ON THIS.
NOT US.
"WE'RE OUT OF OUR LEAGUE NOW."

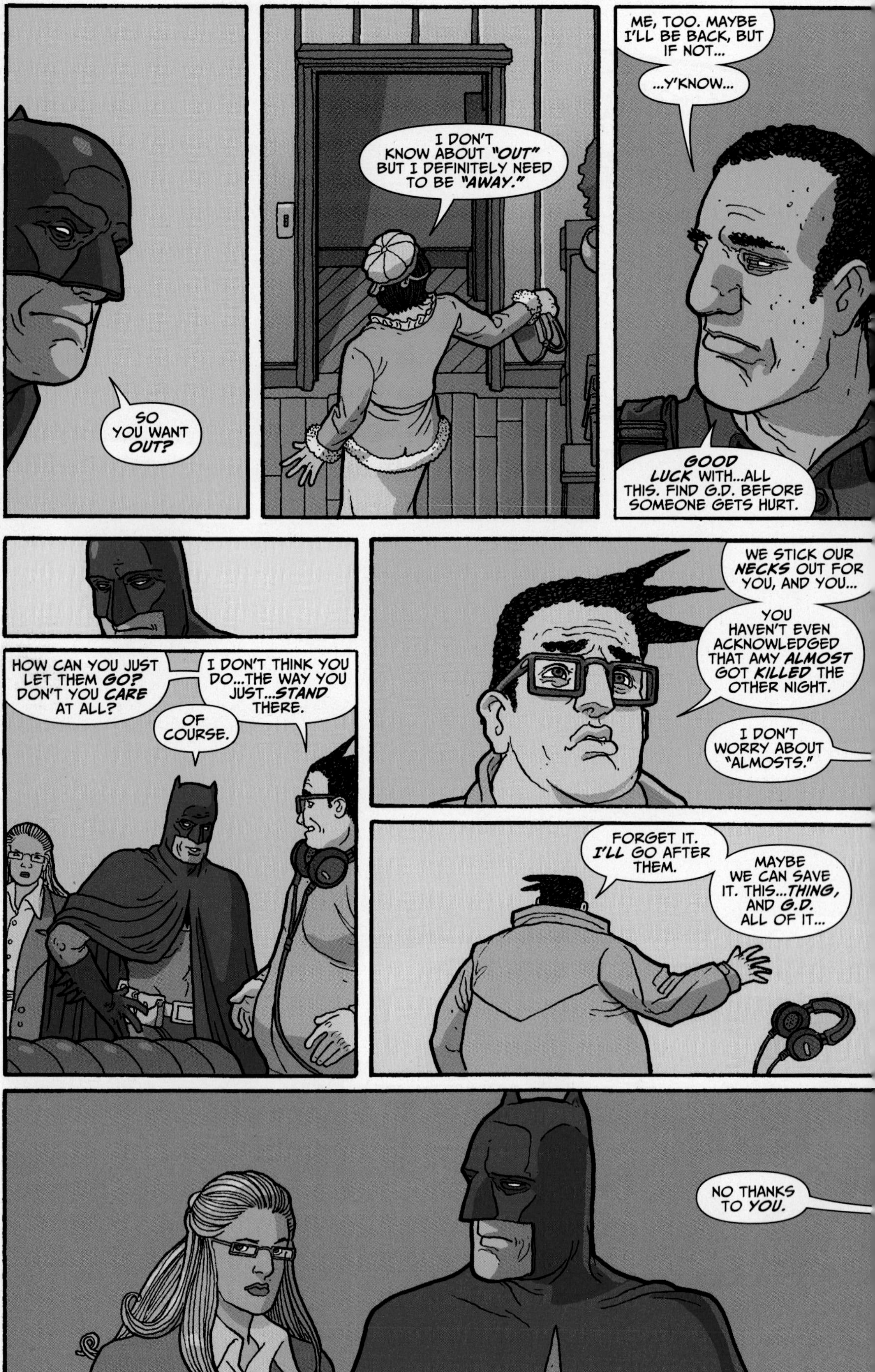
SO YOU WANT OUT?
I DON'T KNOW ABOUT "OUT" BUT I DEFINITELY NEED TO BE "AWAY."
ME, TOO. MAYBE I'LL BE BACK, BUT IF NOT...
...Y'KNOW...
GOOD LUCK WITH...ALL THIS. FIND G.D. BEFORE SOMEONE GETS HURT.
HOW CAN YOU JUST LET THEM GO? DON'T YOU CARE AT ALL?
OF COURSE.
I DON'T THINK YOU DO...THE WAY YOU JUST...STAND THERE.
WE STICK OUR NECKS OUT FOR YOU, AND YOU...
YOU HAVEN'T EVEN ACKNOWLEDGED THAT AMY ALMOST GOT KILLED THE OTHER NIGHT.
I DON'T WORRY ABOUT "ALMOSTS."
FORGET IT. I'LL GO AFTER THEM.
MAYBE WE CAN SAVE IT. THIS...THING, AND G.D. ALL OF IT...
NO THANKS TO YOU.

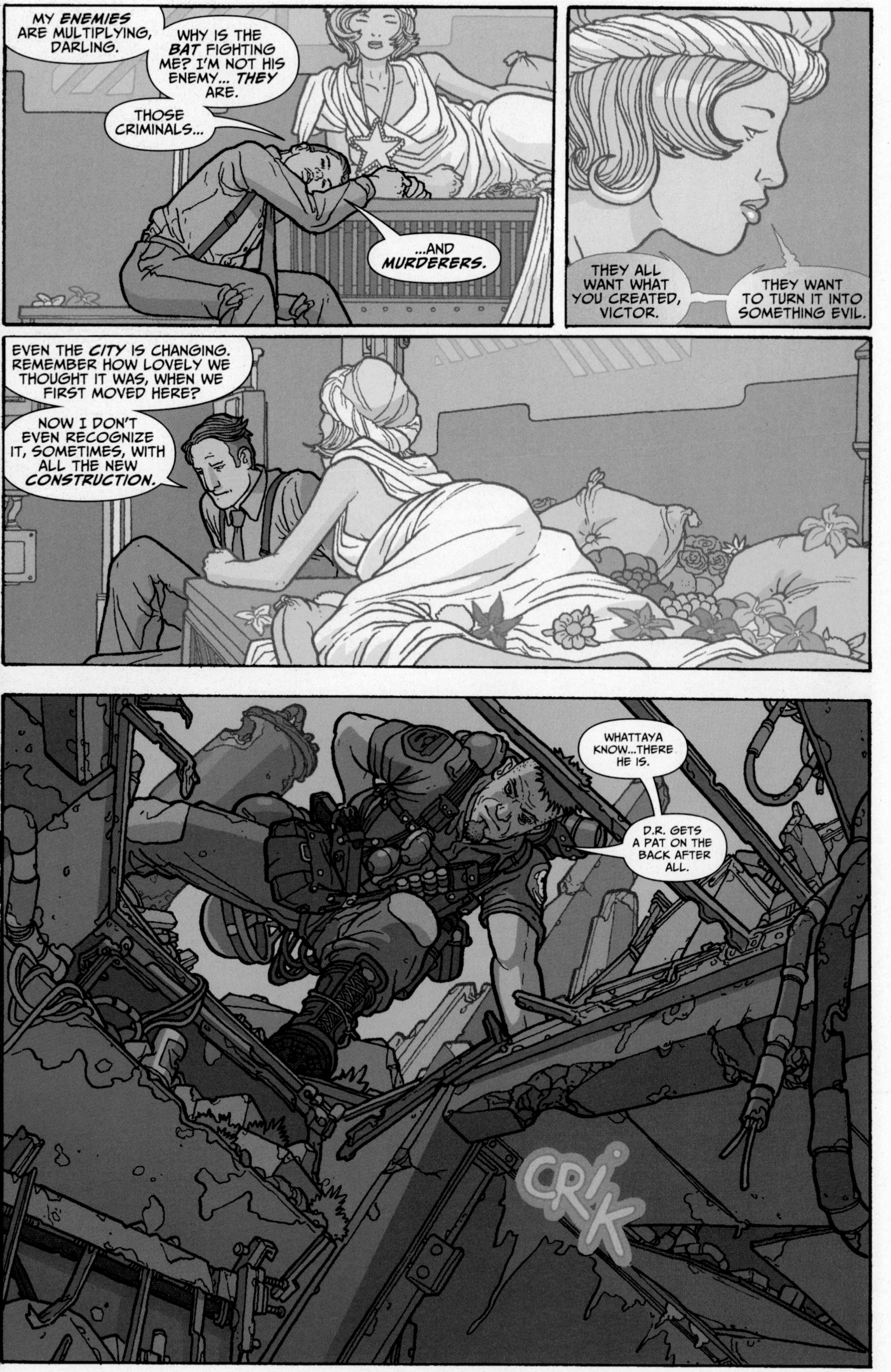
MY ENEMIES ARE MULTIPLYING, DARLING.
WHY IS THE BAT FIGHTING ME? I'M NOT HIS ENEMY... THEY ARE.
THOSE CRIMINALS...
...AND MURDERERS.
THEY ALL WANT WHAT YOU CREATED, VICTOR.
THEY WANT TO TURN IT INTO SOMETHING EVIL.
EVEN THE CITY IS CHANGING. REMEMBER HOW LOVELY WE THOUGHT IT WAS, WHEN WE FIRST MOVED HERE?
NOW I DON'T EVEN RECOGNIZE IT, SOMETIMES, WITH ALL THE NEW CONSTRUCTION.
WHATTAYA KNOW...THERE HE IS.
D.R. GETS A PAT ON THE BACK AFTER ALL.
CRIK

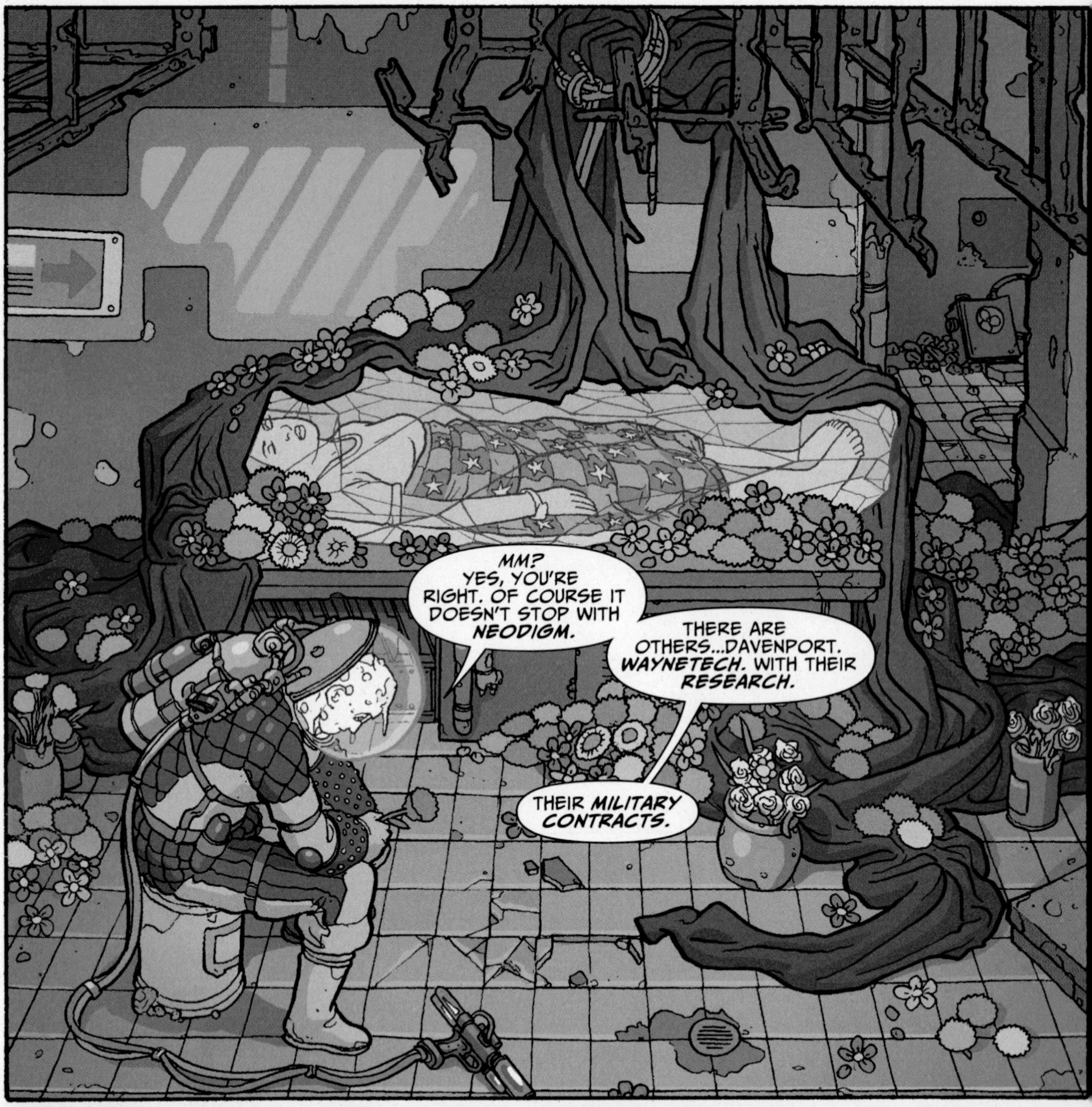
MM? YES, YOU'RE RIGHT. OF COURSE IT DOESN'T STOP WITH NEODIGM.
THERE ARE OTHERS...DAVENPORT. WAYNETECH. WITH THEIR RESEARCH.
THEIR MILITARY CONTRACTS.

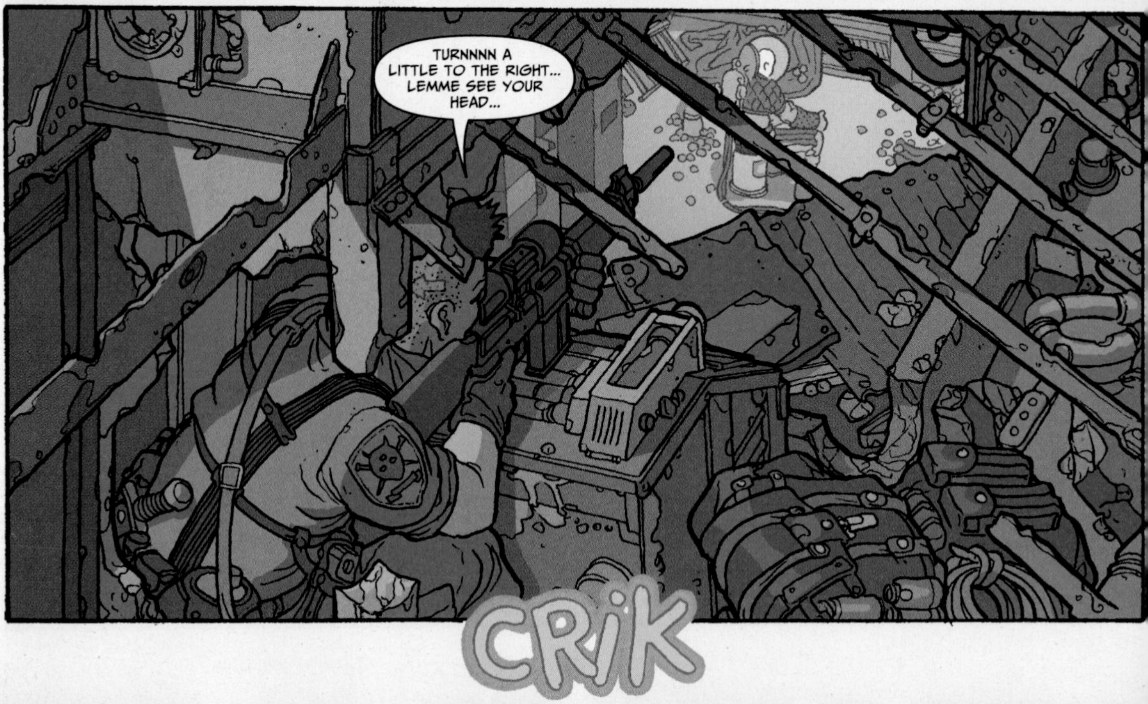
TURNNNN A LITTLE TO THE RIGHT... LEMME SEE YOUR HEAD...
CRIK

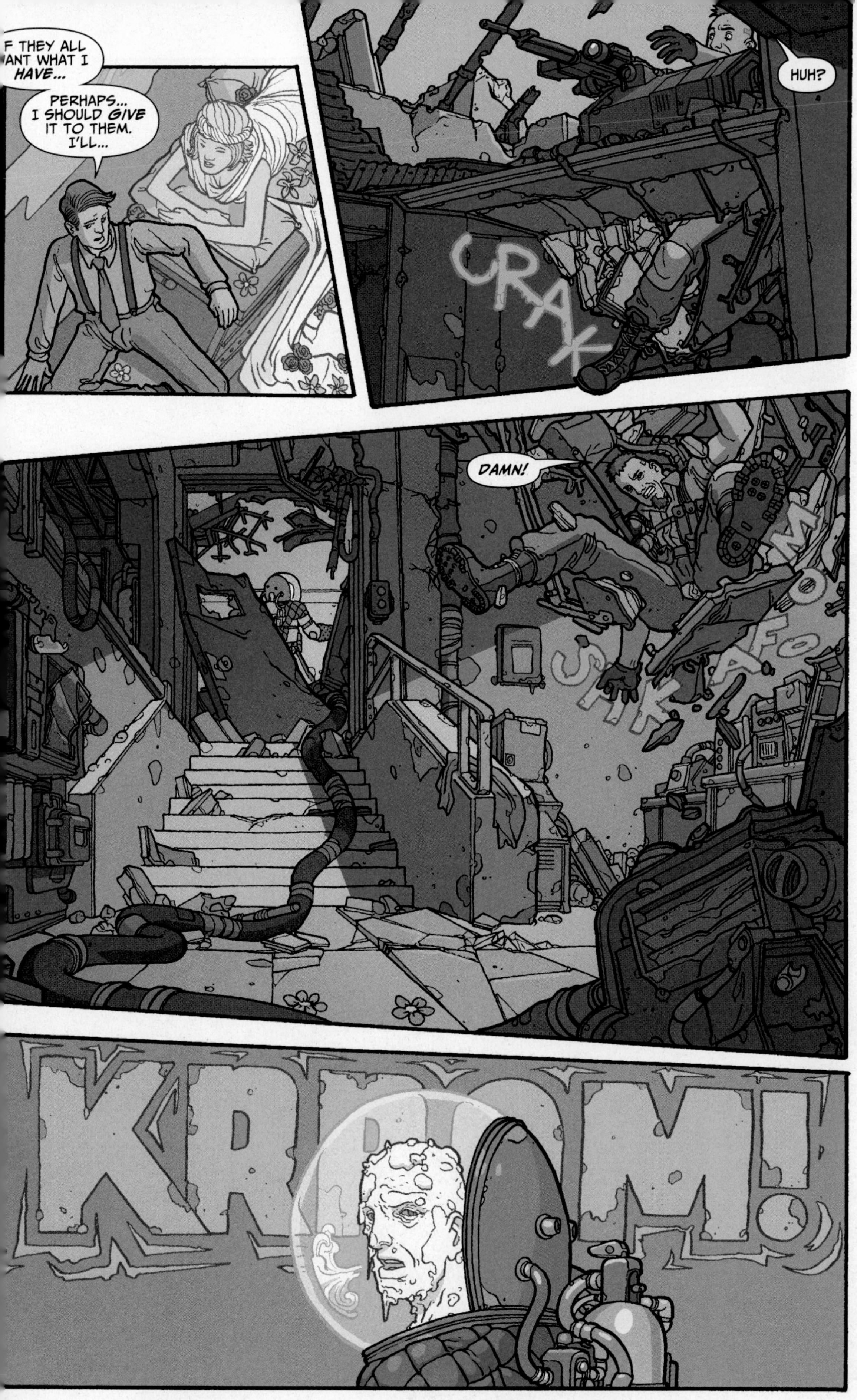
F THEY ALL
ANT WHAT I
HAVE...
PERHAPS...
I SHOULD GIVE
IT TO THEM.
I'LL...
HUH?
CRAK
DAMN!
SHKAFOOM
KRDOOM!

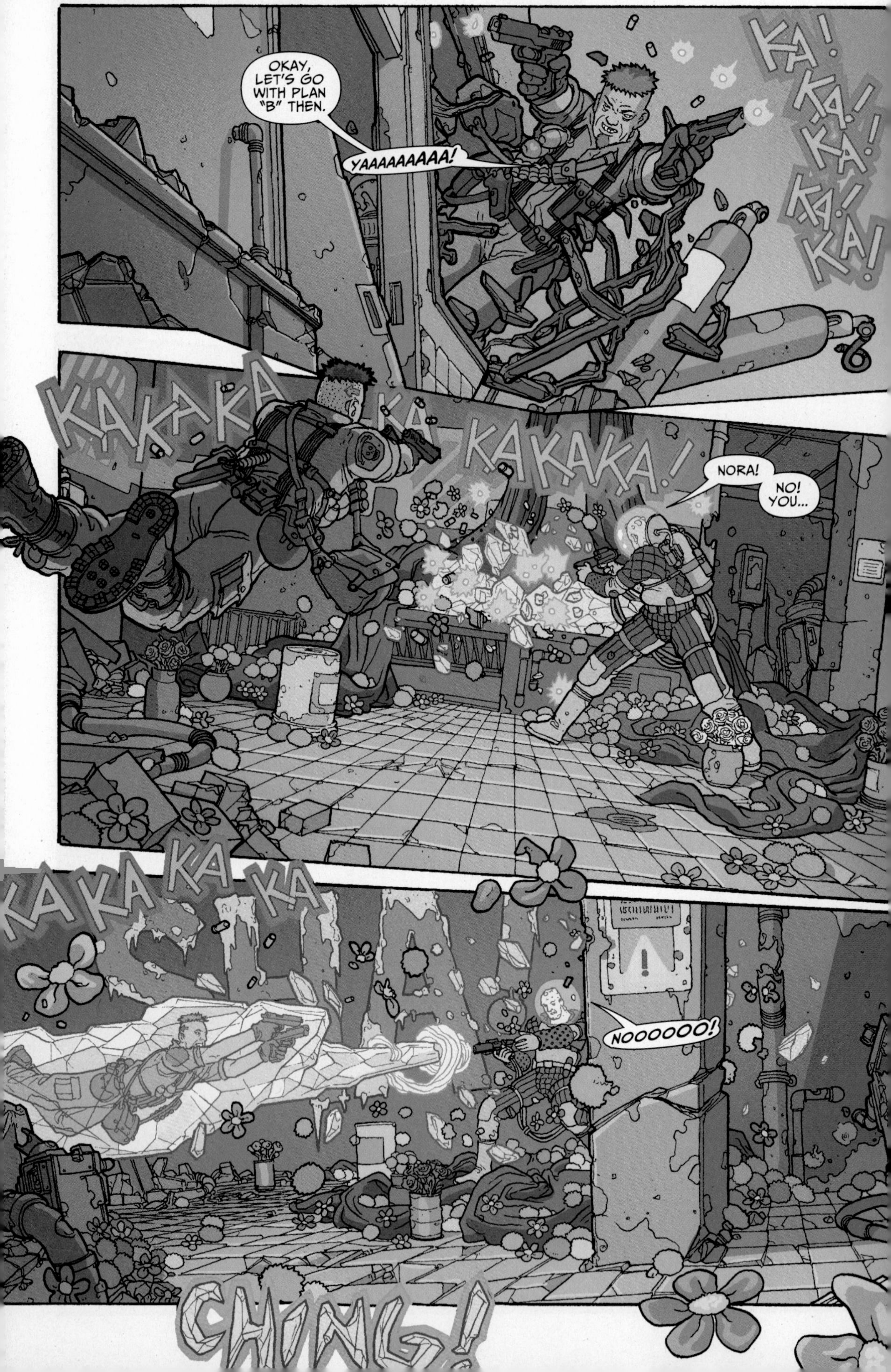
OKAY, LET'S GO WITH PLAN "B" THEN.
YAAAAAAAAA!
KA! KA! KA! KA! KA!
KAKAKA KA
KAKAKA!
NORA!
NO! YOU...
KAKA KA KA
NOOOOOO!
CHING!

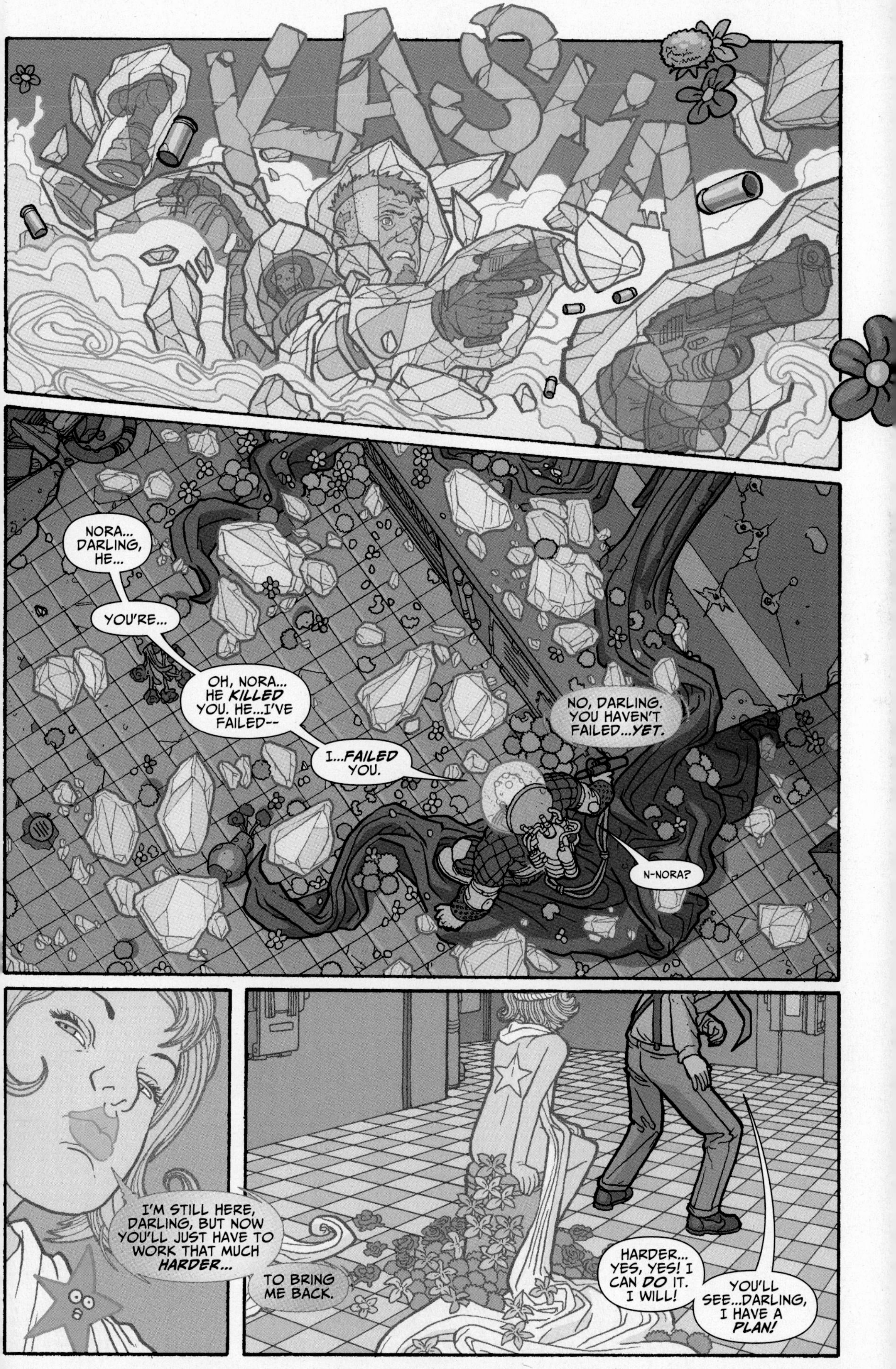
NORA... DARLING, HE...
YOU'RE...
OH, NORA... HE KILLED YOU. HE...I'VE FAILED--
I...FAILED YOU.
NO, DARLING. YOU HAVEN'T FAILED...YET.
N-NORA?
I'M STILL HERE, DARLING, BUT NOW YOU'LL JUST HAVE TO WORK THAT MUCH HARDER...
TO BRING ME BACK.
HARDER... YES, YES! I CAN DO IT. I WILL!
YOU'LL SEE...DARLING, I HAVE A PLAN!

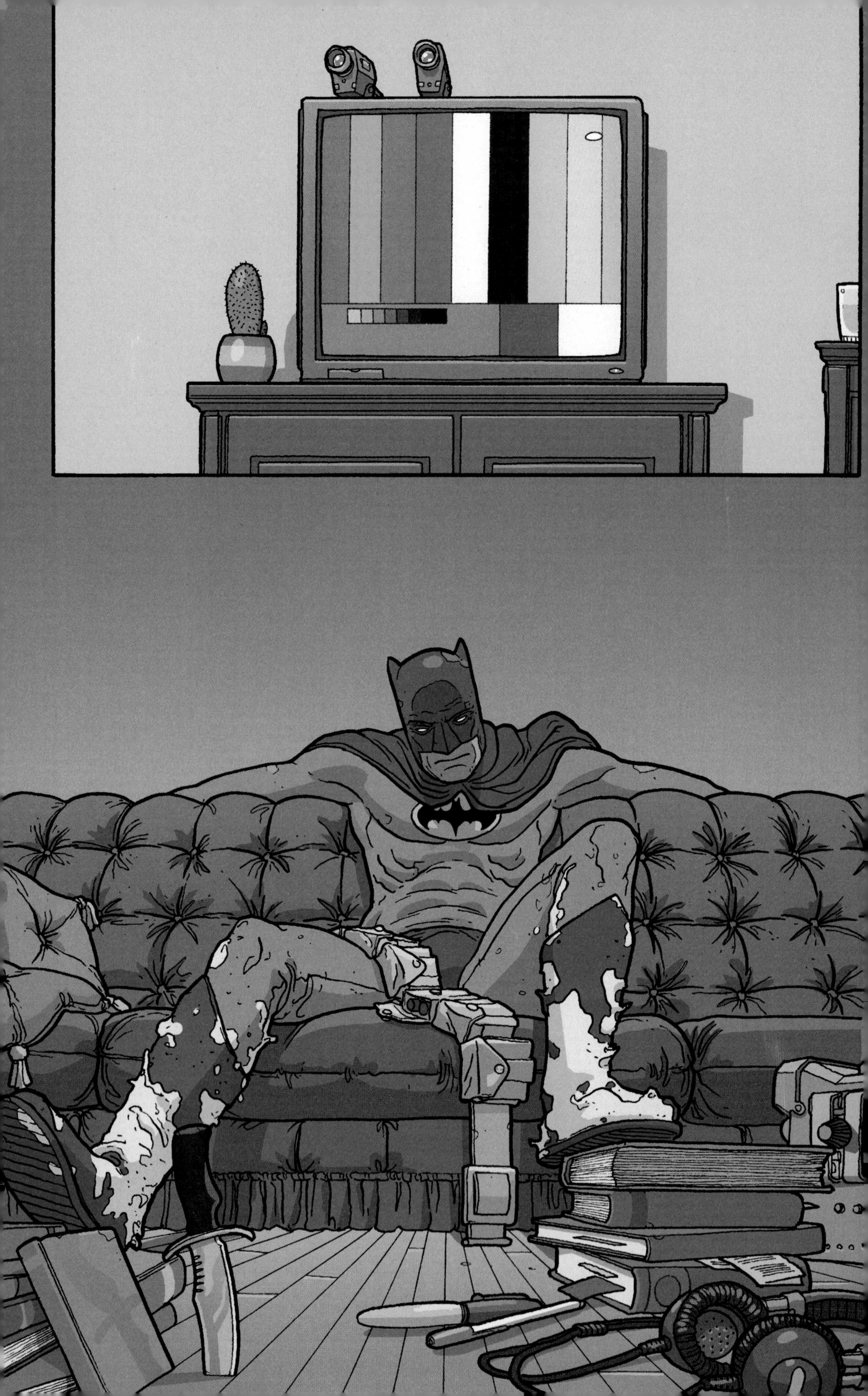

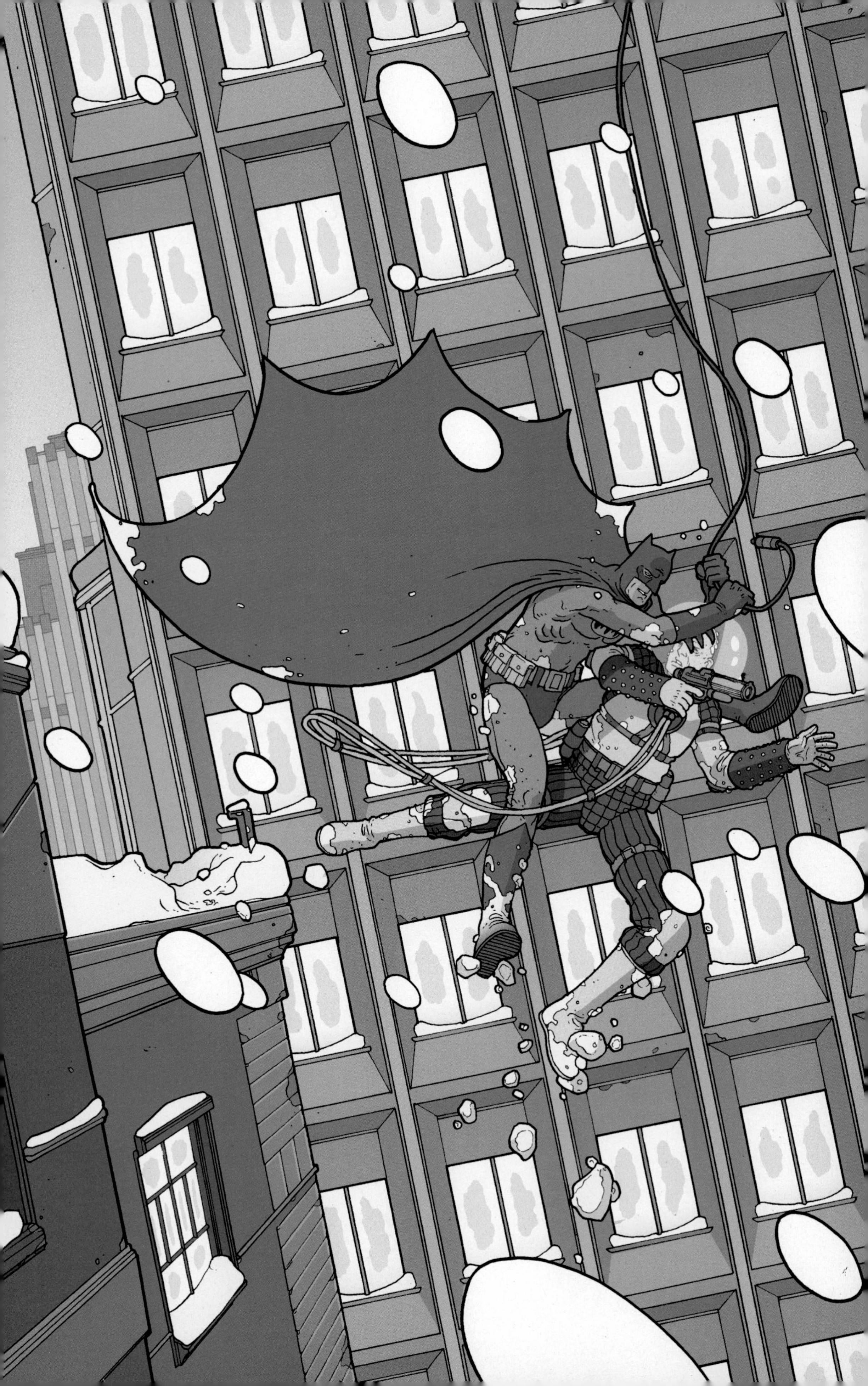

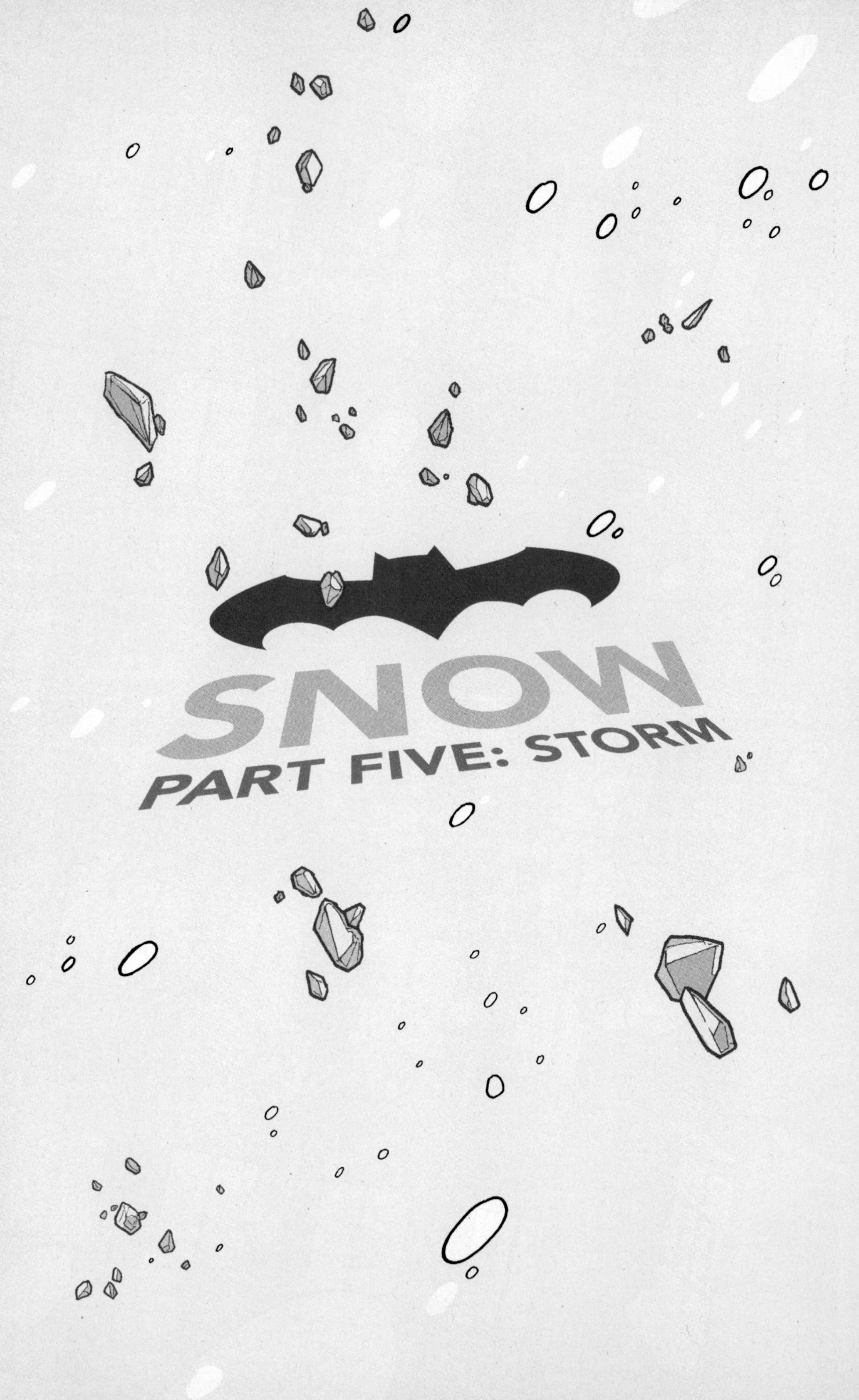
SNOW
PART FIVE: STORM

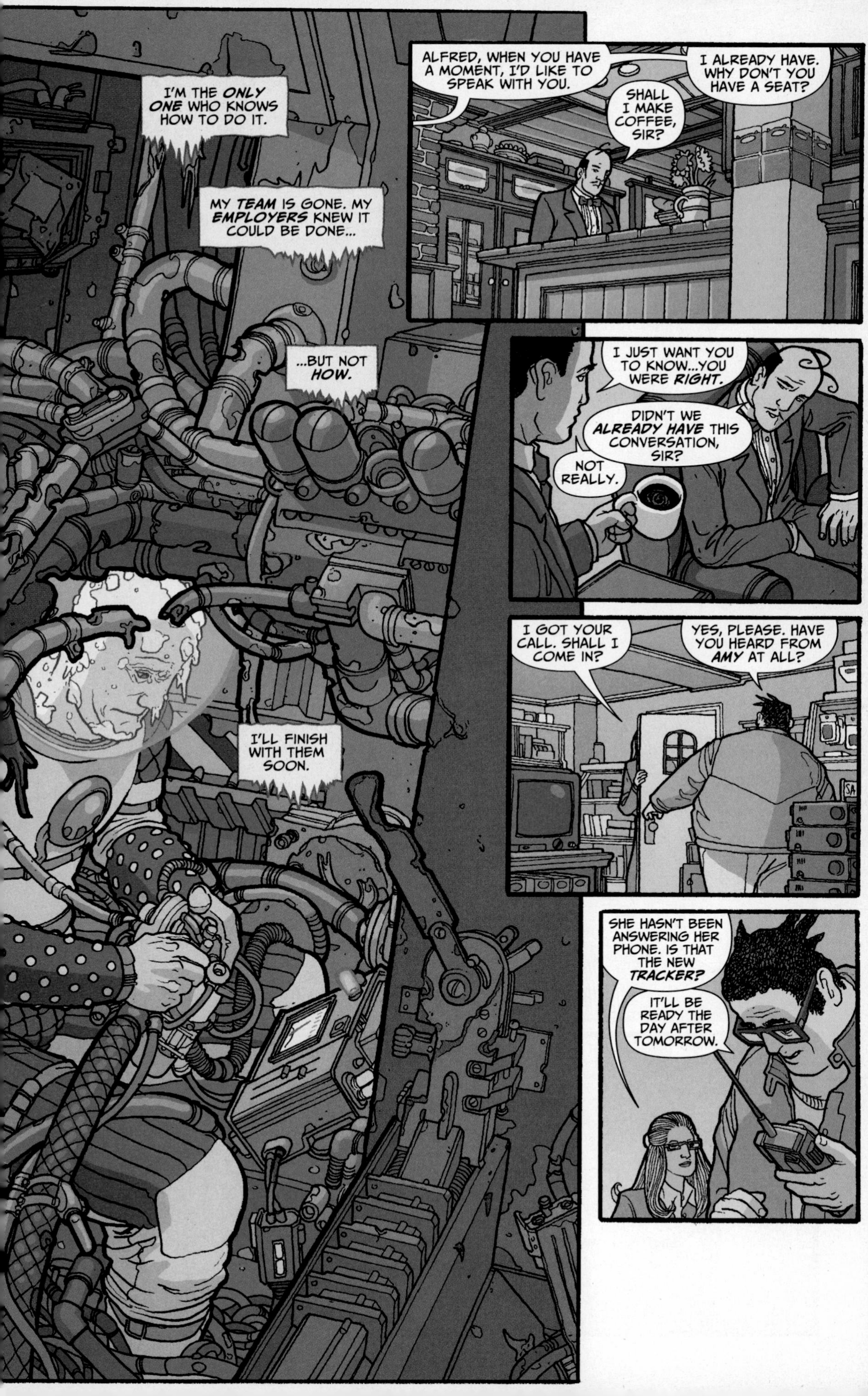
I'M THE ONLY ONE WHO KNOWS HOW TO DO IT.
MY TEAM IS GONE. MY EMPLOYERS KNEW IT COULD BE DONE...
...BUT NOT HOW.
I'LL FINISH WITH THEM SOON.
ALFRED, WHEN YOU HAVE A MOMENT, I'D LIKE TO SPEAK WITH YOU.
I ALREADY HAVE. WHY DON'T YOU HAVE A SEAT?
SHALL I MAKE COFFEE, SIR?
I JUST WANT YOU TO KNOW...YOU WERE RIGHT.
DIDN'T WE ALREADY HAVE THIS CONVERSATION, SIR?
NOT REALLY.
I GOT YOUR CALL. SHALL I COME IN?
YES, PLEASE. HAVE YOU HEARD FROM AMY AT ALL?
SHE HASN'T BEEN ANSWERING HER PHONE. IS THAT THE NEW TRACKER?
IT'LL BE READY THE DAY AFTER TOMORROW.

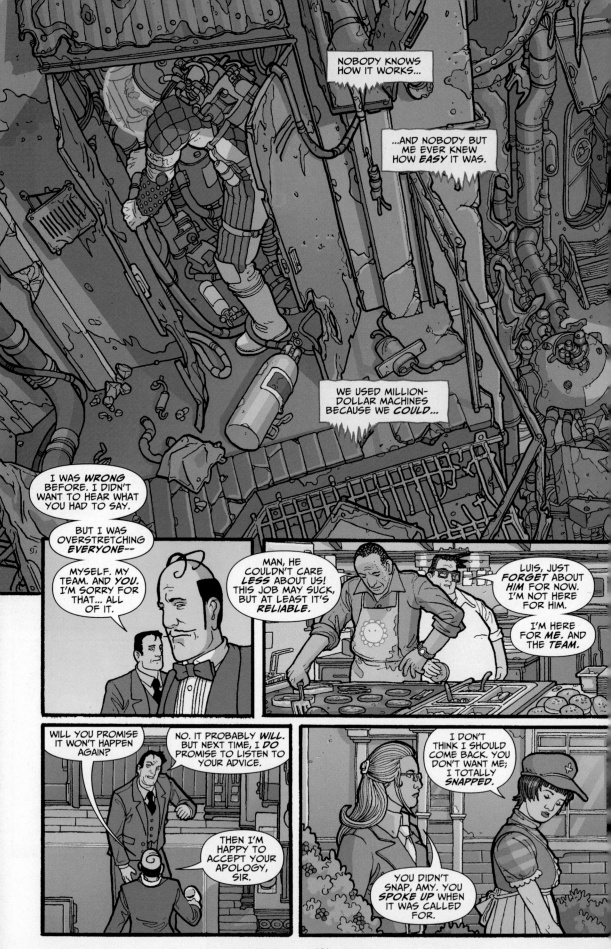

NOBODY KNOWS HOW IT WORKS...

...AND NOBODY BUT ME EVER KNEW HOW *EASY* IT WAS.

WE USED MILLION-DOLLAR MACHINES BECAUSE WE *COULD*...

I WAS *WRONG* BEFORE. I DIDN'T WANT TO HEAR WHAT YOU HAD TO SAY.

BUT I WAS OVERSTRETCHING *EVERYONE*--

MYSELF. MY TEAM. AND *YOU.* I'M SORRY FOR THAT... ALL OF IT.

MAN, HE COULDN'T CARE *LESS* ABOUT US! THIS JOB MAY SUCK, BUT AT LEAST IT'S *RELIABLE.*

LUIS, JUST *FORGET* ABOUT *HIM* FOR NOW. I'M NOT HERE FOR HIM.

I'M HERE FOR *ME.* AND THE *TEAM.*

WILL YOU PROMISE IT WON'T HAPPEN AGAIN?

NO. IT PROBABLY *WILL.* BUT NEXT TIME, I *DO* PROMISE TO LISTEN TO YOUR ADVICE.

THEN I'M HAPPY TO ACCEPT YOUR APOLOGY, SIR.

I DON'T THINK I SHOULD COME BACK. YOU DON'T WANT ME; I TOTALLY *SNAPPED.*

YOU DIDN'T SNAP, AMY. YOU *SPOKE UP* WHEN IT WAS CALLED FOR.

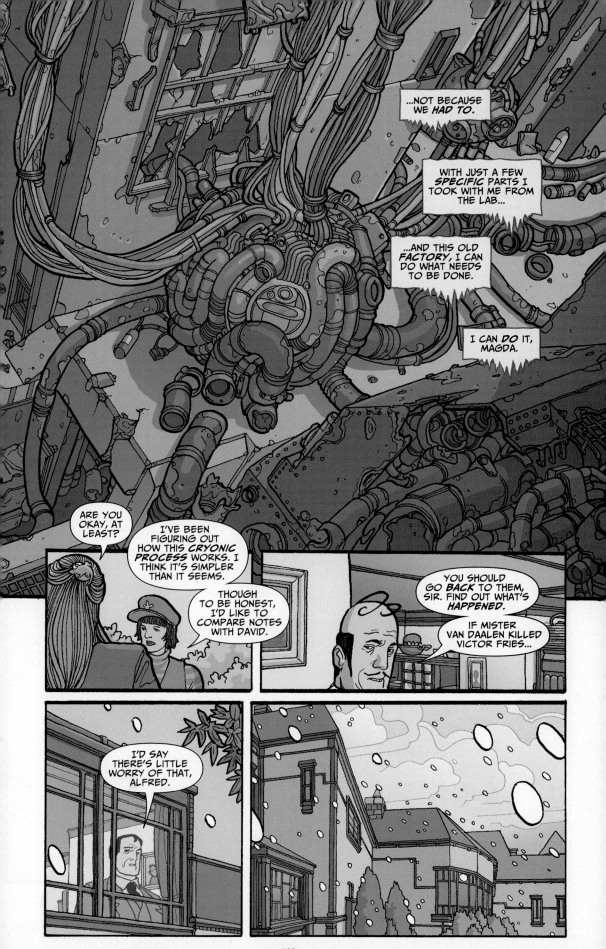

...NOT BECAUSE WE *HAD TO.*

WITH JUST A FEW *SPECIFIC* PARTS I TOOK WITH ME FROM THE LAB...

...AND THIS OLD *FACTORY,* I CAN DO WHAT NEEDS TO BE DONE.

I CAN *DO* IT, MAGDA.

ARE YOU OKAY, AT LEAST?

I'VE BEEN FIGURING OUT HOW THIS *CRYONIC PROCESS* WORKS. I THINK IT'S SIMPLER THAN IT SEEMS.

THOUGH TO BE HONEST, I'D LIKE TO COMPARE NOTES WITH DAVID.

YOU SHOULD GO *BACK* TO THEM, SIR. FIND OUT WHAT'S *HAPPENED.*

IF MISTER VAN DAALEN KILLED VICTOR FRIES...

I'D SAY THERE'S LITTLE WORRY OF THAT, ALFRED.

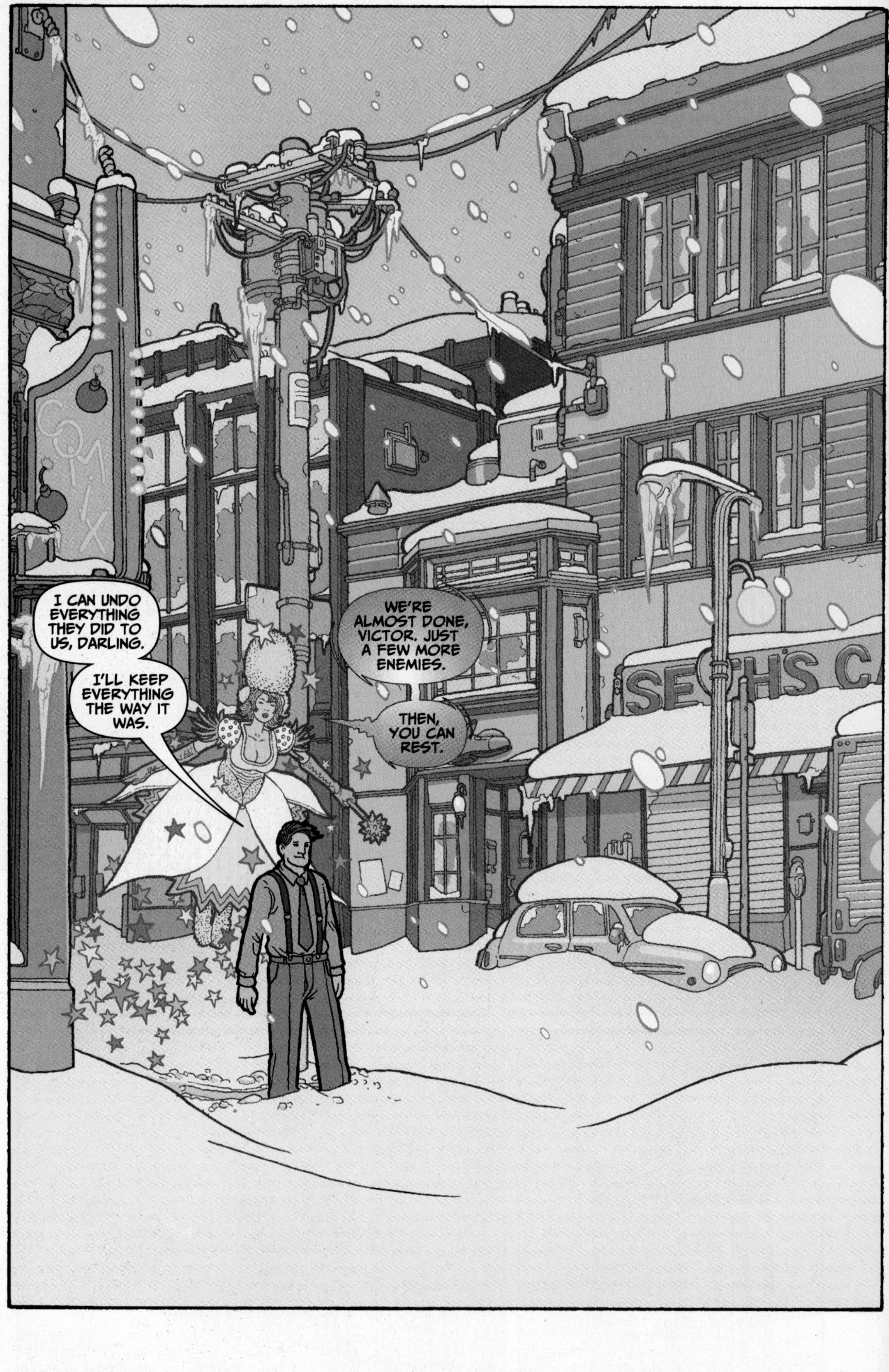
I CAN UNDO EVERYTHING THEY DID TO US, DARLING.
I'LL KEEP EVERYTHING THE WAY IT WAS.
WE'RE ALMOST DONE, VICTOR. JUST A FEW MORE ENEMIES.
THEN, YOU CAN REST.
COMIX
SETHS CA

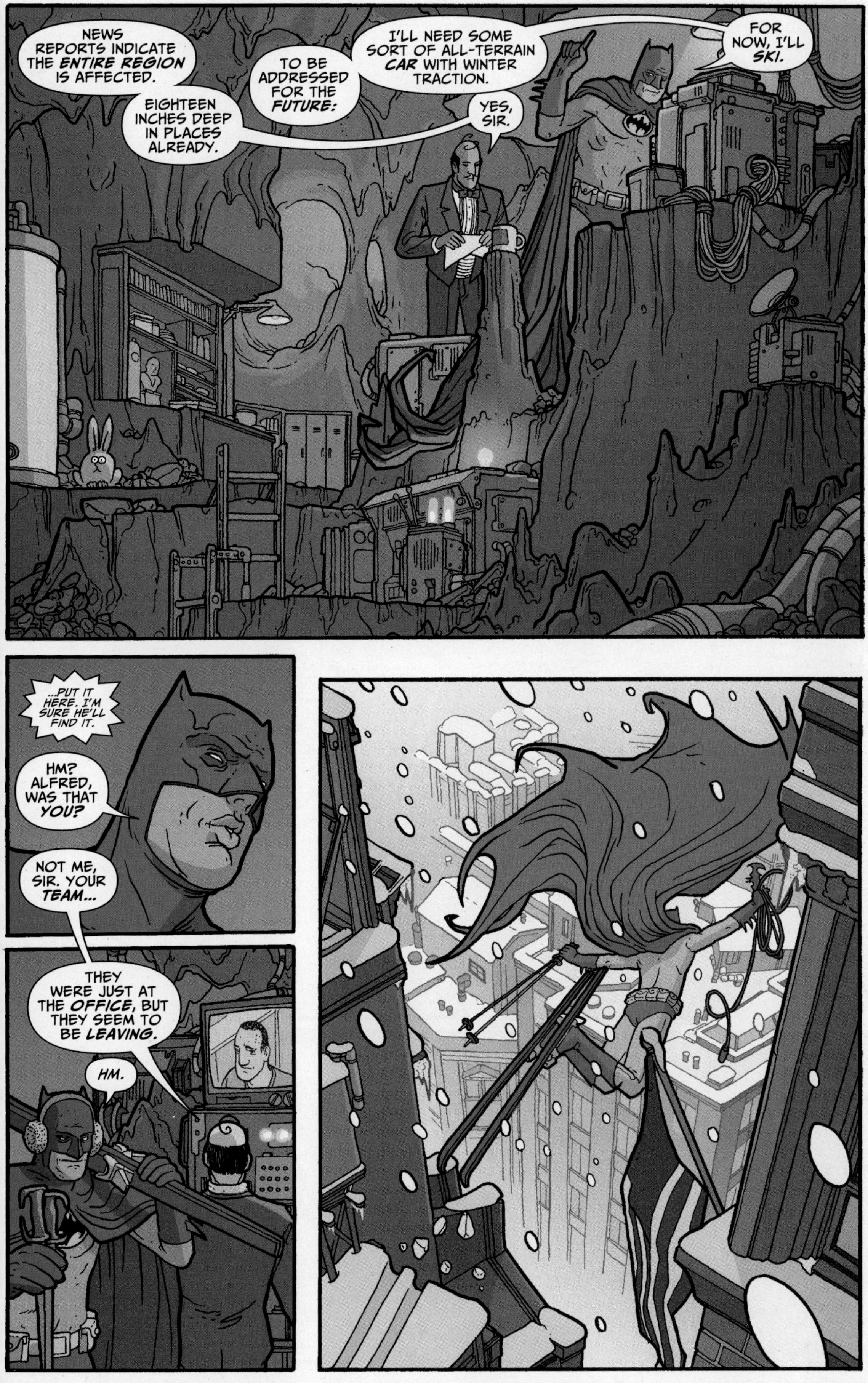
NEWS REPORTS INDICATE THE ENTIRE REGION IS AFFECTED.
EIGHTEEN INCHES DEEP IN PLACES ALREADY.
TO BE ADDRESSED FOR THE FUTURE:
I'LL NEED SOME SORT OF ALL-TERRAIN CAR WITH WINTER TRACTION.
YES, SIR.
FOR NOW, I'LL SKI.
...PUT IT HERE. I'M SURE HE'LL FIND IT.
HM? ALFRED, WAS THAT YOU?
NOT ME, SIR. YOUR TEAM...
THEY WERE JUST AT THE OFFICE, BUT THEY SEEM TO BE LEAVING.
HM.

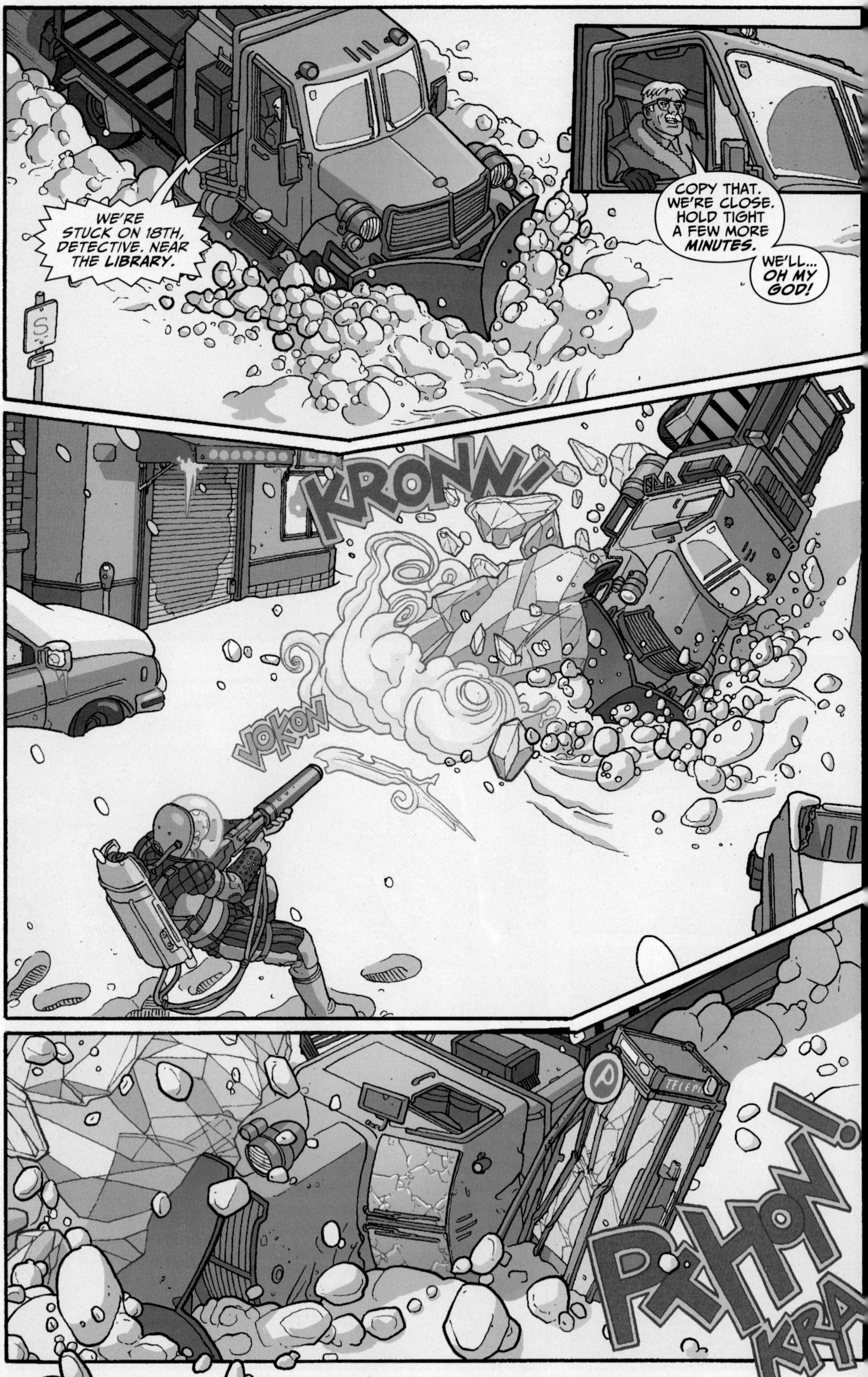
WE'RE STUCK ON 18TH, DETECTIVE. NEAR THE LIBRARY.
COPY THAT. WE'RE CLOSE. HOLD TIGHT A FEW MORE MINUTES.
WE'LL... OH MY GOD!
KRONN!
VOKON
PAHON!
KRA

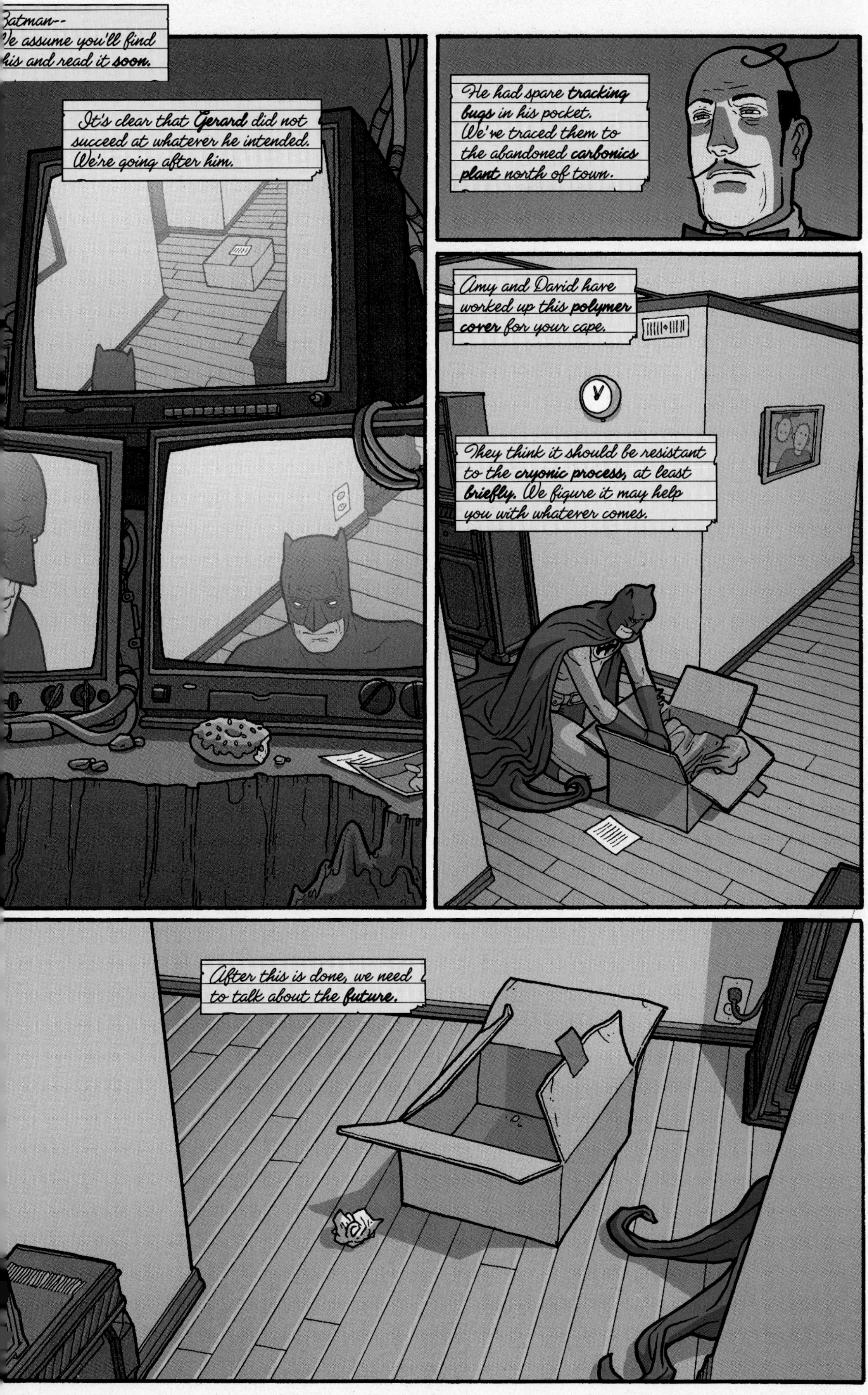
Batman--
We assume you'll find
this and read it soon.
It's clear that Gerard did not
succeed at whatever he intended.
We're going after him.
He had spare tracking
bugs in his pocket.
We've traced them to
the abandoned carbonics
plant north of town.
Amy and David have
worked up this polymer
cover for your cape.
They think it should be resistant
to the cryonic process, at least
briefly. We figure it may help
you with whatever comes.
After this is done, we need
to talk about the future.

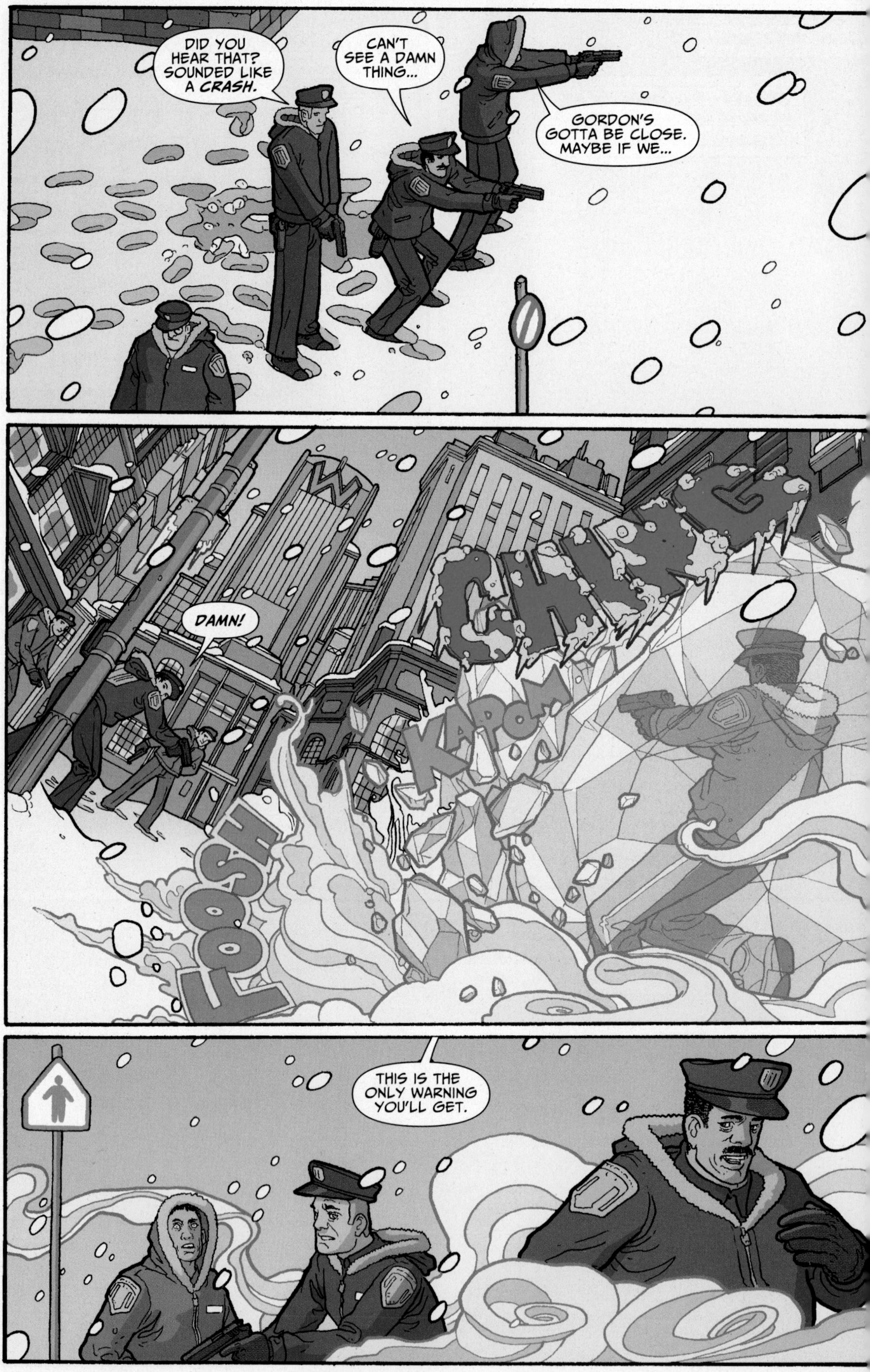
DID YOU HEAR THAT? SOUNDED LIKE A *CRASH.*
CAN'T SEE A DAMN THING...
GORDON'S GOTTA BE CLOSE. MAYBE IF WE...
DAMN!
CHUNG
KAPOW
FOOSH
THIS IS THE ONLY WARNING YOU'LL GET.

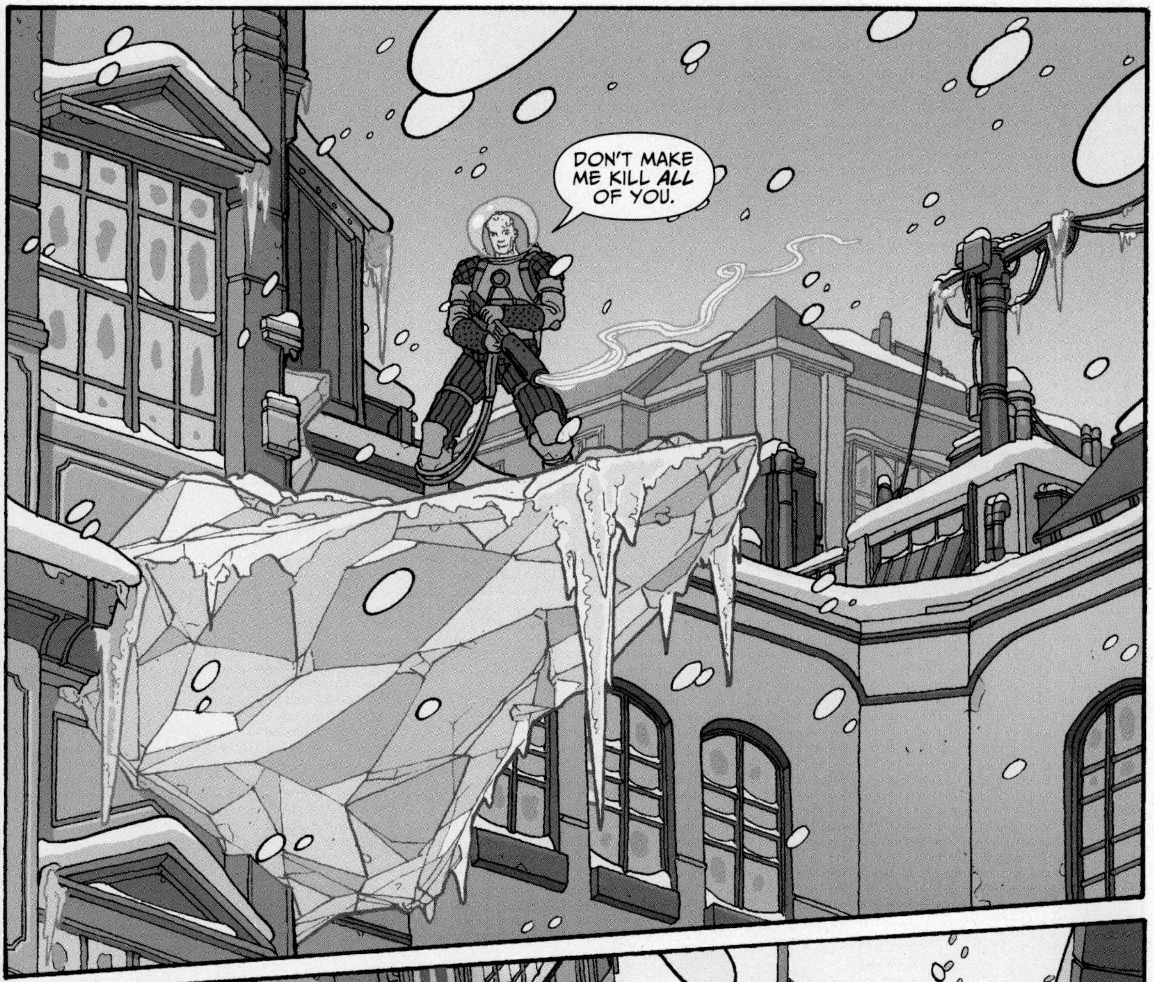
DON'T MAKE ME KILL ALL OF YOU.

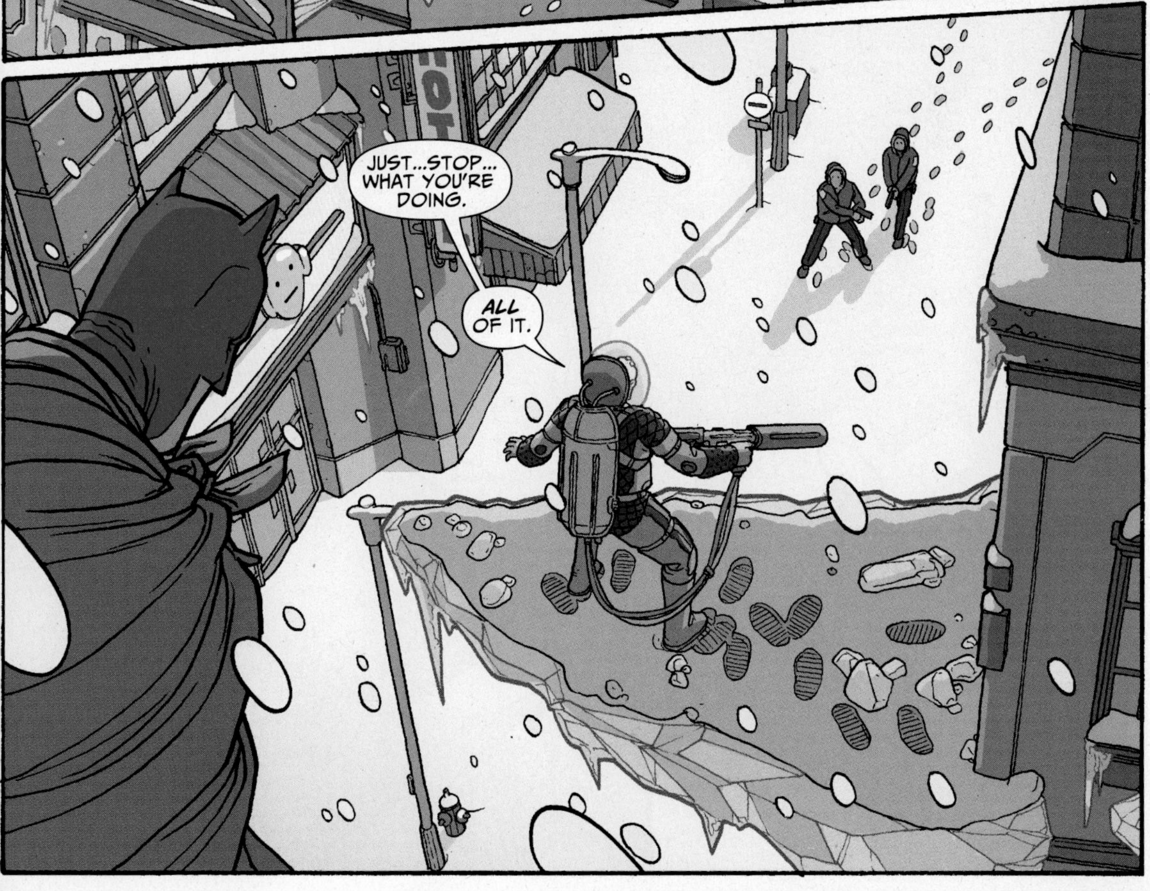
HOT
JUST...STOP... WHAT YOU'RE DOING.
ALL OF IT.

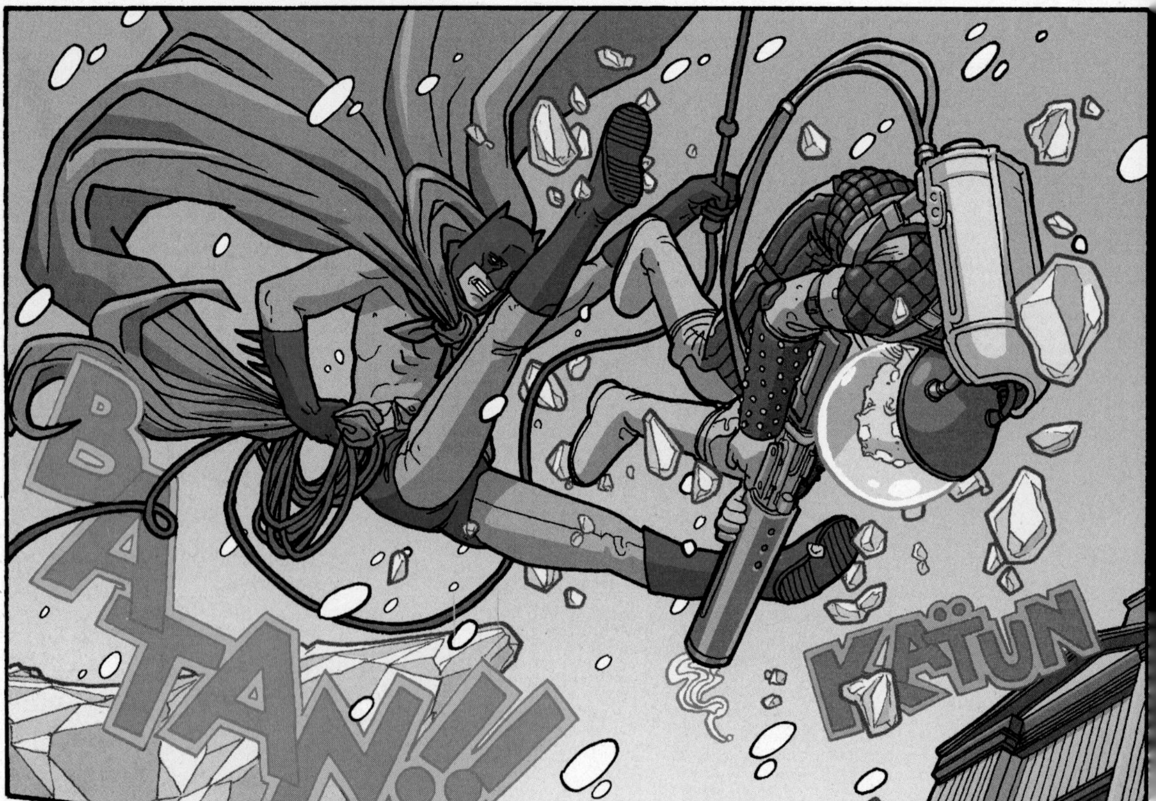
BATAN!!
KÄTUN

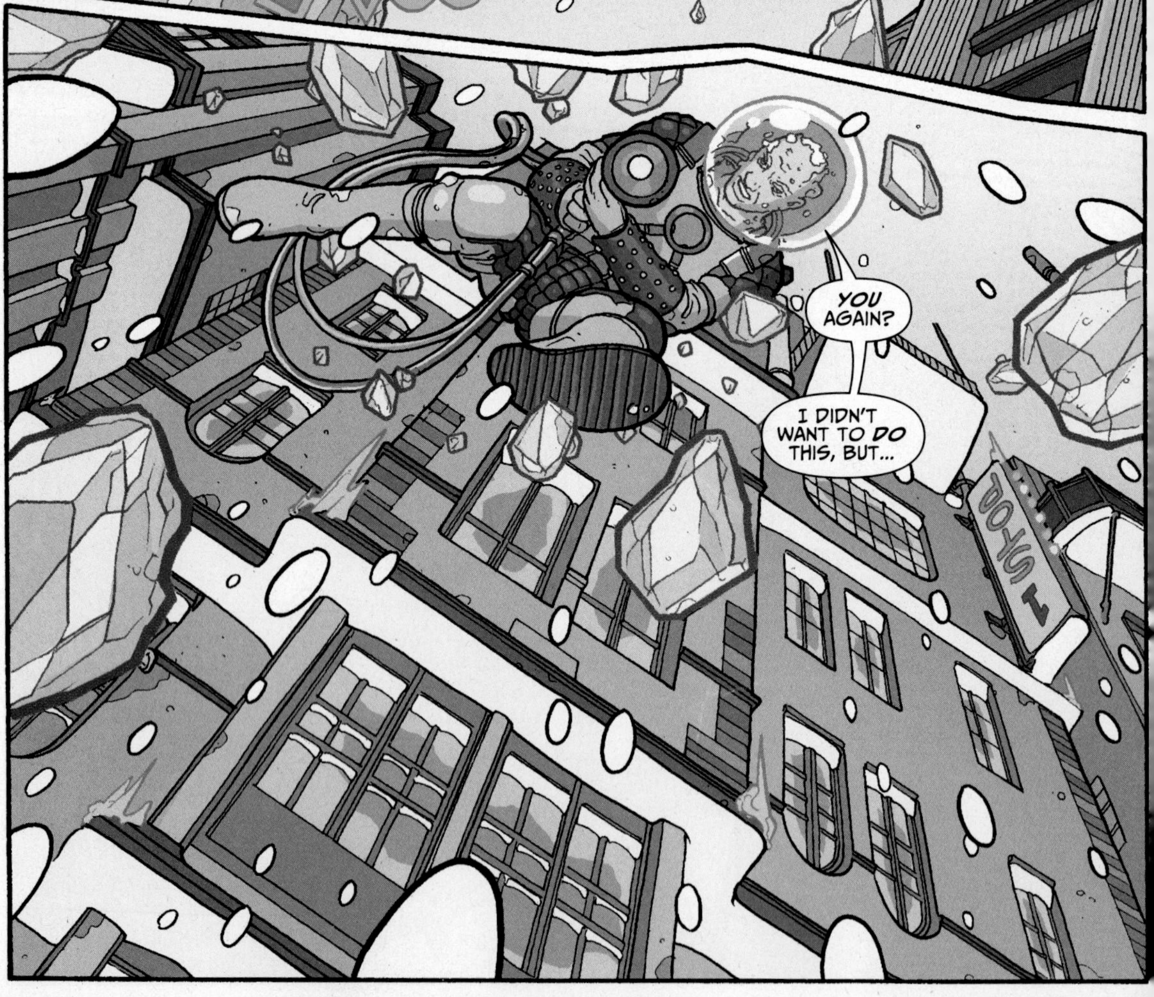
YOU AGAIN?
I DIDN'T WANT TO DO THIS, BUT...

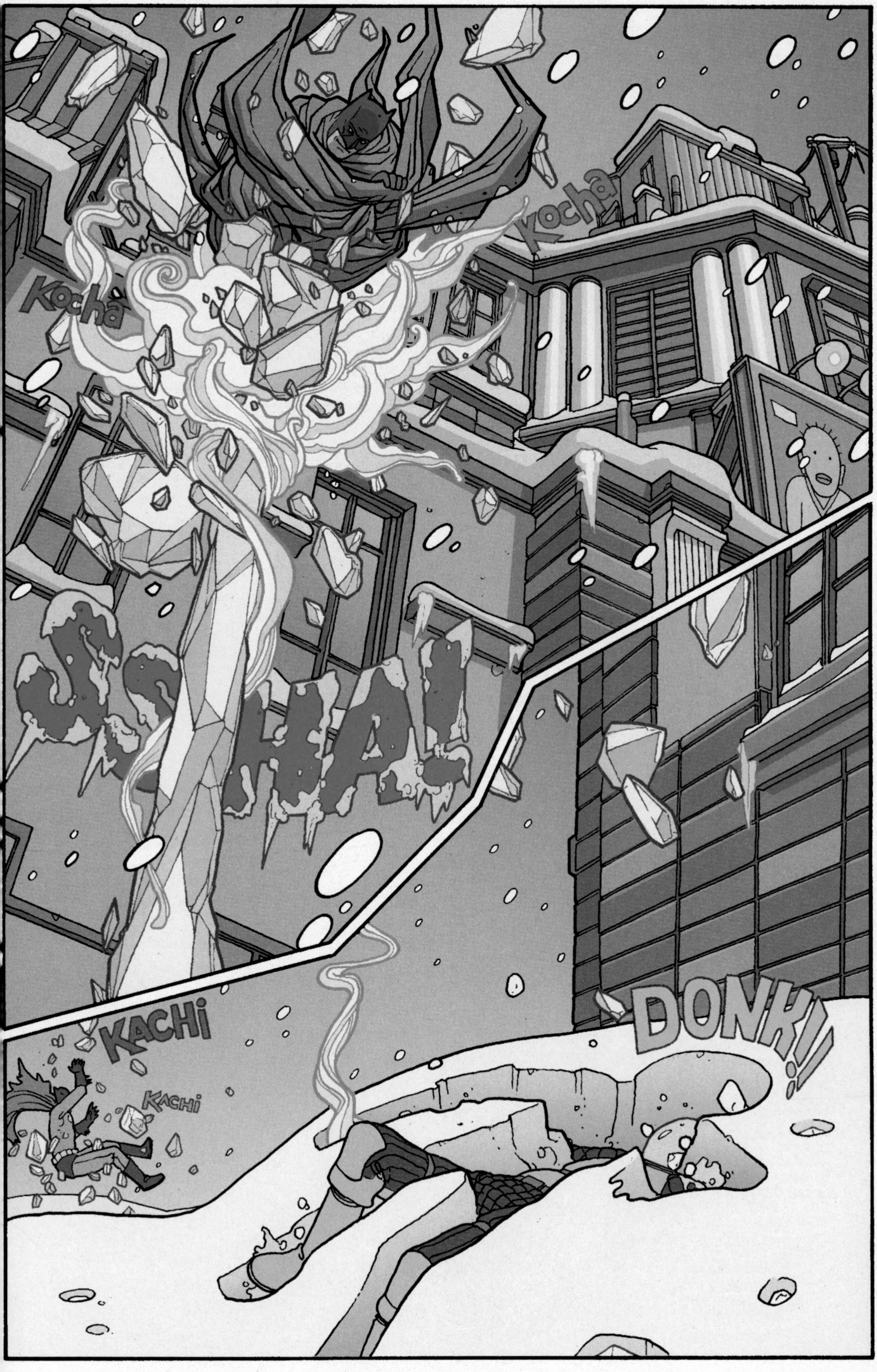

Kocha
Kocha
SSHA!
KACHi
KACHi
DONK!!

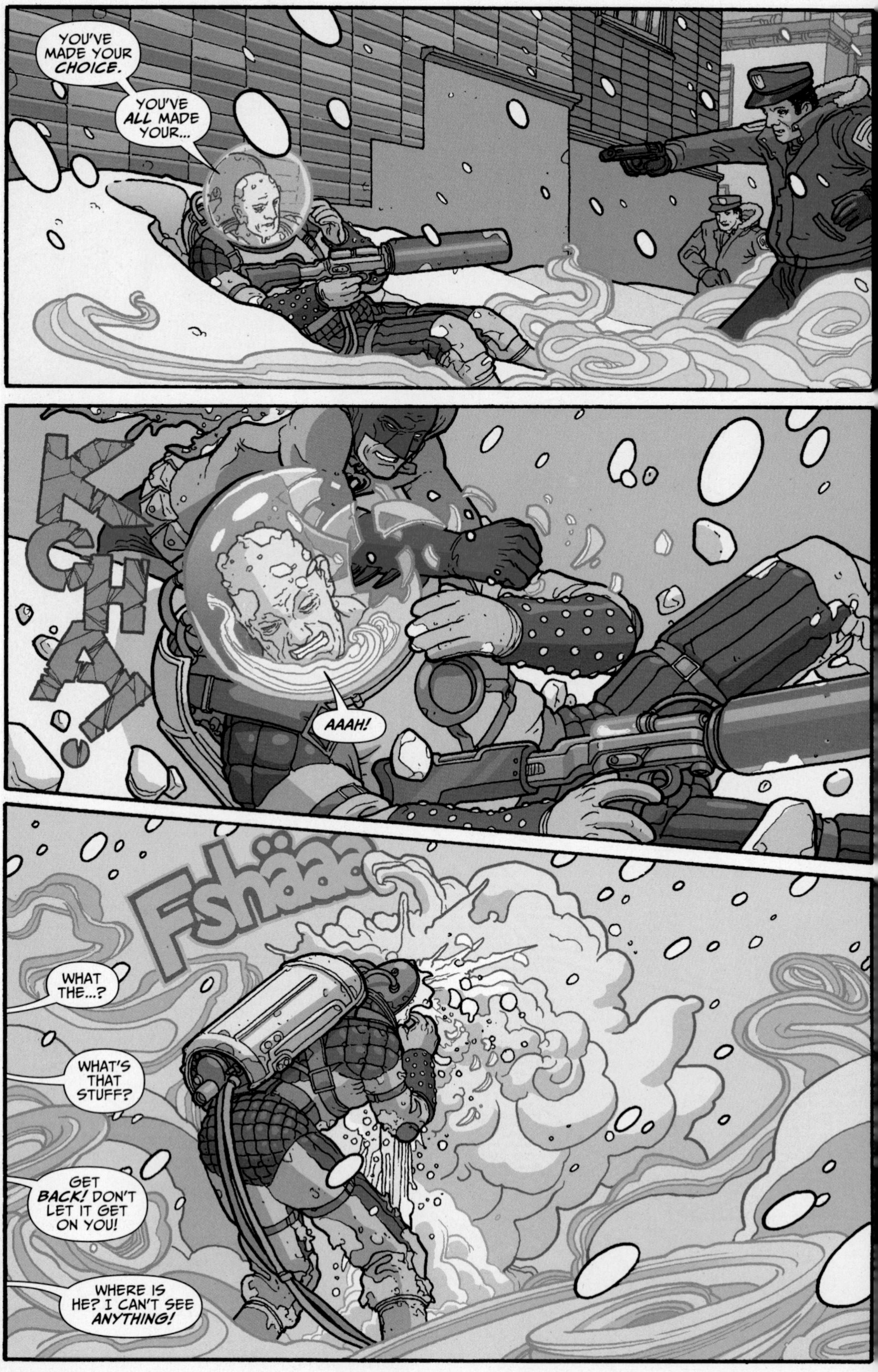
YOU'VE MADE YOUR CHOICE.
YOU'VE ALL MADE YOUR...
KACHAK
AAAH!
Fshäää
WHAT THE...?
WHAT'S THAT STUFF?
GET BACK! DON'T LET IT GET ON YOU!
WHERE IS HE? I CAN'T SEE ANYTHING!

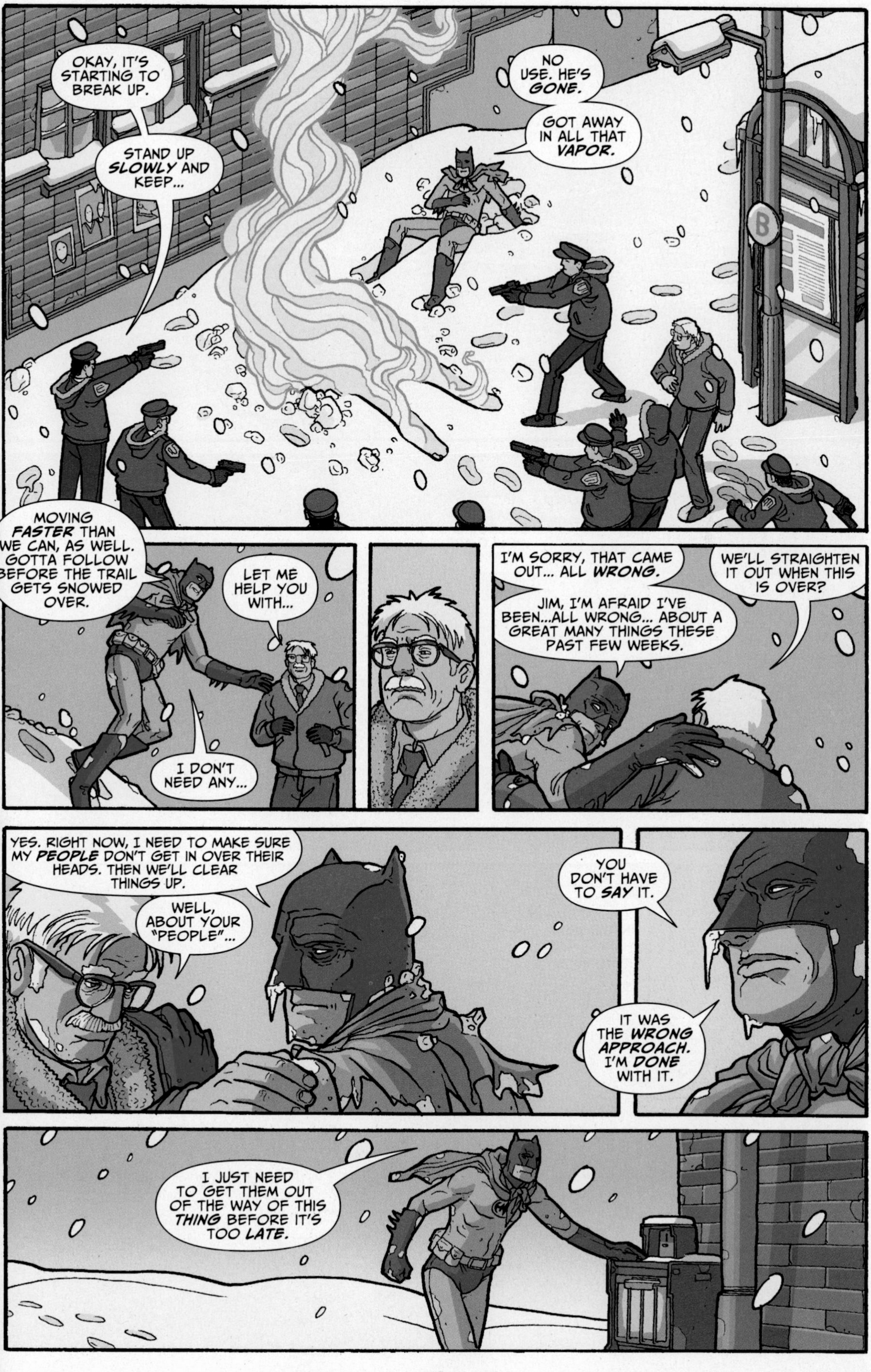

OKAY, IT'S STARTING TO BREAK UP.
STAND UP SLOWLY AND KEEP...
NO USE. HE'S GONE.
GOT AWAY IN ALL THAT VAPOR.
MOVING FASTER THAN WE CAN, AS WELL. GOTTA FOLLOW BEFORE THE TRAIL GETS SNOWED OVER.
LET ME HELP YOU WITH...
I DON'T NEED ANY...
I'M SORRY, THAT CAME OUT... ALL WRONG.
JIM, I'M AFRAID I'VE BEEN...ALL WRONG... ABOUT A GREAT MANY THINGS THESE PAST FEW WEEKS.
WE'LL STRAIGHTEN IT OUT WHEN THIS IS OVER?
YES. RIGHT NOW, I NEED TO MAKE SURE MY PEOPLE DON'T GET IN OVER THEIR HEADS. THEN WE'LL CLEAR THINGS UP.
WELL, ABOUT YOUR "PEOPLE"...
YOU DON'T HAVE TO SAY IT.
IT WAS THE WRONG APPROACH. I'M DONE WITH IT.
I JUST NEED TO GET THEM OUT OF THE WAY OF THIS THING BEFORE IT'S TOO LATE.

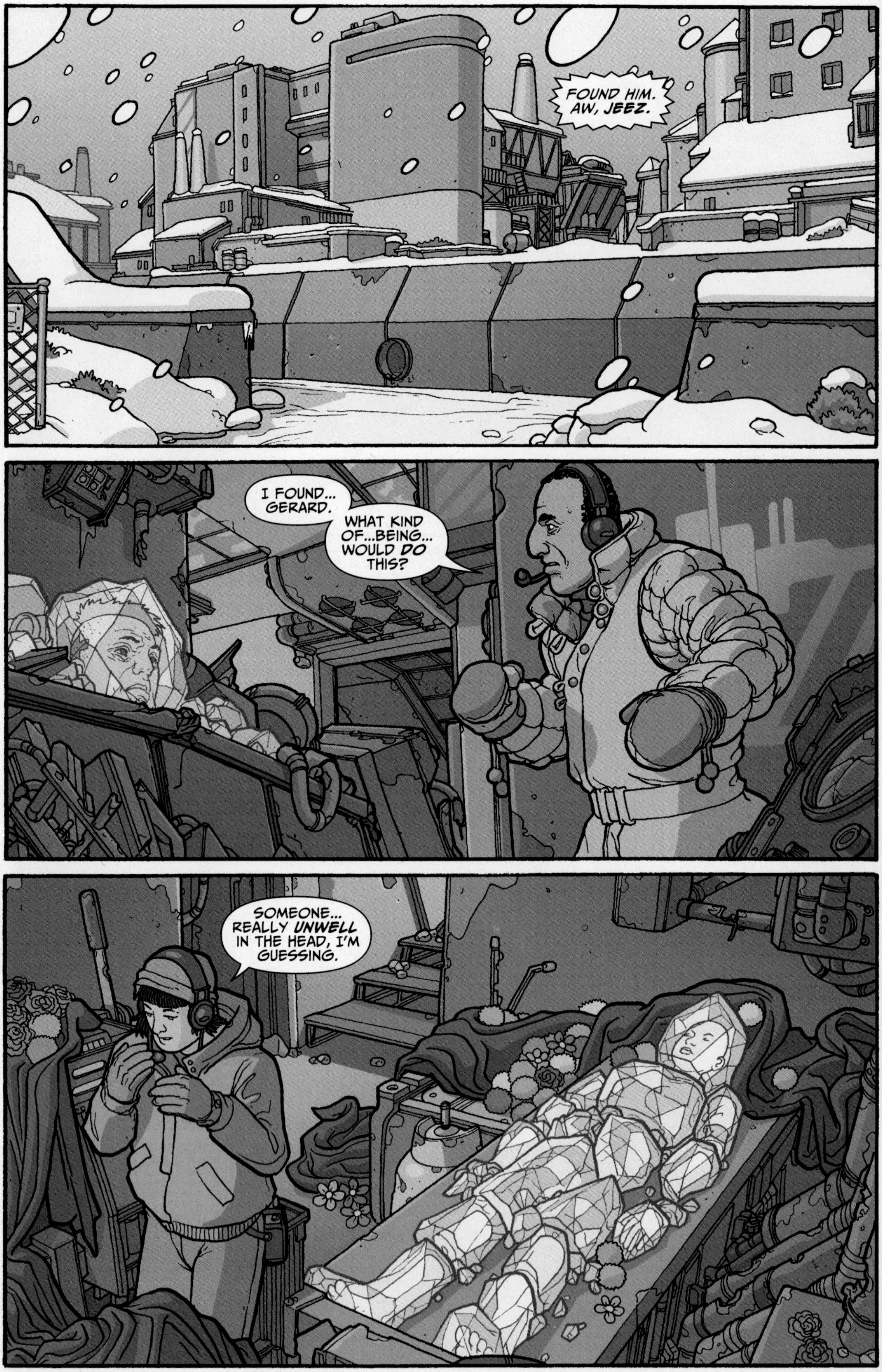
FOUND HIM. AW, JEEZ.
I FOUND... GERARD.
WHAT KIND OF...BEING... WOULD DO THIS?
SOMEONE... REALLY UNWELL IN THE HEAD, I'M GUESSING.

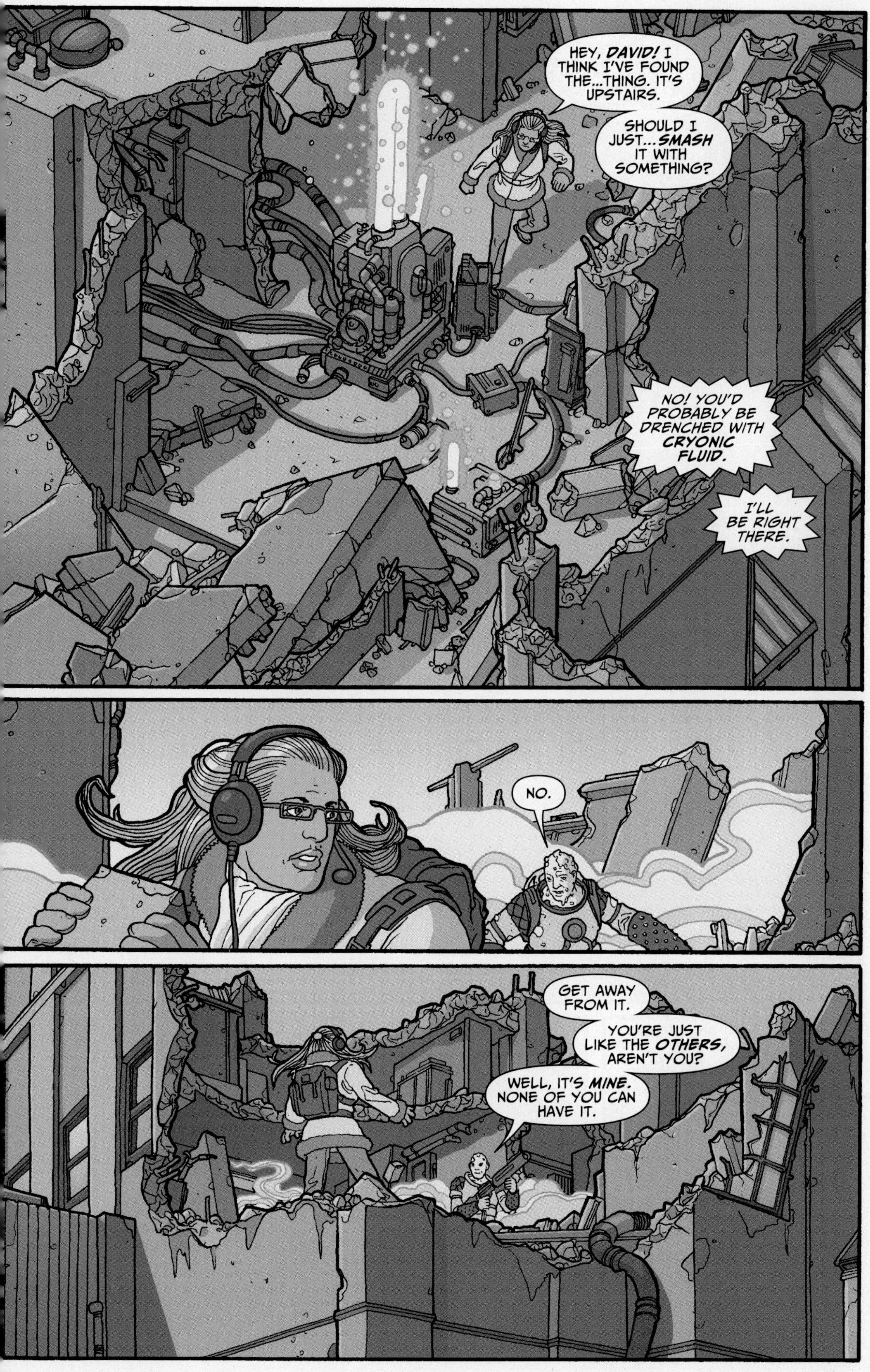
HEY, DAVID! I THINK I'VE FOUND THE...THING. IT'S UPSTAIRS.
SHOULD I JUST...SMASH IT WITH SOMETHING?
NO! YOU'D PROBABLY BE DRENCHED WITH CRYONIC FLUID.
I'LL BE RIGHT THERE.
NO.
GET AWAY FROM IT.
YOU'RE JUST LIKE THE OTHERS, AREN'T YOU?
WELL, IT'S MINE. NONE OF YOU CAN HAVE IT.

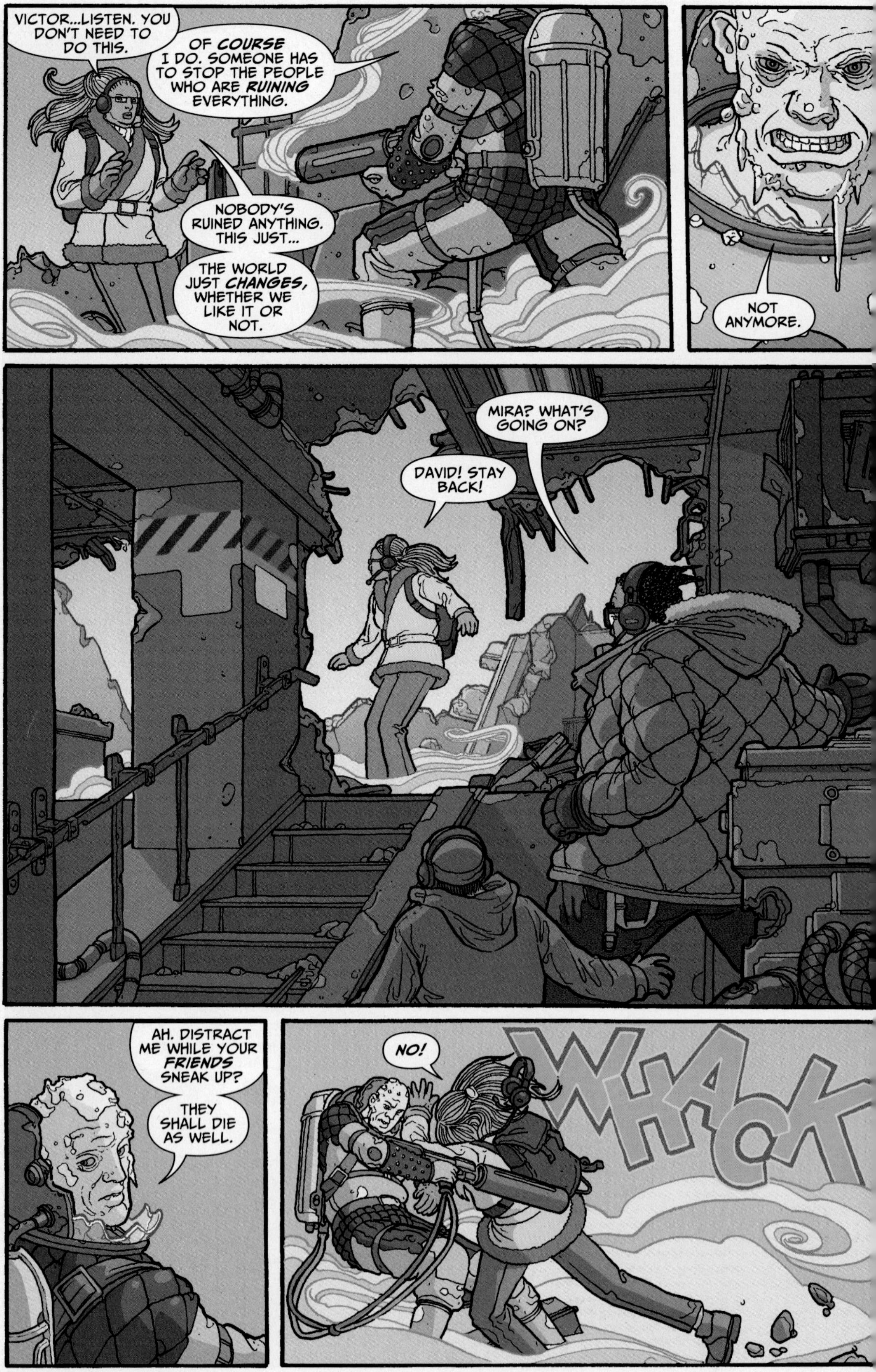
VICTOR...LISTEN. YOU DON'T NEED TO DO THIS.
OF COURSE I DO. SOMEONE HAS TO STOP THE PEOPLE WHO ARE RUINING EVERYTHING.
NOBODY'S RUINED ANYTHING. THIS JUST...
THE WORLD JUST CHANGES, WHETHER WE LIKE IT OR NOT.
NOT ANYMORE.
MIRA? WHAT'S GOING ON?
DAVID! STAY BACK!
AH. DISTRACT ME WHILE YOUR FRIENDS SNEAK UP?
THEY SHALL DIE AS WELL.
NO!
WHACK

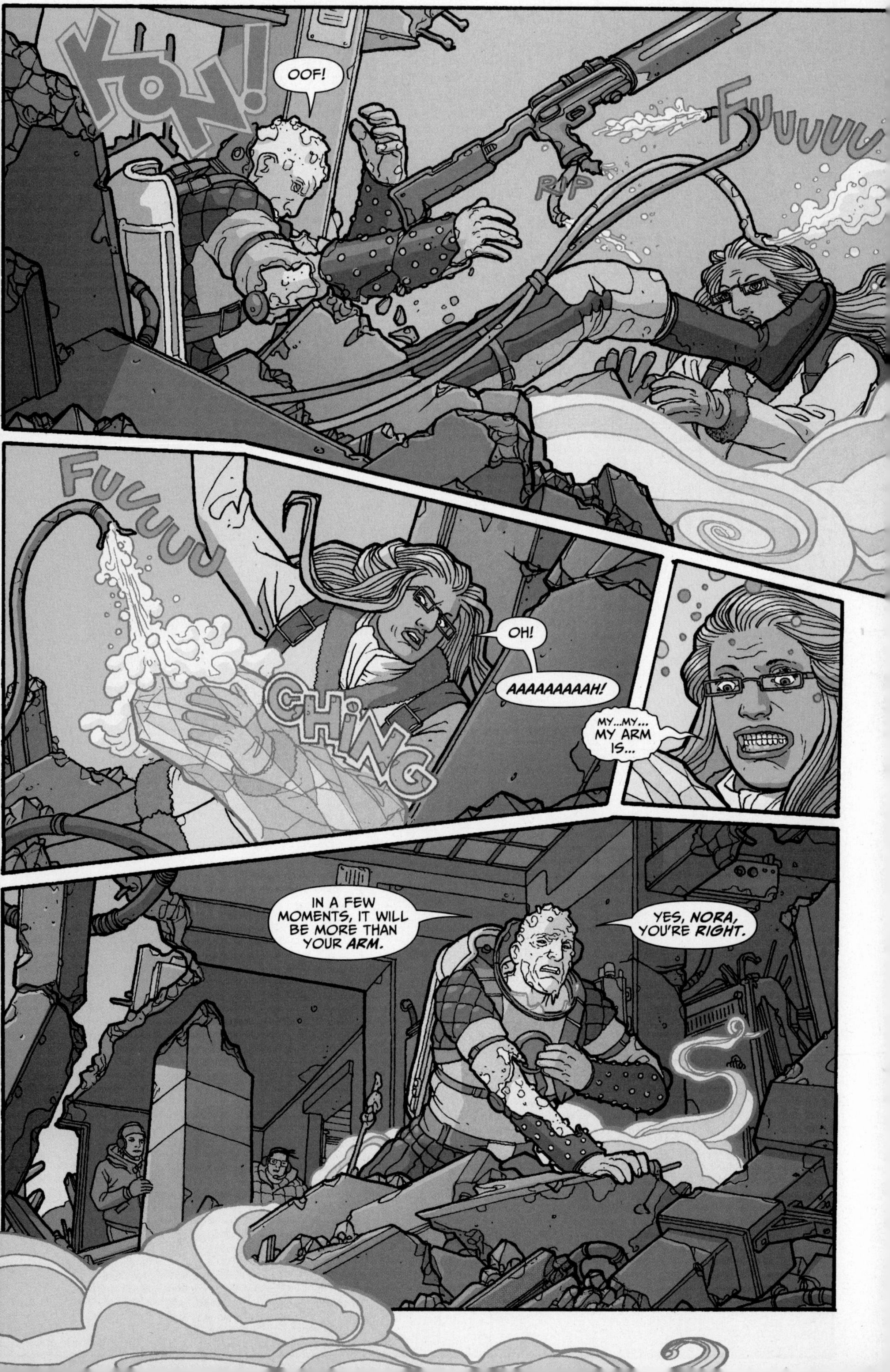
KOW!
OOF!
FUUUUU
RIP
FUUUUU
OH!
AAAAAAAAAH!
CHING
MY...MY... MY ARM IS...
IN A FEW MOMENTS, IT WILL BE MORE THAN YOUR ARM.
YES, NORA, YOU'RE RIGHT.

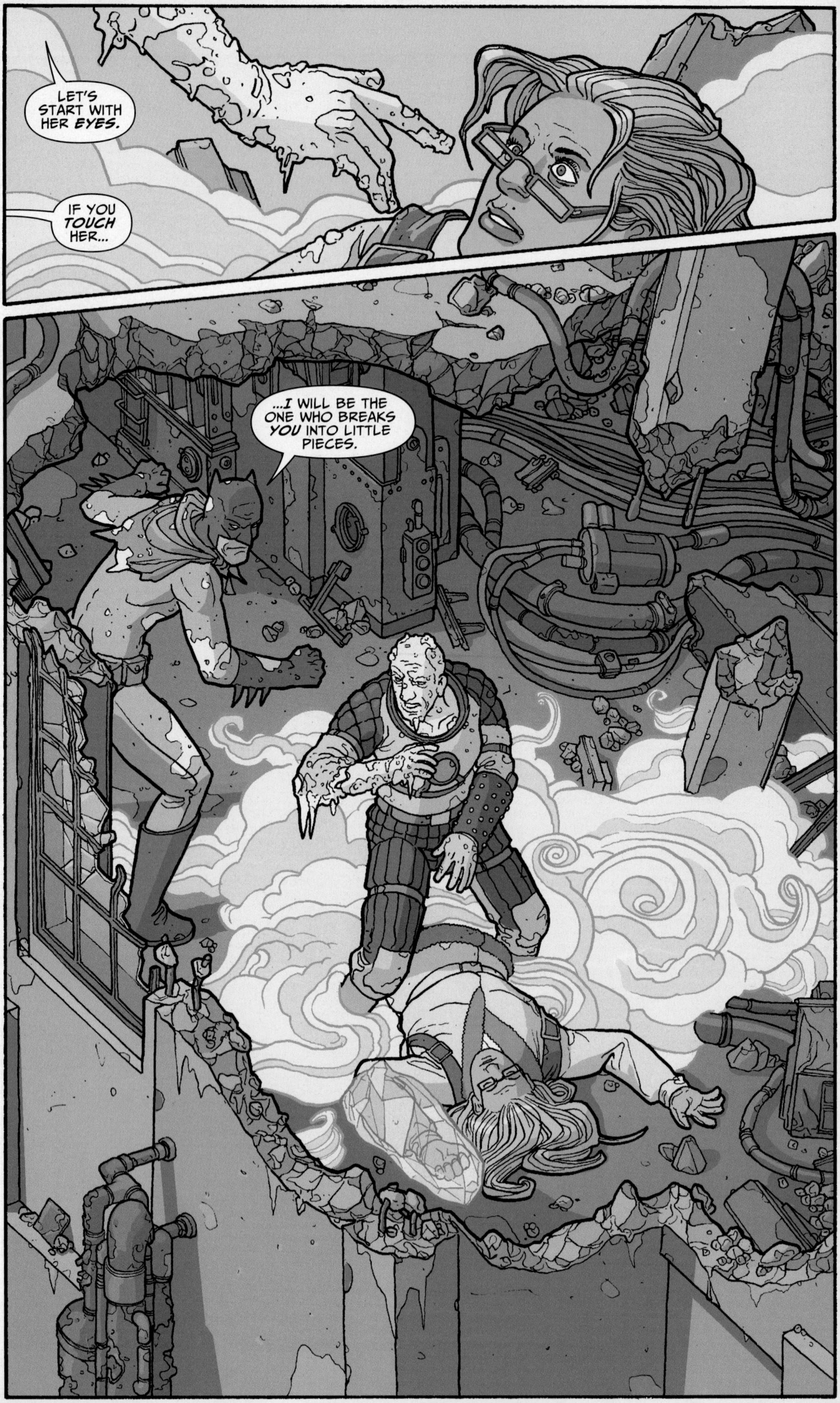
LET'S START WITH HER EYES.
IF YOU TOUCH HER...
...I WILL BE THE ONE WHO BREAKS YOU INTO LITTLE PIECES.

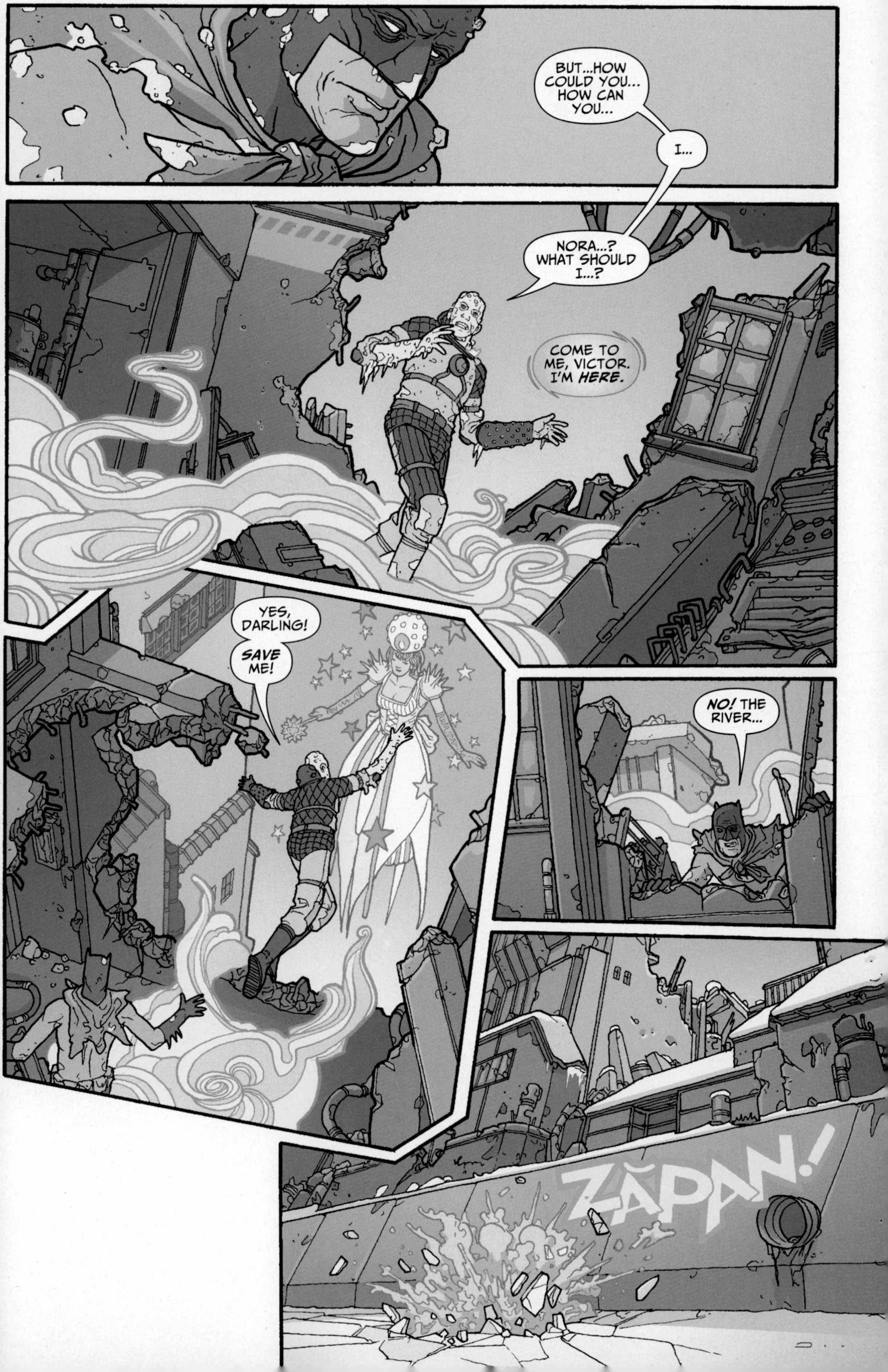
BUT...HOW COULD YOU... HOW CAN YOU...
I...
NORA...? WHAT SHOULD I...?
COME TO ME, VICTOR. I'M HERE.
YES, DARLING!
SAVE ME!
NO! THE RIVER...
ZAPAN!

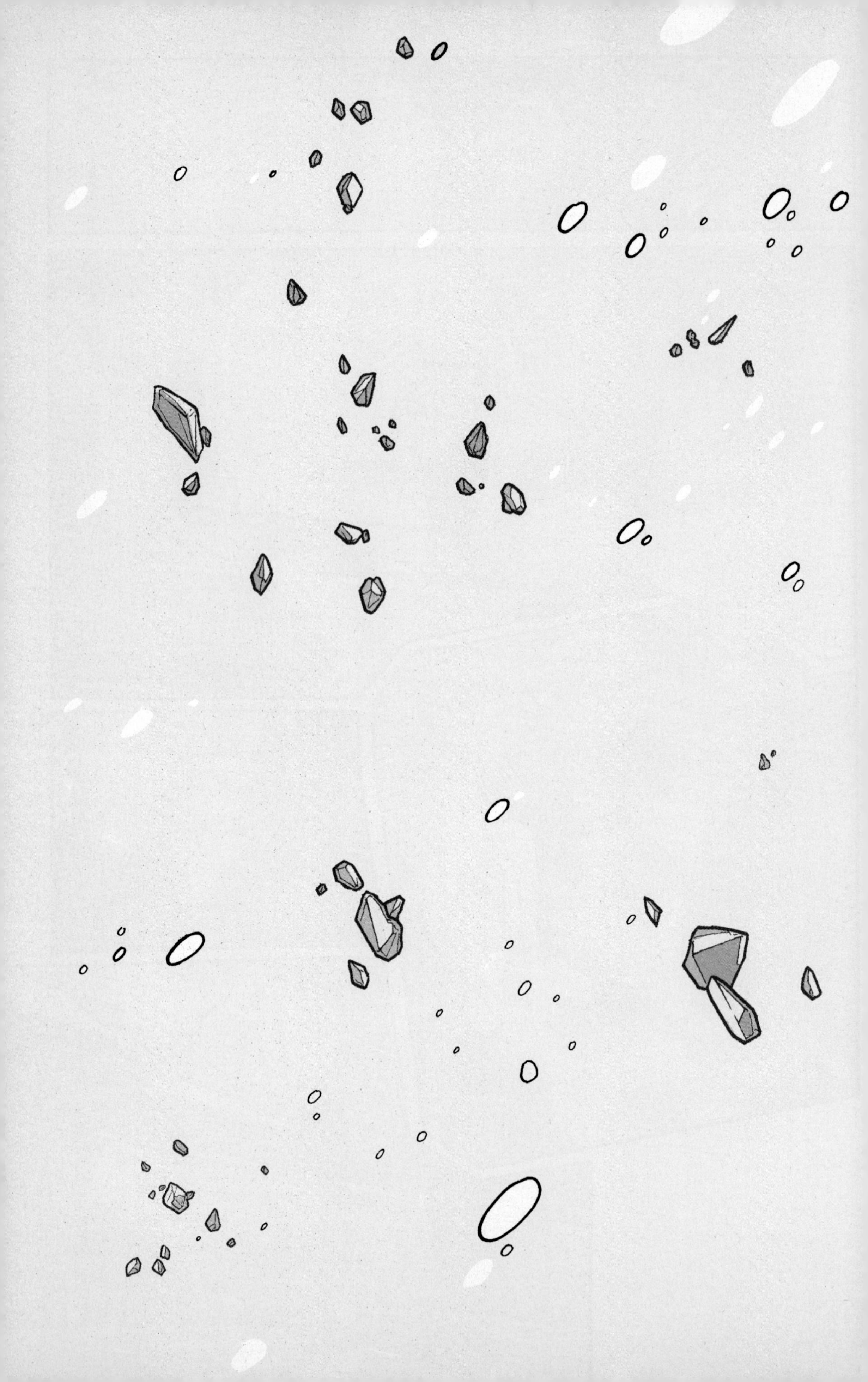

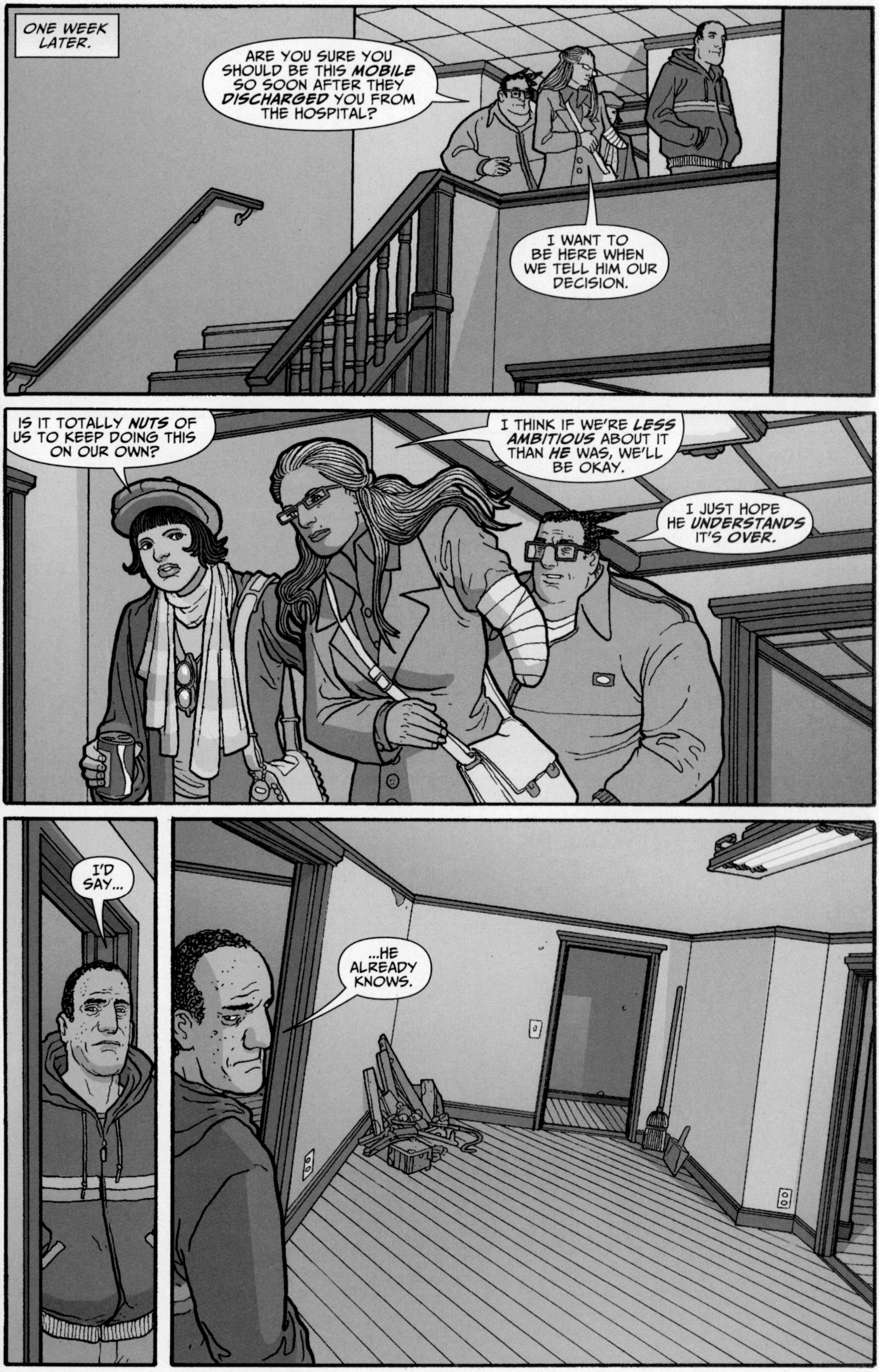
ONE WEEK LATER.
ARE YOU SURE YOU SHOULD BE THIS MOBILE SO SOON AFTER THEY DISCHARGED YOU FROM THE HOSPITAL?
I WANT TO BE HERE WHEN WE TELL HIM OUR DECISION.
IS IT TOTALLY NUTS OF US TO KEEP DOING THIS ON OUR OWN?
I THINK IF WE'RE LESS AMBITIOUS ABOUT IT THAN HE WAS, WE'LL BE OKAY.
I JUST HOPE HE UNDERSTANDS IT'S OVER.
I'D SAY...
...HE ALREADY KNOWS.

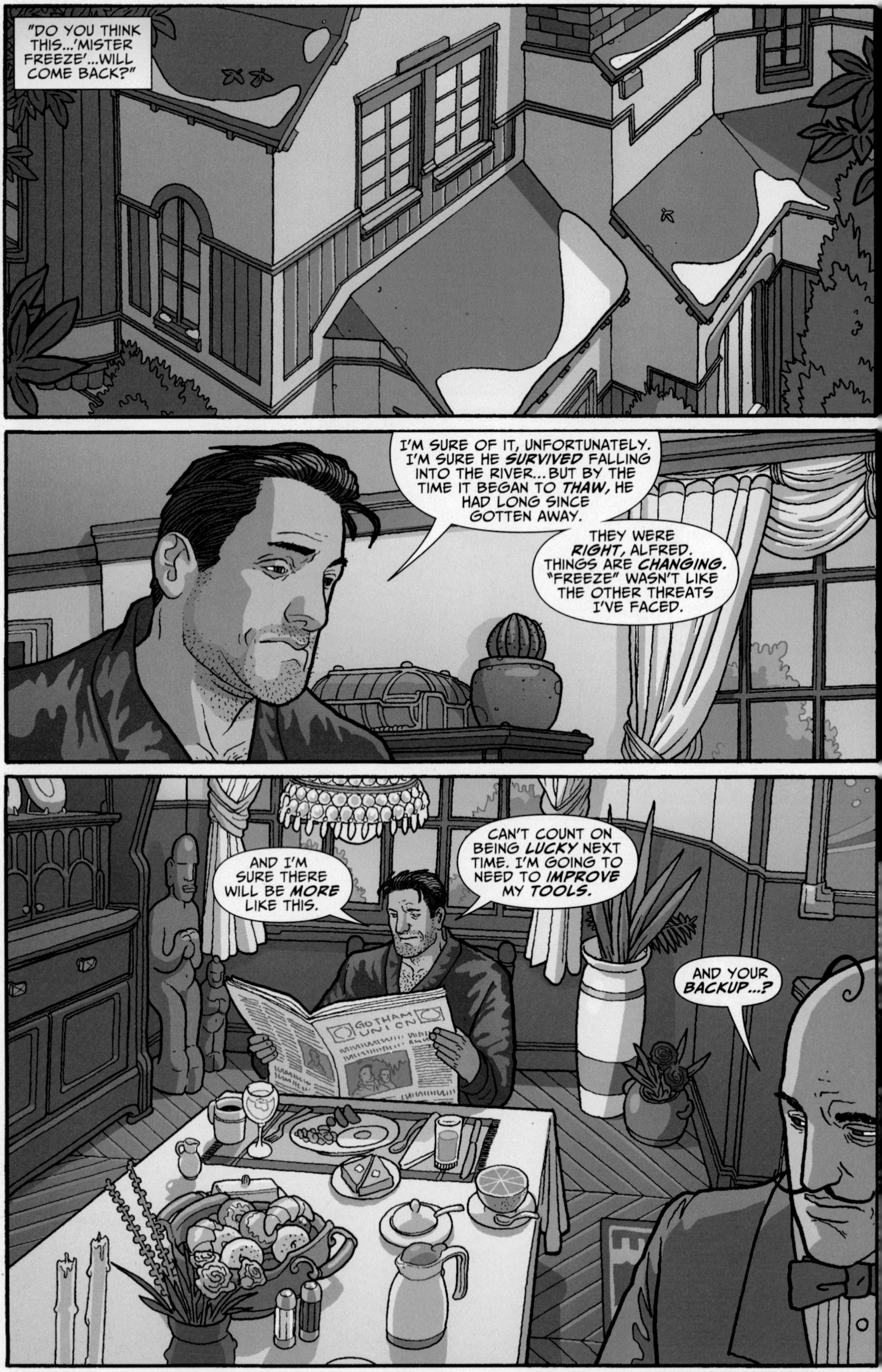
"DO YOU THINK THIS...'MISTER FREEZE'...WILL COME BACK?"
I'M SURE OF IT, UNFORTUNATELY. I'M SURE HE SURVIVED FALLING INTO THE RIVER... BUT BY THE TIME IT BEGAN TO THAW, HE HAD LONG SINCE GOTTEN AWAY.
THEY WERE RIGHT, ALFRED. THINGS ARE CHANGING. "FREEZE" WASN'T LIKE THE OTHER THREATS I'VE FACED.
AND I'M SURE THERE WILL BE MORE LIKE THIS.
CAN'T COUNT ON BEING LUCKY NEXT TIME. I'M GOING TO NEED TO IMPROVE MY TOOLS.
AND YOUR BACKUP...?
GOTHAM UNION

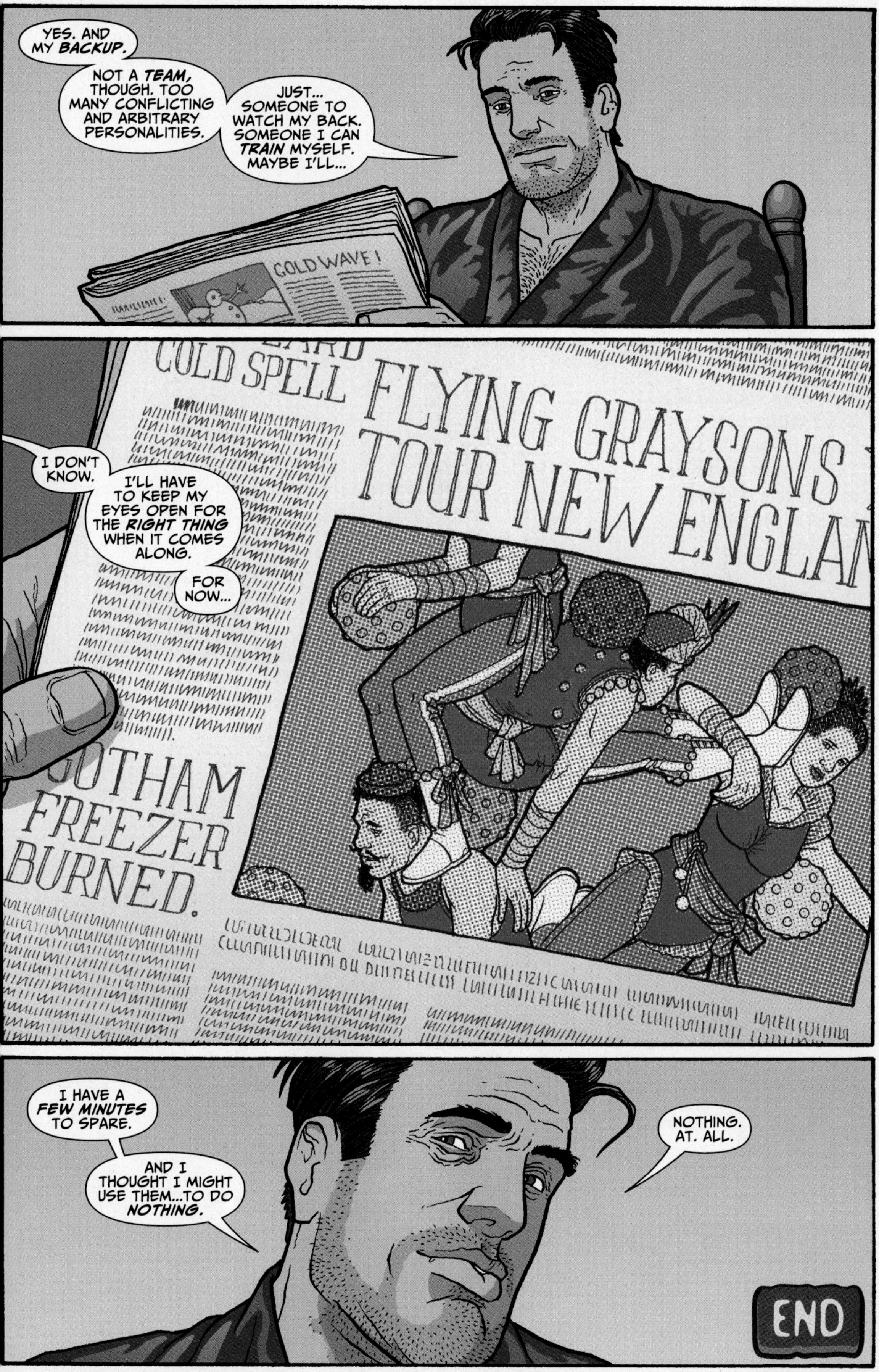
YES. AND MY BACKUP.
NOT A TEAM, THOUGH. TOO MANY CONFLICTING AND ARBITRARY PERSONALITIES.
JUST... SOMEONE TO WATCH MY BACK. SOMEONE I CAN TRAIN MYSELF. MAYBE I'LL...
COLD WAVE!
COLD SPELL
FLYING GRAYSONS TOUR NEW ENGLAN
I DON'T KNOW.
I'LL HAVE TO KEEP MY EYES OPEN FOR THE RIGHT THING WHEN IT COMES ALONG.
FOR NOW...
GOTHAM FREEZER BURNED.
I HAVE A FEW MINUTES TO SPARE.
AND I THOUGHT I MIGHT USE THEM...TO DO NOTHING.
NOTHING. AT ALL.
END

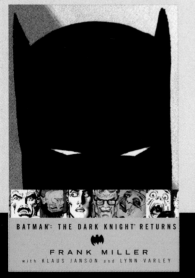

READ MORE ADVENTURES OF YOUR FAVORITE HEROES IN THESE COLLECTIONS FROM DC COMICS:

KINGDOM COME

THE GREATEST SUPER HERO EPIC OF TOMORROW!
ELSEWORLDS
KINGDOM COME
Mark WAID Alex ROSS

Mark Waid and **Alex Ross** deliver a grim tale of youth versus experience, tradition versus change and what defines a hero. KINGDOM COME is a riveting story pitting the old guard — Superman, Batman, Wonder Woman and their peers — against a new uncompromising generation.

WINNER OF FIVE EISNER AND HARVEY AWARDS, INCLUDING BEST LIMITED SERIES AND BEST ARTIST

IDENTITY CRISIS

NEW YORK TIMES BEST-SELLING AUTHOR OF THE ZERO GAME
BRAD MELTZER
RAGS MORALES MICHAEL BAIR
IDENTITY CRISIS
Introduction by JOSS WHEDON, creator of BUFFY THE VAMPIRE SLAYER and FIREFLY

BRAD MELTZER
RAGS MORALES
MICHAEL BAIR

CRISIS ON INFINITE EARTHS

CRISIS
ON INFINITE EARTHS
MARV WOLFMAN
& GEORGE PÉREZ

MARV WOLFMAN
GEORGE PÉREZ

DC: THE NEW FRONTIER VOLUME 1

DC: The New Frontier
VOLUME ONE
BY DARWYN COOKE WITH DAVE STEWART

DARWYN COOKE
DAVE STEWART

SEARCH THE GRAPHIC NOVELS SECTION OF

www.DCCOMICS.com

FOR ART AND INFORMATION ON ALL OF OUR BOOKS!

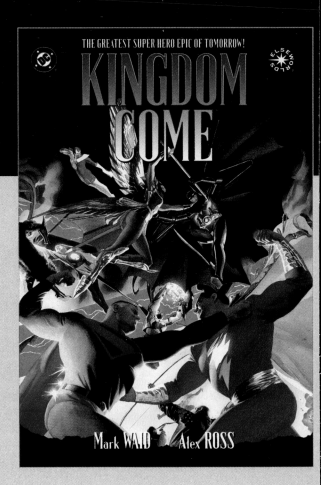